# The Beat
# Generation

# The Beat Generation

BRUCE COOK

Charles Scribner's Sons
New York

Printed in the United States of America
Library of Congress Catalogue Card Number 73-143950
SBN 684-12371-1

## Acknowledgments

Atheneum Publishers
   for excerpt from *Alone With America* by Richard Howard.
   Copyright © 1969 by Richard Howard.
City Lights Books
   for lines of poetry from *Gasoline, The Vestal Lady on Brattle*
   by Gregory Corso. Copyright © 1958, 1969 Gregory Corso.
   for lines of poetry from *Howl and Other Poems, Kaddish and Other Poems,
   Planet News* and *Reality Sandwiches* by Allen Ginsberg, copyright © 1956,
   1959, 1961, 1968, 1963 Allen Ginsberg.
Delacorte Press
   for excerpts from *The Pill Versus the Springhill Mine Disaster* by Richard
   Brautigan. Copyright © 1968 Richard Brautigan. A Seymour Lawrence Book.
   for "Critical Can Opener" from *Rommel Drives Deep Into Egypt* by Richard
   Brautigan. Copyright © 1970 Richard Brautigan. A Seymour Lawrence Book.
Grove Press, Inc.
   for "Circus" from *Word Alchemy* by Lenore Kandel.
   Copyright © 1960, 1966, 1967 Lenore Kandel.
   for "Projective Verse" from *Human Universe and Other Essays*
   by Charles Olson. Copyright © 1951, 1959, 1963, 1967 Charles Olson.
Heavy Metal Music Corp.
   for 10 lines from "Supergirl" by Tuli Kupferberg.
New Directions
   for poetry from *The Happy Birthday of Death* (copyright © 1960 New
   Directions Publishing Corporation) *Elegiac Feelings American* (copyright ©
   by Gregory Corso); *Long Live Man* (copyright © 1962 New Directions
   Publishing Corporation) all by Gregory Corso.
Slick, Grace
   for "White Rabbit"
Sterling Lord Agency, The
   for "Ghost Tantra #2" from *Ghost Tantras* by Michael McClure.
   Copyright © 1967 Michael McClure.
   for "43rd Chorus"
   for excerpt from *Lonesome Traveler* by Jack Kerouac.
Viking Press
   for excerpts from *The Dharma Bums* by Jack Kerouac.
   Copyright © 1958 by Jack Kerouac.

# Contents

PART I

# CHAPTER 1

# Somebody's Niggers

I remember buying a copy of *Esquire* when the plane on which I was returning from my army stretch in Germany landed in Gander, Newfoundland. Transatlantic flights no longer stop there to refuel, so you will have guessed that this was a while ago, and it was—January 1958, to be more precise. The magazine had an article in it by John Clellon Holmes, a name new to me then, and it was all about the Beat Generation, Jack Kerouac, and a novel that had everyone talking just then called *On the Road*. I did know a little about Kerouac. I had read a wild prose piece of his a couple of years before in *New World Writing*, said then to be from an unpublished work that must have been this same novel. And just a few months before my return to the United States, I had gotten my hands on a copy of the *Evergreen Review* devoted to the San Francisco Renaissance, and I had read in it of Kerouac and a number of the óthers they were calling Beats; it gave me the sense that something was about to happen. This article by John Clellon Holmes assured me that it was now happening. I remember that the thought of becoming a civilian again at just this moment in time seemed exciting to me then. And I managed to stay excited for quite some time to come, for about the first thing I did on returning home was to buy a copy of *On the Road*.

That started it for me. I soon came to regard the Beats as my generation. I felt the same keen sense of identification with them that thousands of others my age did, and I had the same feeling that I was lucky to be in on the beginning of something big, if only as a spectator. For yes, even in January 1958, it was possible to detect the vague shape of change on the horizon.

3

And if the Beats meant anything to complacent, conformist Eisenhower America, it was change.

But if the Beats were "my" generation, it should be emphasized, probably, that this did not make me a member of the Beat Generation. I got to know them just as did the rest of those who were my age—by reading their books, attending their poetry readings, and following the hectic accounts of their misadventures in magazines and newspapers. Eventually I came to know personally a couple of the writers associated with the Beat movement—but only a couple; this was a few years after that initial exciting moment when the Beats seemed to be everything—and the only thing—that was happening.

And yet I retained the sense of identification with them that I first began to feel on that trip back to the States. This was because I was in fundamental agreement with what I perceived, in broad outline, to be their program. Which meant that I was against the same things they were against—elitism on the one hand, mass movements on the other, and that if I had been pressed to characterize my personal aesthetic in a single word, that word would have been "populist." (A sculptor named Jack Burnham says, "The goal of a democratic society should be to make every man an artist." I like that.) This by way of declaring my bias.

Because of the affinity I felt for the Beats, I kept an eye on them long after the public had forgotten them and what they stood for. And it was because I never forgot that, really, that I was never quite as surprised as I might otherwise have been at how the 1960s turned out. For the almost schizophrenic change that has been worked in the temper of our times was predicted a decade before, implicit in every poem, novel, and prose piece produced by the Beat Generation.

Indeed there has been a change. The single most conspicuous fact of the present time is the great alteration that has come about in the character and attitudes of the under-thirty generation. They *are* different. Who could deny it? No longer docile, as we were, they present their demands where we submitted our requests in triplicate. Or more impressive still, they drop out in disgust from a culture we slavered to serve.

I must say that I am impressed by this new lot. Yet not so impressed that I am convinced, as many seem to be, that those under thirty are a new breed entirely, a generation without forebears, precursors, or precedents. No, even though many of the young themselves seem unaware of it, the present generation is caught in the usual umbilical relationship to the past. And it may give us some idea of the future in store for us if we give their cord a tug and see where it leads. When we do, we will find that it goes back directly to that legion of artists and frustrated artists, novelists and would-be novelists, poets and poets manqué, those mothers (maintaining the metaphor) known then and ever after as the Beat Generation.

During their moment in the spotlight they received the full treatment from the media—coverage in the news magazines, special attention in *Life,* lots of time on the talk shows, and even a television documentary or two devoted to them. And now, although nearly all the writers who emerged from the movement are still being published, the Beat Generation, if remembered at all today, is recalled as some distant phenomenon, an isolated cultural event of the 1950s. And those of the present generation who have inherited so much from them have only the haziest notion of the Beat Generation, why, what, or even who it was.

All right, *who* were the Beats? Were they truly, as they called themselves, a generation? A movement? Or were they merely—as was said so often of them by members of the literary establishment of that day—a fad, a phenomenon of publicity, a creation of the Luce publications?

If you had gone out and asked who the Beats were on any college campus in, say, 1958, you would have heard the same three names mentioned over and over again in response. The first of them would surely have been that of Jack Kerouac. Now dead, Kerouac was the victim of his own restless urgings and of the deep-seated alienation he felt from the culture that created him and from the counterculture he helped create. His death, which came in the fall of 1969 wrote a sort of full stop to the Beat episode. Once the obituaries and memoirs of Kerouac had come in, many who were a part of it all felt that

5

the Beat Generation was finally a thing of the past. For hadn't he been the star of the show? Wasn't it his ruggedly handsome Canuck face that had appeared in the magazines and been seen so often on television? Hadn't he even been the first to dub his generation Beat?

Yes, according to John Clellon Holmes, it was Kerouac who christened them all, though no one would ever claim that he originated the term. Beat, in the sense of beaten, frustrated, played out, has been around for many, many years. Its fustian, ungrammatical quality suggests it may have originated in the nineteenth-century West or rural South. In the 1940s it had a vogue among jazz musicians who used to embellish it with little variations, such as "I'm beat right down to my socks." A friend of Kerouac's, Herbert Huncke, who was then living an underground life as a Times Square hustler, petty thief, and drug addict, had picked it up from the jazzmen and used it often with frequent variations. So there was nothing really remarkable in Jack Kerouac using the word in that way when he attempted to characterize the new attitude he saw in his contemporaries. "It's a sort of furtiveness," Clellon Holmes quotes him as saying, "like we were a generation of furtives. You know, with an inner knowledge there's no use flaunting on that level, the level of the 'public,' a kind of beatness—I mean being right down to it, to ourselves, because we all *really* know where we are—and a weariness with all the forms, all the conventions of the world. . . . It's something like that. So I guess you might say we're a *beat* generation."

A version of this speech found its way into John Clellon Holmes' novel *Go,* a book particularly important for the picture it provides of the early Beat scene in New York in the 1940s. Published in 1952, it has the distinction of being the first Beat Generation novel. But apart from good reviews, it received no real notice and certainly started no movements. It took Jack Kerouac's *On the Road,* published five years later, to do that.

It is difficult, separated as we are by time and temper from that period, to convey the liberating effect that *On the Road* had on young people all over America. There was a sort of instantaneous flash of recognition that seemed to send thousands of them out into the streets, proclaiming that Kerouac had written their story, that *On the Road* was their book. There was such community of feeling in this response that critics began to speak with some certainty, though without much respect, of Kerouac's as the new literary generation.

Their lack of respect was probably due less to the work produced by Kerouac and his friends than to their public performances. Whether at readings, on panels, or in front of television cameras, they could always be depended upon to shock some and dismay many more. There was a sort of programmatic ruthlessness to their impudence. It was as though they had put aside any notion of revolting against the establishment and had decided merely to thumb their noses at it.

The most avid nose-thumber of them all, and the second of those who would surely have been mentioned on that college campus in 1958, was a young poet from New York who had barely seen the inside of a high school. His name was Gregory Corso. The more sober literary personages of an age noted for its literary sobriety came almost to regard Corso as a nemesis, detesting his hip, easy, wise-guy manner and the direct, artless diction of his poetry. He loved to jape, and would mutter nonsense slogans into a microphone, such as "fried shoes" and "all life is a rotary club." He was the master of the put-on. But beneath it all, below the tough attitude, and down even further, underneath that quality of street-urchin innocence that so often shone through, was something hard and durable that said quite emphatically that Gregory Corso was a poet. And this, more than anything else, infuriated his detractors.

And the third? Allen Ginsberg, of course. The poet of "Howl" and "Kaddish" was not just a new hero to the young, but a new *kind* of hero. When he presented himself before them to read his poems, they found him a sort of self-appointed shaman—intense, voluble, irascible, and obviously convinced of the holiness of his mission as a poet. He was as far as could be from the going "cool" style, just as his poetry—naked, gauche, and crudely confessional as it was—seemed the very antithesis of the dry, precise, and calculated verse of the academic poets who were just then thought to be the only American poets worthy of the name.

7

He was at that time not an altogether attractive personality. "An aggressive, savage young man," recalls novelist Alan Harrington who knew him quite early in New York, "a great hater." But Ginsberg is now greatly changed and Harrington is unreserved in his endorsement of the "new" Allen. "Today," says Harrington, "I think he's a great teacher. The young people seem to think so, too."

Indeed they do. For nobody in America over the age of thirty seems to speak quite so directly to quite so many young people as Allen Ginsberg does today. Call him a guru if you like, for guru is merely Timespeak for "teacher," and he is certainly that to those under thirty. And whether members of that generation know it or not, his real importance to them lies in having done so much to transmit to them the values and myths of the Beats. In his readings, campus appearances, and lectures—such as they are—he has managed to touch and influence many thousands more than he would or could have ten years ago. And there are signs, too, that the influence has been mutual. As a matter of fact, the rather subtle changes that have marked the transition from the Beats to the hippies can also be traced in Ginsberg's own personality. Gentler now and less given to fits of rage and the rhetoric of denunciation, both Ginsberg and his young friends seem more confident today, more aware of their strength, and with a keener sense of direction than before. They seem to know better than most of us where they are headed.

The same sort of gradual change can be perceived in most of the original Beats who are still writing today. It may mean only that they are mellowing with age, but when we consider that we are talking of writers such as Michael McClure, Gary Snyder, and Lawrence Ferlinghetti who have hardly tamed down, this seems highly unlikely. No, these three, and a few others, seem to have achieved, by whatever devious path, something quite like wisdom.

Why not? Nearly all the Beats have displayed to an impressive degree that talent for survival that must always be a prerequisite to wisdom of any sort. And if a few have taken college jobs, gone into publishing, or accepted the foundation grants they jeered at others for accepting only a few years ago

—then what of it? They have in this way managed to survive to transmit in person the spirit of their time to the present generation, and many have come to be regarded as something like mentors by many who are ten, twenty, and even thirty years younger. This is the real importance of a poet like Robert Creeley, teaching today, or of a John Logan, or especially of a battered veteran like Kenneth Rexroth. They keep in touch this way. They are maintaining a sense of continuity from generation to generation, a community of understanding with the young: put simply, they communicate. Thus the much-discussed generation gap seems to be less precisely that than a generalized failure of communication or rapport.

The Beats themselves had precious little rapport with the official culture of their own day. Once they were established, neither Jack Kerouac nor Allen Ginsberg ever received favorable reviews. They were ridiculed, reviled, and scoffed at. Herbert Gold—who may later have come to regret having said so —once suggested solemnly that both were insane. Harold Rosenberg, in one of his more memorable phrases, called the Beats a "herd of independent minds." And Norman Podhoretz, who was then even younger than most of the Beats and just beginning to make his reputation as a critic, labeled them "know-nothing Bohemians," and set forth his judgment in what was soon to become his characteristic stentorian tone of disapproval: "The plain truth is that the primitivism of the Beat Generation serves first of all as a cover for an anti-intellectualism so bitter that it makes the ordinary American's hatred of eggheads seem positively benign."

Anti-intellectualism was, as we shall see, a charge often tossed in their direction. And though we shall deal with it again in passing, let us note with particular reference to Podhoretz's severe judgment that an intellectual, if he is anything, is a man who is in touch with his own time, one who knows what's happening and why. And by that modest standard, any one of the Beat writers was as much an intellectual as he. Why? Because the Beats had perceived and managed to touch something essential that was only then beginning to take shape in the America of the 1950s. It was a very important and widespread something, compounded of a deep hunger for individ-

9

ual recognition, a desire to speak frankly and honestly about things that mattered, and, finally, a need for passionate personal involvement in major undertakings.

Perhaps these are not unusual qualities at all. Perhaps they can be found in Americans of any decade. They may be merely the common needs and characteristic qualities of the young at any time or in any place. But they were of special importance to the Beats and their followers because these, after all, were the 1950s—the era of Joe McCarthy, the HUAC hearings, and a series of spy trials that together spread a brooding pall of suspicion over all of American society. It was a time during which most of the adult population was trapped in an intricate edifice of social conformity built of fear, suppressed hostility, and the simple desire to get along. And finally, it was also a time when many adult Americans experienced personal prosperity and some degree of affluence for the first time in their lives; the middle class was expanded in that decade by many millions who could well remember extreme poverty from the depression years. Most of them had worked hard and waited a long time to get where they were. And once comfortably established, they embraced the values and symbols of middle-class life with all the fervor of religious converts.

In this context the Beats were of considerable social importance to the 1950s, for they soon came to be regarded as a threat to all this because they questioned the conservative, corporate, and suburban values that were then so widely and publicly extolled. The Beats not only questioned, they challenged them, and were soon widely publicized as rebels against the system. And if, as a revolt, theirs may have had serious inadequacies in shape, definition, and direction, still it attracted thousands—tens of thousands—of young people in a very short time.

In the literary culture, as well, this was a period of stasis and conformity. Two groups—the New Critics of the colleges and universities and that group of New York intellectuals known variously as the Family and the *Partisan Review* crowd—dominated the arena without themselves ever really falling into serious contention. They shared. A sort of polite trust prevailed between the two that was based on overlapping interests and

10

mutual advantage. Outsiders—and there were many of
—spoke wryly of this coalition as the *"Kenyon Review-Parti-
san Review* axis."

But make no mistake: the two groups were quite distinct.
For their part, the New Critics were academic in about every
way it was possible for them to be. They were schoolmen who
devoted their time and intellectual energies to the close reading of texts, from which they drew conclusions on points so fine
as to often seem irrelevant. Their poetry—to generalize recklessly—was crabbed, pinched, and reticent, and their fiction
introspective and oblique. Politically, they were either indifferent or conservative. Socially, there was a definite disposition
to the Ciceronian ideals of the ante-bellum South and a tendency to share a fantasy of the agrarian past at the expense of
the urban present. They were elitists at heart, and they drew
their strength from the sudden rise of the universities in America following World War II and from the growing popular faith
that through education a new elite would be created that
might be expected to solve all the problems and guide the way
into that brave new world of the future.

The New York crowd, on the other hand, was intensely
political. No matter what the text at hand, they could be
counted on to examine it fundamentally as a political document. Their style had survived from the 1930s. Nearly all had
at that time gone through a period of keen enthusiasm for
Marxism. One by one, however, they all became disenchanted
and dissociated themselves from orthodox Marxism. This was
the case, certainly, with the *Partisan Review* itself, which was
well known in the 1930s as an independent Marxist political
journal, though it was then categorized as "Trotskyite." Gradually, however, as the personal political commitment of its editors and contributors began to cool—for most this happened
during the war—their attention became focused more and
more on literary subjects. Yet while the content of their articles had gradually changed, their manner and fundamental
concern had not. These have remained essentially political.
Criticism for this group consisted largely in gathering a certain
number of recent novels within a generalization and denounc-
11  ing it as evidence of some especially pernicious social ten-

dency. Their rhetoric is the sort that invariably seems to draw them into intellectual demolition of their opponents. They specialized in feats of literary overkill, and their favorite targets have always been sitting ducks. Yet if nothing more, the New York group was, is, and always will be *serious*—concerned with the great issues, refusing steadfastly to be amused.

Thus the scene is set. Here are the two groups—New Critics and New Yorkers—occupying center stage. They perform their familiar routines to the scattered applause of an indifferent audience. All right, the show may *not* be very interesting but respect and good feeling prevail: a sense of order and authority is present in the world of letters. Suddenly, from the wings there appears onstage a wild, shabbily dressed, and unshaven bunch who mill in disorder about the stage, shouting obscenities, jeering, and making light of all the heavy weight of intellect assembled there. Where order was, there is now anarchy.

That wasn't how it really happened, but that is how members of the literary establishment *thought* it was happening. For these who held so tenaciously to their position in center stage, the keenest irritation of all was not that the Beats, who were now crowding them out, were so ill-mannered and unserious. No, what bothered them most was that the audience they had been boring had suddenly become intensely interested.

This was quite literally apparent whenever the Beats gave a reading or made any sort of public appearance. I remember being present at such an event held at a Loop hotel in Chicago early in 1959. It was a reading given as a benefit to launch a new magazine with Beat leanings, *Big Table*, edited by the poet Paul Carroll. Attendance at the event in every way exceeded the expectations of the academic crowd that usually made up the audience at local poetry evenings such as this. The audience of over 700 completely filled the ballroom they had engaged, and in no time at all the aisles were packed and people were being turned away from the door. But the character of the audience must have surprised the regulars, too, for it was not the modest crowd of college students and young teachers who usually showed up. They were both younger and

12

older than that, ranging from about mid-teens to grizzled middle age. And while there were certainly many there from the area's many colleges, the outsiders seemed to dominate, giving the audience a distinctly nonacademic, almost proletarian appearance.

The most eminent representative of the literary establishment present was the late Henry Rago, an academic in all but point of fact, who was then editor of *Poetry* magazine. He was there seated in the midst of a group of young university teachers. As it happened, I was introduced to him by one of the university teachers I knew and took a seat quite nearby. I couldn't help noticing Mr. Rago's reactions during the reading, and although they were never put into words, they were so expressive in their own way that I think they are worth noting here. When, for example, Gregory Corso began reading his poem, "Hair,"

> My beautiful hair is dead
> Now I am the rawhead
> O when I look in the mirror
> the bald I see is balder still
> When I sleep the sleep I sleep
> is not at will
> And when I dream I dream children waving goodbye—
> It was lovely hair once
> it was
> Hours before shop windows gum-machine mirrors with great
> combs
> pockets filled with jars of lanolin. . . .

I watched Mr. Rago sink deeper and deeper into his seat. He was clearly disturbed by what he heard, perhaps unhappy that he had even come, but he made no move to leave. As I recall, he endured the entire program, perhaps too much of a gentleman to leave (for he was always that), or more likely frozen in consternation at this awful new thing that was happening. In any case he did stay, but by the time Allen Ginsberg was reading his even then famous poem "Howl" ("I saw the best minds of my generation destroyed by madness, starving hysterical naked,/dragging themselves through the negro

13

streets at dawn looking for an angry fix . . ."), Henry Rago's face wore an expression of almost physical pain.

Yet this was clearly not how the rest of the audience heard it. They not only applauded at the appropriate places, they applauded at *in*appropriate places and did a bit of cheering and stamping, too. The response to the poems read and to the remarks made by the poets was so open and spontaneous that the feeling that night was quite like that of a jazz concert. This, of course, was precisely the open and swinging effect that the Beat poets strove for in all their readings, with or without musical accompaniment. The response was there. No doubt about it: Corso and Ginsberg had touched something real that night.

On another similar occasion, the two were in New York to give a reading at Columbia University's McMillin Theater. It seemed that when Ginsberg had been a student at Columbia about ten years before, he had taken a loan from the university for a modest amount and had never paid it back. His new-found fame as a poet brought him, along with everything else, a dun from the Columbia University bursar's office for the delinquent loan. Since a Columbia student club, the John Dewey Society, had already been in contact with him to read at the university, Ginsberg suggested they go even-steven on it: he would give a reading without fee if the university would forgive him the debt. And those were evidently the terms under which he and Gregory Corso subsequently appeared.

These facts have been extracted from Diana Trilling's account of the reading in her essay, "The Other Night at Columbia: A Report." It is a remarkable piece of work, well worth reading in her collection of a few years aback, *Claremont Essays.* Nothing quite so well expresses the attitude of the intellectual establishment (in this case the New York intellectual community) to the Beats. It is an almost perfectly sustained exercise in condescension whose tone is altered only occasionally when she lapses into outright contempt as she certainly does here: "Allen Ginsberg, with his poems in which there was never quite enough talent or hard work, and with his ambiguous need to tell his teacher exactly what new flagrancy had opened to his imagination as he talked about Gide with his

14

friends at the West End Cafe, had at any rate the distinction of being more crudely justified in his emotional disturbance than most."

The reason for the personal tone of these remarks of Mrs. Trilling's, and for that matter, her reason for writing the essay in the first place, is that Allen Ginsberg was a student of her husband's while at Columbia, and he was a student who caused particular trouble. Ginsberg, who was about as reckless in his college years as one might suppose from his later career, left behind him a unique record of mishaps, mistakes, and misunderstandings into which we shall go in some detail a little later on (the delinquent loan from the bursar was the least of it). He was remembered by all the members of the faculty he had come in contact with and by many others he had not. He was notorious.

During this period at Columbia, Ginsberg became particularly attached to Mark Van Doren and Lionel Trilling because, according to Mrs. Trilling, he was trying to get them to play father to him. Yet, perversely, he had the *chutzpah* to address them as equals: "I suppose I have no right to say now, and on such early and little evidence, that Ginsberg had always desperately wanted to be respectable, or respected, like his instructors at Columbia, it is so likely that this is a hindsight which suits my needs. . . . Not that Ginsberg had ever shown himself as a potential future colleague in the university; anything but that. Even the implied literary comradeship had had reference, not to any possibility of Ginsberg's assimilation into the community of professors, but to the professor's capacity for association in the community of rebellious young poets."

Did Mrs. Trilling read too much into the relationship? Probably not, for at the reading Ginsberg dedicated a poem to her husband, one that she calls "Lion in the Room." It must surely be "The Lion for Real," which appears in the Ginsberg collection, *Kaddish and Other Poems.* The lion, of course, is the most obvious sort of symbol for Ginsberg's Columbia experience—"Roar, Lion, Roar" and all that—but, characteristically, he treats it as a very real flesh-and-blood lion that invades his room and simply remains there to menace him: " 'Terrible presence!' I cried 'Eat me or die!' " But no. One day the lion leaves: "Pushed the door open and said in a gravelly voice 'Not this time Baby—but I will be back again.' " And the poem ends with four lines of unmistakable, though slightly ambiguous, significance:

> Lion that eats my mind now for a decade knowing only
>     your hunger
> Not the bliss of your satisfaction O roar of the
>     Universe how am I chosen
> In this life I have heard your promise I am ready
>     to die I have served
> Your starved and ancient Presence O Lord I wait in
>     my room at your Mercy.

But whether the lion in the poem referred directly to Mr. Trilling or whether it was meant as a more generalized symbol of Columbia and all the poet associated with that episode in his life does not matter much, for Mrs. Trilling clearly took it all quite personally.

She was, she said, moved by the poem and Ginsberg's dedication of it to Lionel Trilling. She describes coming home after the reading: "There was a meeting going on at home of the pleasant professional sort which, like the comfortable living room in which it usually takes place, at a certain point in a successful modern literary career confirms the writer in his sense of disciplined achievement and well-earned reward." She tells the guests where she has been, and she is chided by one of them, W. H. Auden, when she confesses that she was moved by what she heard. But before she leaves the room she tells her husband, "Allen Ginsberg read a love poem to you, Lionel. I liked it very much." And then she concludes rather coyly, "It was an awkward thing to say in the circumstances, perhaps even a little foolish as an attempt to bridge the unfathomable gap that was all so quickly and meaningfully opening up between the evening that had been and that evening that was now so surely reclaiming me. But I'm certain that Ginsberg's old teacher knew what I was saying, and why I was impelled to say it."

"The Other Night at Columbia: A Report" is, after all, only

16   one essay among scores of pieces written about the same time

on the Beats. Why dwell on it? Because I think its considerable importance lies in what it tells us of the attitude of the New York intellectual community to the Beats and their protest. They saw Ginsberg, Corso, Kerouac, and company not so much as a threat, but as writers of little intrinsic worth whose importance to them lay in their relation as inferiors to the senior group. (And they saw themselves—Mrs. Trilling makes this painfully clear—as defenders of the True Faith.) Or perhaps more realistically, the ultimate significance of the Beats to the Family was that they served them as convenient whipping boys. Everybody—as the saying in Chicago has it—is somebody's nigger. The Beats were theirs.

The single exception here was Norman Mailer, who at the time the Beats appeared on the scene possessed no more than an associate membership in the Family. He was always thought to be a bit extreme, unstable, given to indecorous behavior and vulgar writing. Except for him, the overwhelming majority of the New York intellectuals ranged from indifferent to bitterly hostile in their reaction to the Beat protest.

And yet the Beats survived. They not only survived, they prevailed. Why? And how, when neither Kerouac nor Ginsberg nor any of the rest received much more than muttered encouragement from critics, did they manage to pull off the sort of cultural revolution they boasted they would? If that seems excessive, then just think how different things are today from what they were when the Beats came along. Socially, culturally, even politically, the drift was set long before in their direction. The Beats simply managed to accelerate the pace so wildly that less than a decade after they had begun to amuse the readers of *Time, Life,* and *Newsweek,* America was so radically changed that those who had done the laughing could hardly believe it was the same country. ("Something's happening, but you don't know what it is, do you, Mr. Jones?")

It was not only that they touched something essential and responsive in their younger readers and listeners. The Beats also had behind them the force of a long, rich, and deeply American tradition.

# CHAPTER 2

# An American Protest

No writer of the older generation had a greater or more direct influence on the Beats than did William Carlos Williams. Born in 1883 of an English father and a Puerto Rican mother, he had a long active life as a poet, novelist, and short-story writer, spanning decades, movements, and countermovements, and ending only with his death in 1963. Throughout his life he maintained his poetic gift as few American poets before or after have managed to do—developing it, maturing as a man as he gained in his art. He did his best work in the latter half of his life. He was the poet of the direct statement, the plain man who spoke plainly of the things that mattered most to him. He withstood the influence of Eliot, ignored the New Critics and the academic poets who followed their lead, and simply went his own way, his lines growing shorter, more austere, more pointed with each poem.

In this way, a whole generation of poets grew up looking to William Carlos Williams as an established poet who wrote simply and directly from the heart. His theories of versification greatly influenced Charles Olson in the formulation of his own theory of "projective verse." And the spirit of Williams' poetry permeated that of a great many younger poets—Robert Creeley, Denise Levertov, Robert Duncan, and others of the so-called Black Mountain group. But it is on Allen Ginsberg that his influence was keenest and most certain.

Throughout his career as a poet, William Carlos Williams practiced medicine in Paterson, New Jersey, an industrial suburb of New York City, where Ginsberg was born and grew up. At a very rough period in Ginsberg's life—he had just been thrown out of Columbia University and had spent a short session as a patient in the Columbia Psychiatric Institute—he went to some trouble to meet Dr. Williams. He asked the editors of the Paterson paper to send him to interview the local celebrity. "I was too shy just to see him as a poet, so I went as a kind of humble newsman," Ginsberg told his biographer, Jane Kramer. "We had a lovely conversation, and I began sending him poems and letters about Céline and Burroughs and Kerouac, and all the different influences I was interested in. It was sort of like a big responsibility for Williams—my being a younger poet from Paterson. We'd take walks occasionally. He'd show me his Paterson, and I'd show him what my epiphanous places were. Places like by the river, under the bridge, where I masturbated for the first time. Where I kissed that girl who moved away. Where I saw a gang fight. Where I always felt ashamed for some reason. The hedge where I was lonely. And I showed him the library where I first read Dostoevski. So that while there was like a whole other scene going on in New York—around the Cedar Bar and the San Remo, where all the writers and the abstract expressionists and the musicians were hanging out—which was like a big new influence on me, there was also Williams in Paterson talking about native ground."

And, perhaps surprisingly, the influence was mutual. Allen Ginsberg must have made a deep impression on William Carlos Williams for the older poet, then in the middle of writing his long poem, *Paterson,* introduced him and those walks they took together into the text. The references to the "young poet" and the passages from Ginsberg's letters inserted in the poem clearly suggest that the relationship was just as important to Dr. Williams.

William Carlos Williams was always passionately and self-consciously an *American* poet. Anything but a chauvanist, he resented deeply what was being done *to* America—how the land, the people, and their resources were being plundered for the personal gain of a few—and this resentment spilled out to become one of the dominant themes of *Paterson.* Yes, he cared and thought much about the country and its people, and he was given to sprinkling his writings with abrupt and gratuitous interjections such as "We are a half-mad race, and what we say is not to be trusted." Or, "And this is the opportunity of America! To see large, larger than England can."

He was a man obsessed with America, a poet dedicated to discovering and defining an American tradition. And it is this impulse that quickens that excellent book of his, *In the American Grain*, first published as long ago as 1925. Its brief episodes are not intended so much to recount history as to make it actual, "to re-name the things seen, now lost in chaos of borrowed titles, many of them inappropriate, under which the true character lies hid." And through these vivid scenes, in which we see the figures of such as Eric the Red, Daniel Boone, and George Washington projected against the fluttering backdrop of American history, we also perceive Dr. Williams' intense awareness of the teeming contradictions of American life.

Yes, the contradictions. He later sought to resolve them by organizing them around two opposing principles in an essay of his called "The American Background": "Thus two cultural elements were left battling for supremacy, one looking toward Europe, necessitous but retrograde in its tendency—though not wholly so by any means—and the other forward-looking but under a shadow from the first." Yet this sounds suspiciously as though he were simply balancing the new world against the old. What has he to say about that? "One might go on to develop the point from this that the American addition to world culture will always be the 'new' in opposition to an 'old' represented by Europe. But that isn't satisfactory. What it is actually is something much deeper: a relation to the immediate conditions of the matter in hand, and a determination to assert them in opposition to all intermediate authority. Deep in the pattern of the newcomers' minds was impressed that conflict between present reliance on the prevalent conditions of place and the overriding of an unrelated authority."

Dr. Williams clarifies a great deal simply by suggesting that America's past and present are best understood according to two principles, rather than only one: "two great bands of effort, which it would take a Titan to bring together and weld into one again." This duality is so much a part of America that nearly anyone who has attempted an overview has resorted ultimately to some brand of cultural Manicheism—whether Vernon Parrington with his liberals and reactionaries, Van Wyck Brooks with his highbrows and lowbrows, or Philip Rahv with his palefaces and redskins.

The pull of opposites—it is a fact of American life so evident that to most of us it has come to seem almost palpably real. We feel the "torsion" that William Carlos Williams spoke of in our own contradictory impulses—in the hostile and essentially violent feelings, for example, that overwhelmed many in the peace movement. We see evidence of it in the fissures that seem to be opening up all around us—not only the so-called generation gap, but also the splits between sections of the country, colors of the people, and styles of life here in America. We perceive this persistent pull through our history in the record of the abrupt and traumatic changes in our national temper that we as a people seem condemned to undergo every decade or so.

This pull can be felt, certainly, in all the writings of the Beats, especially in those from the late 1950s onward. There is in them the same keen sense of a past lost and a present squandered that is to be felt in the works of William Carlos Williams. Like him, they were deeply conscious of themselves as *American* writers, and the Beat Generation can only be understood and appreciated in the context of the American literary background.

An accident of time brought a group of young English writers—which their press had dubbed the Angry Young Men —before the public at just about the same moment the Beats came on the scene. There was a great, futile effort to unite the two in some generalization about a great new wave of international protest sweeping the world. One publisher even issued a sort of joint anthology made up of the writing of the two groups that was held together by no more than the weak mucilage of this very premise.

But it wouldn't work. The Angry Young Men—John Wain, Kingsley Amis, John Braine, et al.—were too well rehearsed in their own English tradition ever to try beyond the merest half-hearted echo the sort of metaphysical yowl of protest that came so naturally to the lips of the Beats. They were embarrassed by Jack Kerouac, baffled by Allen Ginsberg and Gregory Corso, frightened by William S. Burroughs, and felt themselves intimidated by Norman Mailer. There is an old scenario of challenge and acceptance that is played out at decent intervals in England. It puts the young outsiders against the old members of the literary establishment in what looks very much like a real rebellion, an every-man-for-himself, free-for-all punch-up that nevertheless always seems to end with the new men being welcomed into the establishment by the old. That process may even be part of what T. S. Eliot described as the interaction of tradition and the individual talent—"What happens is a continual surrender of himself as he is at the moment to something which is more valuable. The progress of an artist is a continual self-sacrifice, a continual extinction of personality"—but it certainly is not protest.

Protest is a word whose meaning has become somewhat twisted through careless use over the years. Its fundamental meaning, of course, is to "witness for" something, to make a solemn affirmation of an idea, a cause, or a proposition. Yet it has now lost its positive connotations almost completely, and today protest is usually understood to mean witnessing *against* something, voicing objections strenuously, noisily, and conspicuously. To accept such a definition completely is to give tacit assent to society's negative view of protest, to cooperate in the judgment of the majority upon the minority. For if it is to have value at all, protest must stand for something positive —if only to the protester himself.

"The notion of the community," Daniel Boorstin tells us, "is one of the most characteristic, one of the most important, yet one of the least noticed American contributions to modern life." Probably so. Boorstin has recently written often and eloquently on this theme, pointing out that mutual dependence enforced by the privations and hardships of the frontier brought the early Americans together into natural social units —communities—long before any sort of firm political identity had been established. Thus communities here had—and to some extent still have—a peculiar strength that derives not just from law but from the power of community opinion. To oppose this power—here we leave Boorstin—meant testing your strength against that community. You may only have been "standing up for your rights" or "voicing an opinion," but before long it was you against them, and you were then engaging in an act of protest, that is, witnessing for yourself, for your beliefs, for your ideas—ultimately, for your right to be different from the rest.

And that, of course, is where the Beats fit in—not just as recent representatives of an odd-ball rebel strain in the American tradition, the latest in a line of eccentrics who have danced a quickstep through American history, hopping along in time to their different drummer. No. For the tradition of protest and dissent, of the beleaguered minority against the majority, the individual against the community—this *is* the American tradition. What worthwhile thing has been accomplished here that was not accomplished by a spirited minority over the reluctant submission of a sullen majority? What American writer worth his salt has not had to struggle against the community that contained him? This was one—perhaps the most abundant—source of "torsion" in the writing of the Beats, and the one that best accounts for the shrill tone of so much of it. The Beats were different from what they saw around them and what they felt smothering them. They knew they were, and they spent a good deal of their time and energy protesting their right to be different.

Related to all this, too, was their vision of the America that could be. Each of them seems to have come separately to some similar notion of the awful gap that lay between promise and fulfillment. And this perception provided them with whatever social "message" they had to offer. And if it was a message that was sometimes put all too artlessly in their work, there were some eloquent and original things said by some of them about all this. Allen Ginsberg, for instance, wrote often on this theme and said some fine things in his poem "America," which comes across simply as a statement of real concern. It begins with lines that seem to echo Jack Kerouac's description of their generation ("a kind of beatness—I mean being right down to it"). But this is Ginsberg:

23

America I've given you all and now I'm nothing.
America two dollars and twentyseven cents January 17, 1956

Starting thus from ground zero, the poem develops into a jeremiad along the lines of "Howl," in which national follies and failings are exposed line by line to Ginsberg's withering scorn. Yet it ends on this somewhat more hopeful note:

I'd better get right down to the job.
It's true I don't want to join the Army or turn lathes in precision
       parts factories, I'm nearsighted and psychopathic anyway.
America I'm putting my queer shoulder to the wheel.

Call it an upbeat ending, if you will—but not a cop-out, for all through the poem can be felt Ginsberg's sense of commitment to the *idea* of America. There is here a kind of dialectic by which he proceeds, careening on, as he does, between reality and possibility—this is what gives the poem its thrust. Its authority comes from Ginsberg's inclusion of himself in his own indictment. Just before he waxes bitterest, he asserts parenthetically:

I'm addressing you.
Are you going to let your emotional life be run by Time Magazine?
I'm obsessed by Time Magazine.
I read it every week.
Its cover stares at me every time I slink past the corner
       candystore.
I read it in the basement of the Berkeley Public Library.
It's always telling me about responsibility. Businessmen
       are serious.
     Movie producers are serious. Everybody's serious but me.
It occurs to me that I am America.
I am talking to myself again.

All of this sounds a little like Walt Whitman—"It occurs to me that I am America"—revised and updated: the great, gray poet given an unceremonious goose.

    Allen Ginsberg has, of course, been so often likened to Whitman that there is really not much reason to make the point again—that is, *unless* we can draw something new from such a comparison. I think we can. What needs to be emphasized finally is the extent to which Ginsberg consciously imitated Whitman in a number of ways. The Whitman influence was there in the poetry, of course, and was particularly strong at the time the early collection, *Howl and Other Poems*, came out. It can be seen particularly in the long lines and the hortatory style of most of these poems, and in the eager way that the young poet seeks out the very greatest themes on which to make the very largest pronouncements. One of these poems, "A Supermarket in California," is even addressed to Whitman —quite appropriately, as it turns out, for it concludes with just the sort of *quo vadimus* apostrophe that Whitman himself, the newspaper editorial writer, was so fond of:

Where are we going, Walt Whitman? The doors close in
an hour. Which way does your beard point tonight?
    (I touch your book and dream of our odyssey in the
supermarket and feel absurd.)
    Will we walk all night through solitary streets? The trees add
shade to shade, lights out in the houses, we'll both be lonely.
    Will we stroll dreaming of the lost America of love
past blue automobiles in driveways, home to our silent cottage?
    Ah, dear father, graybeard, lonely old courage-teacher,
what America did you have when Charon quit poling his ferry
and you got out on a smoking bank and stood watching the boat
disappear on the black waters of Lethe?

Yet there is in this—as in all these poems, even including the brutal "Howl"—a kind of facetiousness, an ironic self-consciousness, a continuing sense communicated by the poetry that the poet himself is playing a role.

And the role that Ginsberg plays is the one described at great length by Walt Whitman in his rambling Preface to the first (1855) edition of *Leaves of Grass*—the role of the American poet. Old Walt has such an exalted—even inflated—notion of the poet's vocation that he seems to glorify this new breed of supermen out of all measure: "The American poets are to enclose old and new for America is the race of races. Of them a bard is to be commensurate with a people." And of the poet, "His brain is the ultimate brain. He is no arguer . . . he is judgment. He judges not as the judge judges but as the sun falling around a helpless thing." And again, further on: "He is a seer. . . . he is individual . . . he is complete in himself . . . the others are as good as he, only he sees it and they do not. He is not one of the chorus. . . . he does not stop for any regulation . . . he is the president of regulation." And on and on. He gushed unconscionably, of course, but it was always possible to forgive him, for he truly believed it all, and what is more, he acted on his beliefs.

Allen Ginsberg believed it, too, and perhaps—even probably—still does. Although, as we shall see, he is less inclined today to stress in his own work the sense of national identity that so obsessed Walt Whitman, he is certainly willing to accept the idea of the poet as judge, as prophet and seer. And in the 1950s, of course, he was more than willing to accept this notion; he embraced it and to some extent rearranged himself to suit it. From his college days to the present, in fact, the very real alterations that have taken place in Ginsberg's personality have had the effect of bringing him closer and closer to the Whitman ideal—and even to the Whitman image. Lately, with his flowing beard and balding pate, he has even come to resemble old Walt physically. Just remember that picture of Allen Ginsberg in the Uncle Sam hat.

Why Whitman? What was his attraction for Ginsberg? It must have been partly, let us be frank, because of Walt's supposed homosexuality. There are, after all, no two poets in English who show themselves to be more body conscious than this Jew and this Quaker who were born within a hundred miles of one another but nearly a hundred years apart. To read either of them is to feel oneself overwhelmed by the pressing flesh and breathing closeness of the poet between the lines. Ginsberg's poems sometimes give the impression that they are just the sort Whitman himself might have written had he survived into an age of more liberal expression. Allen Ginsberg himself once suggested something quite like this in an interview: "Whitman was constantly reflecting his subjective nature, and if you read Whitman aloud, it's pretty shocking. And he also had to deal with the repression of the time, and I don't.

We have fought against that and beaten it down."

But sexuality aside, what then? What was it that drew Ginsberg to Whitman when the latter was being so diligently discredited by so many? At the moment Ginsberg embraced him, after all, Walt was considered at worst a charlatan and at best an embarrassment. To some extent it must have been this very unpopularity, the disrepute into which the old poet's name had fallen, that initially attracted Allen Ginsberg to Walt Whitman. His intuition may indeed have followed the line that any poet whom Lionel Trilling so despised might be worth looking into.

And having looked, he must have been attracted by the very American-ness of Walt's poetry—its loose, plain quality and its apparent artlessness, the way that it shucked off the outer restraints and so gladly accepted those imposed from within. But it must finally have been Whitman's vision of America that won Ginsberg over, for he saw it as the great land of the openhanded, where men could speak openly to one another without being thought gauche or vulgar:

> To be absolv'd from previous ties and conventions, I from
> mine and you from yours!
> To find a new unthought—of nonchalance with the best of Na-
> ture!
> To have the gag remov'd from one's mouth!

That is Whitman, of course, but it could well be Ginsberg, too, for this passage became a sort of motto by which to interpret his role in the whole Beat movement. Walt became for Ginsberg a kind of model as the great American truth-sayer, the man who never hesitated to speak frankly. And in no time Allen Ginsberg became a kind of Walt Whitman to them all— the inspired blabberer of the Beat Generation and a favorite of every reporter and tape-recording critic who pursued them, for he would have thought it an absolute sin to mutter a cold "no comment" to another human being and simply walk on. To this day, he nurtures a deep and very real belief in the spiritual efficacy of direct and open communication. He sees in it the future of America and the hope for the survival of the world.

And if Allen Ginsberg was the Beat Generation's Walt Whitman, then Gary Snyder was its Henry David Thoreau. Or, to put it even more emphatically, Snyder is the present generation's Thoreau, for far from diminishing, his popular influence has increased over the last ten years. It would be wrong to speak of him in the past tense; as a poet, he is better known and more widely respected today than any other associated with the Beat movement. It is worth mentioning that he is given an enthusiastic presentation in Richard Howard's study of the post-1950 generation of American poets, *Alone with America*. And because it supports my Thoreau thesis so well, it seems worth quoting a sentence from Mr. Howard's eloquent and energetic essay on Snyder: "We are reminded that Snyder is the true heir of that Thoreau who retired to Walden in order to discover the meaning of the word 'property' and found it meant only what was proper or essential to unbound human life."

Yes, Gary Snyder has become a sort of prophet of the essential in human life, and in his own way a great liberator, too. His concern with ecology and the physical environment of America—to cite an important example—is not just fashionably recent. It is and has been as fundamental to his own thought and expression as it was to Thoreau's a hundred years before. And he, unlike Thoreau, was born to the pioneer life. Gary Snyder's childhood in Oregon was lived by necessity under the same sort of backwoods circumstances that Thoreau set about rather programmatically to create for himself at Walden Pond, which was two miles from his mother's home in Concord, Massachusetts.

As Jack Kerouac first described him to the world, Gary Snyder was a poet of many and impressive parts. He "was a kid from eastern Oregon brought up in a log cabin deep in the woods with his father and mother and sister, from the beginning a woods boy, an axman, farmer, interested in animals and Indian lore so that when he finally got to college by hook or crook he was already well equipped for his early studies in anthropology and later in Indian myth and in actual texts of Indian mythology. Finally he learned Chinese and Japanese and became an Oriental scholar and discovered the greatest

Dharma Bums of them all, the Zen lunatics of China and Japan. At the same time, being a Northwest boy with idealistic tendencies, he got interested in old-fashioned I.W.W. anarchism and learned to play the guitar and sing old worker songs to go with his Indian songs and general folksong interests."

The tipoff phrase here, of course, is "Dharma Bums," for that is the title of the novel from which this passage has been lifted. And the character thus described is Japhy Ryder, a name that translates directly from Kerouacese as Gary Snyder. (The phrase "Dharma hobos," incidentally, occurs in Snyder's own notebooks as early as 1956, roughly the same year covered by Kerouac in his novel.) *The Dharma Bums* is that most selfless act of creation, a book about a friend, and reading it should make clear the important influence that Snyder had not just on Kerouac, but on the whole Beat movement.

This importance has not been sufficiently appreciated. The reason for this, I think, is that during the time the Beat Generation was most avidly publicized, Snyder was out of the country. He was neither seen nor interviewed by most of those writers and reporters who were sent out to San Francisco to get that story. He was in the Orient—in Japan most of the time, and some of that in a Buddhist monastery in Kyoto. But he was on hand to greet Allen Ginsberg when Ginsberg arrived in India and to show him around the country.

And that, symbolically, was what Gary Snyder did for many of the Beats and for many times more of the generation that followed them: he introduced them to the East. It was his influence, more than Kenneth Rexroth's and certainly more than Alan Watts' (who was really outside the Beat circle), that was responsible for the introduction of the distinct taste of the East that flavored the whole Beat movement. His anecdotes and poems of the wandering Zen Buddhist monks, those original "truth bums," had immense appeal to this bunch of born wanderers. They gave a sense of intellectual, even religious justification to the Beats' deep natural impulse to freedom, their wish to stay unattached and on the move.

Anyone who supposes Gary Snyder's Oriental proclivity separated him from the American literary mainstream in general, or from Henry David Thoreau in particular, simply has no appreciation of the widespread early influence of eastern philosophy and religion on our literature. Most of this, of course, came from the Transcendentalists, and chiefly from Emerson. His idea of the "Over-Soul" as God, an idea which Thoreau accepted, was largely borrowed from the Hindus. And Thoreau himself was a great reader of and quoter from the *Bhagavad-Gita*. In his first book, *A Week on the Concord and Merrimack Rivers*, for instance, there is a lengthy comparison of that Hindu holy book with the New Testament, that he sums up: "The New Testament is remarkable for its pure morality; the best of the Hindu scripture for its pure intellectuality. The reader is nowhere raised into and sustained in a higher, purer, or *rarer* region of thought than in the *Bhagavad-Gita.*" And then, taking this as his opportunity to quote passages at length, he concludes, "Beside the vast and cosmoganal philosophy of the *Bhagavad-Gita*, even our Shakespeare seems sometimes youthfully green." This dialectic between East and West is maintained through all Thoreau's work, and it is certainly true that he would not have written the books he did were it not for his reading of Confucius and the Hindu holy books. There is some justice, however, for eventually the debt was repaid to the East. Thoreau's famous essay, "On Civil Disobedience," when it was first read by Mohandas K. Gandhi, became the basis for the Mahatma's whole philosophy of passive resistance.

In just such a way, too, there has been a continual conversation between East and West in the work of Gary Snyder. Both voices in this dialogue are rightly his own. And although the accents of the Orient have been learned, they are no less properly his. A man of remarkable intellect and flexibility, he seems less interested in hammering out a snythesis drawn from the best of East and West, than he does simply in containing both within himself. There is a key passage in Snyder's essay, "Buddhism and the Coming Revolution," that suggests the width and power of his embrace: "The mercy of the West has been social revolution; the mercy of the East has been individual insight into the basic self/void. We need both. They are both contained in the traditional three aspects of the Dharma path: wisdom (prajna), meditation (dhyana), and morality (sila)."

He is one of the very few American contemporary poets who can speak with authority about wisdom. For he seems to possess it to some degree himself. There is a plain-speaking quality to his poetry that suggests this. The large thoughts and bold statements of his essays certainly support it. And a face-to-face encounter with him leaves no doubt.

I met Gary Snyder in front of his small apartment in an old but well-kept frame house on Pine Street in San Francisco's Japanese section. Even a casual passer-by would have noticed him that afternoon, for here was a wiry, bearded man of indeterminate age washing a Volkswagen bus at the curb—and washing it in the single-minded way of a man who fully enjoys what he is doing and doesn't mind getting himself wet in the bargain. By the time I arrive on the scene, in fact, he is pretty well soaked. Barefoot, sailor's blue denims rolled up to his knees, he splashes and hoses away until the job is done and then turns to me, makes a pass at drying his palm on his shirt, then gives me a firm, wet handshake.

Inside his place, he introduces me to his wife Masa, and then excuses himself to change into something dry. In stocking feet I follow Masa Snyder into their small living room and take the place on the pillow and mat she indicates for me. She excuses herself and leaves me alone to register my impressions of the place.

It is quite a room. There are Japanese prints around the room and a scroll or two, and this seems quite proper; yet opposite them on another wall are a coyote pelt and a bracket-mounted Winchester 30-30 carbine, that seems equally in place. There is a typewriter in one corner, but it is set on a very low Japanese writing table of no more than a foot and a half in height. There is a tea table of about the same size and shape in the middle of the room and no other furniture except, of course, for the bookcases. And of course there are many, many books in them, about half of them in Japanese (including, as it turns out, a translation of *The Commonsense Book of Child Care* by Dr. Benjamin Spock); those in English are works on the American Indian, and a few basic items like *The Standard Dictionary of Folklore*, and yes, there is also *Walden* by Henry David Thoreau.

Gary Snyder comes in and takes a place across the tea table from me. As we talk—at least in the beginning—he has the rather disconcerting habit of performing stretching exercises, sitting cross-legged before me, pushing and pulling away with his arms and shoulders. To him, at least, there seems nothing remarkable in this, for he gives the impression that he does this sort of thing during most of his "idle" moments.

I asked him about his own background, what it had been like growing up as he did where he did. "I always think of mine as a very typical western family," he explains. "Although probably it was not. My grandfather homesteaded in Kitsap County, Washington and that's where my father was born. My mother's family was from down around Leadville, Colorado, although she was born in Texas. They were all westerners, though. My father's five brothers were seamen. He was a logger. My mother's brothers were all railroad men.

"Formative influences?"—he grinned through his beard—"well, that's kind of funny. I guess my grandfather, the one up in Washington, was pretty important. He was a Wobbly, dues-paying member of the Industrial Workers of the World—that was from back in his days as a logger—and he voted straight socialist as long as he had the chance. The old I. W. W. mythology became very important to me as I grew up in the Northwest. But these were all romantic feelings and a little confused. As a matter of fact, I remember that in my mid-twenties I felt sort of torn apart because I was drawn in two different directions. On the one hand I identified with the I.W.W. and the frontier, and all those good old feelings about the American West. And on the other hand I had a deep admiration for the American Indians. It was a very interesting conflict while it lasted. But I finally kicked the whole thing and joined the Indians."

Gary Snyder's interest in the American Indians, their folk-lore and religion, and his sympathy for the Indian way of life led him eventually to consider Oriental culture. He recalls that he was in San Francisco then in 1952, working on the docks and backpacking in all directions on weekends during the good months. It was then he decided he would like to go to Japan and enrolled at Berkeley to learn Japanese and Chinese.

While he was there at the University of California, he met his first poets—Kenneth Rexroth, and through him, Allen Ginsberg and Jack Kerouac. And although he was writing poetry himself, what involved him most at this juncture, was sorting out his own feelings of alienation from Western culture, from his own background. Gary Snyder, who had sprung from pioneer stock and who had come about as close to living the pioneer life as anyone of his generation could, began to regard the whole frontier ethos with some degree of suspicion as "basically mercantile." It seemed important to him at that time in his life to choose something different.

"That choice took the form for me of going to study Buddhism in Japan," he explains. "It was sort of a symbolic journey, I'll admit." He had even then begun to perceive relations, a cultural continuity that he would eventually trace in one of his more important essays, "Passage to More Than India," and dub the "Great Subculture." This subculture's characteristics, as he describes them, are a tribal social structure, a deep respect for man's natural surroundings, and religion that sees God immanent in all nature.

"I guess I wanted to go to Japan, because I wanted to go some place where all this has been developed to a sophisticated level. And I was deeply attracted to Zen Buddhism because of all this. But I see the subculture, of course, as not just in Japan, but a very prevalent, a very widespread thing. It certainly is in the East. In Chinese civilization this can be found very well expressed in Taoism. And today the kids right here in San Francisco and all over the West are embracing tribalism of a kind. I think these elements are all fundamentally interconnected. And I think that certainly for me the American Indians are important in understanding these things and how they relate to each other. It was through them and what I saw in them that I got into all this in the first place. Now that I've come back from Japan, my most pressing desire is to go back to the American Indian thing and try to fit some more of the pieces together."

Masa Snyder came in with tea. She served it quietly and with a minimum of ceremony, taking time to sit at the table and have a cup with us. She listened quietly and intently as her husband talked and only left us when there came from the rear of the house the persistant sounds of their son waking from his afternoon nap.

Gary Snyder talked on, nodding his wife out as she left silently, and then stopping for a moment to consider a question I had just put to him. I had asked if he felt there were something in Western culture that was fundamentally inimical to the Great Subculture he had described.

"No," he said at last, "I don't think so, because there has been an ecologically responsible thread in Western culture all along. You can see it popping up all sorts of places—with the Romantic poets in England, and with our nineteenth-century poets—the Transcendentalists, and Whitman, and of course it's very strong in Thoreau. Oh, and let me see, where else? In the seventeenth century, the Diggers who were a sort of anarchistic communal organization from whom the hippies have taken their other name. And you can see it in the witchcraft cult, too. No, I don't mean the black magic and all those anti-Christian elements, but purged of that, you had in the witchcraft cult a fundamental nature religion that was really older than Christianity, may indeed have gone back to neolithic times.

"In a very real sense, I think this constitutes another culture. These are not altogether unconnected, isolated instances that appear at random, but a strong, basic strain running underground in Western culture and surfacing from time to time. I think there's a continuity here. And the reason it's surfaced in this particular moment in time is that just now people are feeling threatened. There is an instinct for survival involved here."

I asked him if the Indians fit into all this in some special way.

"Oh," he said, "in a very special way—that is, for us. Americans. Here and now. I think the Indians are going to show us the next stage of this other culture. But of course if we had only looked before, they could have shown us earlier. We really had such an opportunity to learn from them—because, of course, the Indian was more civilized than the frontiersmen were when they came along. He lived more cleanly and more intelligently. Indians were well disciplined. They had beautiful, simple homes, and they took baths. And that's more than you could say for most white men back then out on the frontier. They were so busy looting, killing, and cheating the Indians and each other that they didn't take time to find out how to live in this land they were grabbing.

"No, the Indians certainly didn't see the best of the white race. And all this—the Indians and what we did to them—it's coming back to us, you see. It's our Karma as Americans."

I asked him to explain.

"Well, in simpleminded terms it means that when you've done something wrong to someone or something you have to pay them back. And it has to do with the idea that one of the ways an obligation of this sort is discharged is by becoming like that which has been wronged. You see what I mean about the Indians being important to us now?"

Gary Snyder wasn't just talking. He planned to act upon this in a very personal, practical way. He explained that at the end of the week he would be moving his wife and child to a new home in Sierra County, California. "It's just some acres of wilderness I bought with a cabin on it. But I want to get us out there, so we can begin to learn to break the habits of dependence. It's important for me. I think it will mean more consciousness, more awareness. And nothing has more value for the individual than his consciousness, intensifying and refining it."

Or, as he might put it today if you asked him why he took to that cabin in Sierra County:

I went to the woods because I wished to live deliberately, to front only the essential facts of life, and see if I could not learn what it had to teach, and not, when I came to die, discover that I had not lived. I did not wish to live what was not life, living is so dear; nor did I wish to practise resignation, unless it was quite necessary. I wanted to live deep and suck out all the marrow of life, to live so sturdily and Spartanlike as to put to rout all that was not life, to cut a broad swath and shave close, to drive life into a corner, and reduce it to its lowest terms, and, if it proved to be mean, why then to get the whole and genuine meanness of it, and publish its meanness to the world; or if it were sublime, to know it by experi-

35

ence, and to be able to give a true account of it in my next excursion. . . .

But Gary Snyder did not put it that way. Henry David Thoreau did, in explaining why he had gone off to live at Walden Pond.

It may not be literally true, as Ernest Hemingway said it was true, that "all modern American literature comes from one book by Mark Twain called *Huckleberry Finn,*" but nevertheless, there is no denying that that novel has had an influence that is both widespread and deep. For we see in Twain's account of Huck's adventures the purest early treatment of the initiation myth that has been so often repeated through American literature right on through to the present. What happens in the novel of initiation? A young man goes on a trip and learns something. This, in infinite variations and forms, is surely what people mean when they talk about that glittering ideal, the Great American Novel.

What is it that Huck learns on that long journey down the big river? Fundamentally, he learns about freedom, for that, to oversimplify shamefully, is what *The Adventures of Huckleberry Finn* is all about. It communicates the subjective reality, the feeling of it, about as well as any book could any theme so large and amorphous. The metaphors are there, all right, just where you might expect to find them: Jim, who accompanies Huck on that trip down the river, is an escaped slave on the run for his freedom, and Huck himself is a runaway, who leaves after elaborately arranging proof of his own "death." They are fugitives, and together they move through one adventure after another, seeking no more than just to get away a little farther down the river. But it is not their adventures we remember, but *them,* the boy and the black man floating down the Mississippi on that raft. That is the image, the long moment projected by the book. But why? After all, nothing *happens* to them out on the river. The danger is all on the shore, and that is where their adventures take place. But the journey on the river—that is what Mark Twain makes real to us here, an abstract made actual, freedom as a trip out of time, without responsibility.

Once their time on the river is done, their freedom ends with it. Huck finds himself thrust once more back into the community from which he and Jim had thought to have made good their escape. It is too much for him. He finds himself surrounded and stifled by the town and its people, and he vows (in what must be by now the most famous passage in all of American literature) to get out once again, to head west for the freedom of the frontier: "But I reckon I got to light out for the Territory ahead of the rest, because Aunt Sally she's going to adopt me and sivilize me, and I can't stand it. I been there before—"

It is easy to see Jack Kerouac in all this, for it was his refusal to be "sivilized" that sent him out on the road, where he made a Mississippi of those long, broad highways leading west. There was always a clear and conscious affinity in Kerouac's work for Mark Twain and his Huck. But he, of course, is certainly not the *only* writer to show such an affinity. There is, in fact, a whole hobo tradition in American literature that stems from *The Adventures of Huckleberry Finn.* Writers as widely different as Ernest Hemingway and Saul Bellow have celebrated Huck's brand of freedom in their fiction. Hemingway's Nick Adams, in many ways his most attractive hero, can be followed through a series of short stories—feeling, experiencing, observing—yet always on the bum, unattached, refusing to become involved. Free. And Saul Bellow's Augie March, of course. Augie is the very personification of this spirit—this "Columbus of those near-at-hand," restless, moving, consciously and willfully independent. *The Adventures of Augie March*—see how Bellow parodies Twain in the title?—contains one adventure that is perhaps the most satisfying of all, a sort of epiphany in parenthesis among the rest. It is Augie's own sad sample of the hobo life—riding the box cars and thumbing the highway on his way back from Buffalo—and his only brush with the criminal life. A depression Huck Finn, down but not out, up by the count of seven.

In addition, you find the hobo in all the places you would logically expect to find him—in Jack London's novels and documentaries, in the proletarian fiction of the 1930s (Jack

Conroy's *The Disinherited* is about the best and most accessible example of the type), in Steinbeck, and in James Jones, and Nelson Algren's novels of the depression, *Somebody in Boots* and *Walk on the Wild Side,* and on and on through Thomas Pynchon's *V,* and the late Richard Fariña's *Been Down So Long It Looks Like Up to Me.* Jump to film, and you see in Dennis Hopper's *Easy Rider* that the hobo style Huck set a hundred years ago still has plenty of life left in it. Captain America and Billy, vagrant, rootless, and free, could, would, and in a sense always will be Huck and Nigger Jim. The America they were looking for as they cruised the highways on their bikes was the one that Mark Twain knew.

Look where you will today, that America is getting harder and harder to find. And nobody knew that better than Jack Kerouac:

> The American Hobo is on the way out as long as sheriffs operate with as Louis-Ferdinand Céline said, "One line of crime and nine of boredom," because having nothing to do in the middle of the night with everybody gone to sleep they pick on the first human being they see walking. —They pick on lovers on the beach even. They just don't know what to do with themselves in those five-thousand dollar police cars with the two-way Dick Tracy radios except pick on anything that moves in the night and in the daytime on anything that seems to be moving independently of gasoline, power, Army or police. —I myself was a hobo but I had to give it up around 1956 because of increasing television stories about the abominableness of strangers with packs passing through by themselves independently. —I was surrounded by three squad cars in Tucson Arizona at 2 A.M. as I was walking pack-on-back for a night's sweet sleep in the red moon desert:
> "Where you goin'?"
> "Sleep."
> "Sleep where?"
> "On the sand."
> "Why?"
> "Got my sleeping bag."
> "Why?"
> "Studyin' the great outdoors."
> "Who are you? Let's see your identification."
> "I just spent a summer with the Forest Service."
> "Did you get paid?"

"Yeah."

"Then why don't you go to a hotel?"

"I like it better outdoors and it's free."

"Why?"

"Because I'm studying hobo."

"What's so good about that?"

They wanted an *explanation* for my hoboing and came close to hauling me in but I was sincere with them and they ended up scratching their heads and saying "Go ahead if that's what you want." —They didnt offer me a ride four miles into the desert.

Yes, as he warned us in the last line of that excellent piece on "The Vanishing American Hobo" from which I have quoted here, "The woods are full of wardens."

How well Jack Kerouac knew it, and how bitterly he must have regretted it. For he was never more himself and never wrote with more passionate enthusiasm than when he was recounting those hours and days he spent as a hobo out on the road. No writer better than he has ever infused travel—simply getting from one place to another—with such a keen sense of adventure. It is not that what he sees or does along the way is ever especially marvelous; he makes the mere going *seem* marvelous. You can look for a bit of this in nearly every book of Jack Kerouac's—in *Desolation Angels, The Dharma Bums,* and certainly in *On the Road,* nearly every page of it.

There must be nearly a hundred quotably eloquent examples of Kerouac on the art of travel. And in all of them there is such freedom, such an obvious feeling of optimism and joy that it seems almost superfluous to emphasize the deeply and specifically American quality that permeates all his writing. He is what the Beats have most in common with Mark Twain, the Wobblies, Jack London, and all those hobo heroes of American literature. Kerouac, his prodigious memory and his automatic typewriter—without them, America seems not quite as large as before.

# CHAPTER 3

# Between the Sputter
# and the Boom

Those who like to fix dates, who feel it their duty to assign precise beginnings and ends to literary movements and moments, are sure to have some difficulties with the chronology of the Beat Generation. The question is *when* did it all start? Was it in 1955 at that famous reading at the Six Gallery in San Francisco when Allen Ginsberg first proclaimed "Howl" to an astonished, wine-bibbing multitude? Or was it earlier, much earlier, in New York, when the right people got together and found in each other the proper elements for the catalyst, and set swirling into motion all the conflict, love, and psychic energy necessary to sustain a group effort as large and important as this one? What were things like in those years following the first sputter of that long fuse that led up to that big boom at the Six? What happened in the time between?

Jack Kerouac and Allen Ginsberg met in 1945 at Kerouac's place somewhere near the Columbia University campus. Both had been hanging out at the West End bar nearby and had become acquainted independently with William S. Burroughs who also lived nearby. At Burroughs' urging, Ginsberg came by one morning to meet Kerouac, evidently with some trepidation, for he opened the door, stuck his head in, and, according to Kerouac, said, "Well, discretion is the better part of valor." He saw the expression on Kerouac's face and ducked out again. Kerouac, who had seen him around and knew who he was, said, "Aw, shut up, you little twitch." At that, Ginsberg came back into the room giggling. Auspicious the occasion may have been. Solemn it was not.

At that time Jack Kerouac would have inspired awe college freshman, and certainly did in sixteen-year-old Ginsberg. He had come to Columbia five years before on a football scholarship, had his leg broken during a game, and decided without much more ado to chuck football altogether. So he lost his football scholarship and, it being 1942, enlisted in the Navy. But the U.S. Navy took a good hard look at Jack Kerouac and discharged him as a schizoid personality. The merchant marine, he thought, was almost as good, and so he got his A.B. papers and began to make a habit of the dangerous Murmansk run. This saw him through the war, and along the way, some time in 1944, he got married during one of his weeks in port. The war ended, he returned with his wife to Columbia, full of resolve to get himself an education and become a great writer. But neither his marriage nor his pass at education lasted long. His wife left him after six months, and shortly afterward he dropped out of Columbia. But the ambition to be a great writer remained. It was all Kerouac talked about in those days. When he was not raving about the glorious prose of Thomas Wolfe, he was at home trying to produce a reasonable facsimile of it on his own typewriter. That was what he was doing when Ginsberg stuck his head in the door and interrupted him that morning.

Allen Ginsberg, described by Kerouac as "a freshman with his ears sticking out at the time," was then well on his way to acquiring the mad genius label he wore so proudly at Columbia. Although he was a straight A student, then a history major intending to go to law school, he had had a number of scrapes with the dean of Columbia College due to his sloppy appearance and eccentric behavior. Kerouac liked him. The two saw a lot of each other in the months that followed their meeting and became fast friends. When Kerouac fell behind on his rent and was turned out of his apartment, Ginsberg invited him to stay as long as he needed in his Columbia dormitory room. Kerouac, no longer a student at Columbia, was found there the morning that Allen Ginsberg was kicked out of Columbia—the first time.

41      This was not because of Kerouac's unauthorized overnight

stay in the room—a minor infraction worth only a modest fine —but the outcome of a long war of nerves Ginsberg had been waging against the dormitory's Irish cleaning woman. She wouldn't touch his room. She seemed to feel it was too dirty even to bother with. He called her bluff by drawing a few rather explicit pictures in the film of dust that covered the window. But that didn't work. She kept right on ignoring his room, window and all. Finally, in desperation, he etched "Fuck the Jews" deep in the window dust. That worked. That very morning he was hailed before the dean, suspended, and barely given time to pack before he was hustled off the campus.

But by that time it hardly mattered, for he was getting his real education, as opposed to his formal one, from Kerouac, William S. Burroughs, and the gang that hung out with them. Although older than Kerouac or Ginsberg, Burroughs himself had done very little writing at this time. The scion of the Burroughs adding machine family, he had graduated from Harvard in 1936 and had just sort of hung around Boston and New York since that time, meeting people, investigating what interested him, and improving his knowledge in areas such as anthropology, semantics, and psychoanalysis. He was a far better educated man than most of Ginsberg's teachers at Columbia. He was at that time also a heroin addict.

It was Jack Kerouac, according to Ginsberg, who turned Burroughs on to writing. Kerouac had such bubbling enthusiasm for it all that he managed to pursuade Burroughs to collaborate with him on a detective novel in the style of Dashiell Hammett, a Burroughs favorite. They kept at it, writing alternate chapters until Kerouac became too deeply involved in his own novel, *The Town and the City*, to keep it up.

Yes, perhaps in spite of everything, some writing got done. There were plenty of distractions. Burroughs was psychoanalyzing Kerouac and Ginsberg. He had met a Times Square hustler, a desperate, end-of-the-tether intellectual named Herbert Huncke, and brought him to live with them all there. Huncke, an addict and a part-time researcher on the original Kinsey Report, brought through the place a steady succession of petty and not-so-pretty criminals, sex deviates, and desperate men. For Ginsberg, no less for Kerouac, it was quite an education. And what should perhaps be emphasized here is that it *was* an education: neither of them became narcotics addicts, nor did they become criminals. No, they managed to learn from the afflictions of their teachers—in what was perhaps a rather ruthless way—without themselves becoming infected. By the time Ginsberg had sat out his suspension and had been readmitted into Columbia, he was a much different, much wiser, young man.

Gregory Corso made a late arrival on the scene. He did not meet Allen Ginsberg until 1950, and that was by chance at a bar in the Village. "I'd just come out of prison in Clinton, New York," he remembers. "I'd been in from the time I was sixteen until I was nineteen. So in a way I was just a kid, but I was a kid who knew a lot because in prison these were men, by God, and I had to learn to make my own way. I did, and I also started writing poetry in prison."

And so, with the prison experience under his belt and his poems in his pocket, Corso found himself accosted one night in a place called the Pony Stable by a horn-rimmed, bushy-haired Columbia student named Allen Ginsberg. In the way that only he can, Ginsberg swarmed over him, broke down his defenses with his enthusiasm, and soon had Corso admitting that yes, he had written some poems, too, and, well, he supposed it would be all right if somebody took a look at them.

They exchanged manuscripts, and then, according to Jane Kramer's *Allen Ginsberg in America*, Gregory Corso told Ginsberg of his secret, voyeuristic love for a young lady who lived across the street from his room in the Village. He had watched her faithfully every night as she undressed and performed "sexy and complicated dances" before a big mirror in her room. It was, it seemed, just about time for the performance to begin. Would Ginsberg, he asked shyly, care to come up to his room for a look? Ginsberg came along, the young lady made her appearance, and she turned out to be an old girl friend of his. Immediately, he took Corso across the street and introduced him to her. What better circumstances for a meeting of poets?

The most vivid, detailed, and colorful account of the group during this period can be found in John Clellon Holmes' excellent novel, *Go*. Rather than carefully observed and minutely descriptive, *Go* is filled with the pulse and drive that can be sensed in all the best Beat writing. Holmes' portraits of Kerouac and Ginsberg, quick sketches though they be, are probably more frankly accurate than any others available. Here he is, for instance, on David Stofsky, who is quite clearly recognizable as Allen Ginsberg:

> It was Stofsky's habit to burst in full of news, for he was one of those young men who seem always to be dashing around the city from apartment to apartment, friend to friend; staying a few moments to gossip and ingratiate, and then running off again. Although he had no job, his days were crowded with vague appointments up and downtown, and for a large group of people he was the unofficial bearer of all sorts of tidings. His sources were multitudinous and his candor so infectious that it made the more suspicious of his friends question his motives. When entering a room full of people, for instance, he would pass from one to the other, shaking hands with mock gravity, then go directly up to someone he did not know, and say, eyes twinkling with excitement behind the heavy horned-rims: "You're so-and-so, aren't you? Well, I'm David Stofsky. I know *all* about you!" This was said with such eager, guileless smiles that it annoyed almost no one.

Although no single paragraph quite so neatly presents *Go*'s Gene Pasternak, who is identifiable as Jack Kerouac, Pasternak plays a more important role in the novel. He is the foil for the protagonist Paul Hobbes—John Clellon Holmes himself?— natural man to his neurotic, vigorously masculine to Hobbes' neuter, active to his passive. He is above all a *physical* presence, and to Holmes, as to most of the others who knew him then, what evidently seemed most impressive about Kerouac was the way that his impressive physical force—remember, he was a football player and one good enough to attract Lou Little's interest back in the days when they were still producing All-Americans at Columbia—was matched by his intellectual hunger and creative energy. In this, there seemed something peculiarly and purely American.

Much later, John Clellon Holmes put all this quite explicitly in an excellent essay on Kerouac, "The Great Rememberer," in which he calls him "the kind of writer only America could produce, and that only America could so willfully misunderstand." He goes on in that piece to describe the Kerouac of the late 1940s, the period that *Go* covers:

> He was open-hearted, impulsive, candid and very handsome. He didn't seem like any other writer that I knew. He wasn't wary, opinionated, cynical or competitive, and if I hadn't already known him by reputation, I would have pegged him as a poetic lumberjack, or a sailor with Shakespeare in his sea locker. Melville, armed with the manuscript of *Typee*, must have struck the Boston Brahmins in much the same way. Stocky, medium-tall, Kerouac had the tendoned forearms, heavily muscled thighs and broad neck of a man who exults in his physical life.

By this time, Jack Kerouac had already completed *The Town and the City*, and Holmes had read it and was filled with genuine admiration for him. *Go* is filled with that admiration, just as it is filled to bursting with the sense of breathless excitement that Holmes truly felt at being in New York at that moment, at seeing something important take shape—he thought of it as the birth of a new sensibility, a whole new way of feeling—and at being a part of all this himself.

That is what *Go* is about, the new sensibility. Beat. It is perhaps less a novel than one young man's testimony on the turmoil he sensed bubbling around him in the members of his generation. It has no plot in the formal sense, but is rather a chronicle of events—pot parties, intense conversations, confrontations, adventures, and misadventures. The only real development in the novel is Paul Hobbes' gradual estrangement from his wife Kathryn. And in the last scene of the book, as the two of them huddle together on the deck of the ferry peering at the New York skyline (ah, Gotham!), they leave us with the feeling even here that their troubles are less personal than they are the merest sympathetic vibrations set in motion by all the trouble stirring around them. Elsewhere and elsewhen, it

45

might have been different between them.

*Go* is an important book to the Beat movement. Not merely because of the historical interest of the details it provides in such abundance—in addition to those of Ginsberg and Kerouac, you will find recognizable portraits of Herbert Hucke, Neal Cassady, and William S. Burroughs in the book, and there are reasonably accurate accounts of some of Ginsberg's wild early adventures—but it is also important because by any accurate standard, it must be considered the first Beat novel. Jack Kerouac's *The Town and the City* had appeared, it is true, two years before *Go* was published in 1952, but the two books are about as different as they can be. That first novel of Kerouac's should always be set apart from his others, an anomalously "straight" novel that has not much in common with the screaming works of spontaneous prose that followed it. *The Town and the City* is a typical first novel, overlong, derivative, and terribly earnest. There is in this family saga a ponderous heaviness and the sort of willful repetition and inclusiveness that mar the work of so many young novelists. The prose is a strange and uneven blend of James T. Farrell and Thomas Wolfe. To see how much and how fundamentally Jack Kerouac's writing changed over the next two decades, you have only to compare this novel with *The Vanity of Duluoz,* which was published in 1968. It covers roughly the same period in his life and treats much of the same material—growing up in Lowell, Massachusetts, football, the war, and the early years in New York—but does so with a humor, a confessional intensity, and an awareness that is totally lacking in the earlier book. *The Town and the City* is a product of the soft, solemn, early fantasies of Kerouac's boyhood and youth, and is oddly, almost schizophrenically, divorced from the quality of the life he was living while he was writing it.

By contrast, *Go* seems, if not a more mature piece of writing, at least one that is altogether different and better than the usual first novel. It is charged through with the same desperate energy that Holmes perceives in his characters and their milieu. The dark, fugitive quality that pervades *Go* was one that was quite new to the postwar literary scene. It might best be described, borrowing some of John Clellon Holmes' own words, as "the feeling of having been used, of being raw. It involves a sort of nakedness of mind, and, ultimately of soul; a feeling of being reduced to the bedrock of consciousness." This is quoted from a *New York Times Book Review* piece he wrote just after the appearance of his novel. The *Times*, quick to sniff out a cultural novelty, had invited Holmes to write a piece defining his generation and explaining their feelings. In the essay, which Holmes titled, "This Is the Beat Generation," he explained, "A man is beat whenever he goes for broke and wagers the sum of his resources on a single number; and the young generation has done that continually from early youth."

Beat—what did it mean to them then? What could it mean to that first postwar generation? Holmes' good friend, novelist Alan Harrington (who can be recognized as Ketcham in *Go*), tells a story that goes a long way toward defining the difference between the early Beats and other writers around them who were slightly older or slightly more orthodox in their responses. "In the beginning," says Harrington, "I was repelled by them, by some of their ideas. But I was a much different person then, and they did a lot to change my thinking. How did we differ? How can I put it? I remember once walking down Lexington Avenue with Jack Holmes, when across the street a man came running out of a Greek restaurant with a piece of fruit in his hand and the manager close behind, yelling for him to stop. Just as I was thinking, 'I hope the manager catches him,' Jack said out loud, 'I hope the guy gets away.' That's how we were different. And that's how I've changed. Today I'd trip the manager if I could."

Between the years 1945 and 1955 there were a great many articles and even a few books written with the intention of collecting the motley group of literary artists who then dominated the scene into some sort of effective generalization and proclaiming them a generation. But it never really worked. The man who wrote most sensibly about them, John Aldridge, concluded in his survey of the postwar literary scene, *In Search of Heresy,* that about the only thing that the Vidals, the Willinghams, the Capotes, and the Bowles really seemed to have in common was their timidity, their reluctance either to experiment or to take dangerous positions. Theirs was, perhaps, less a literature of introspection, as they so often claimed it to be, as it was one of circumspection.

None of this is to deny that some of the work produced by certain writers who came to be known during this period was very good work indeed. But it was not individual works on which they were all betting so heavily, but on the collective significance of these writers as a generation. They seemed to identify very closely with the Lost Generation of the 1920s. The unspoken rationale here was that Hemingway, Dos Passos, Cummings, et al. went through the very nasty experience of World War I, and we went through the even nastier experience of World War II, so therefore the literature we produce is sure to exceed theirs in importance and depth. If only equations were so reliable in literature and cycles so easy to chart!

There were not only those who did good work, there were also those whose good work foreshadowed in feeling, form, or substance the writing of the Beats. I'm thinking here of Norman Mailer, of course—not so much of *The Naked and the Dead*, which was of course a very considerable novel, but of *Barbary Shore*, a much less successful work that fits almost precisely into the Beat category as delimited and defined by John Clellon Holmes ("the feeling of having been used, of being raw"). I'm thinking also of Chandler Brossard, whose second novel, *The Bold Saboteurs*, had a teen-age hero who seems even today the very model of a hipster. I'm thinking, too, of a writer now all but forgotten, named Robert Lowry whose excellent stories and good novels, particularly *Casualty* and *The Big Cage*, did a lot to keep American writing in contact with the vein of rich, raw experience from which has always been mined the best literary ore. As for poets, those associated with the Black Mountain College group are important, partly because of their close relation to the Beat poets, and among them Robert Duncan and Charles Olson in particular had great and benevolent influence.

A few more perhaps, but there were never very many. How could there be? This was, after all, an age in which the creative impulse was very nearly throttled by the critical spirit. The academics and the *Partisan Review* crowd were then in charge as no group of critics had ever been before. And while it lasted, their domination was so complete that they managed to impose their influence on some literary works even during composition. Who can say how many authors engaged in the sort of self-censorship that led them to write their stories, poems, and novels not merely to the high standards of these critics—which would in its own way have been admirable—but also with an eye fixed firmly on the predilections and prejudices of this school or that clique? Stories were written, then rewritten and salted with symbols. Personal experience, no matter how genuine or deeply felt, was rejected—often most reluctantly—in favor of myth. Poems were refined through draft after draft to the point where they lacked all substance. This one was certainly, as Malcolm Cowley dubbed it, "the new age of the rhetoricians."

But such self-censorship and the virulent epidemic of creative constipation that swept America during the late 1940s and early 1950s were, in human terms, the least of it. This was a period of early deaths—coronaries at the age of thirty-eight—breakdowns and psychosis. Does it seem unlikely to you that intellectual pressures and doubts could produce such results? It shouldn't. Just see into what tight little knots they tied one would-be novelist:

> I had natural sock as a story-teller and was precociously good at description, dialogue and most of the other staples of the fiction-writer's trade, but I was bugged by a mammoth complex of thoughts and feelings that prevented me from doing more than just diddling the surface of sustained fiction-writing. Much of this was personal; some of it was due to the highly critical (how can you write when you haven't yet read *Bartleby the Scrivener?* etc.) period I came of age in; and some of it was due to grave troubled doubts I had that the novel as a form had outlived its vital meaning and was being perpetuated by the dishonesty and lack of imagination of its practitioners. Taken together all these facts threw me off the narrowly uncertain balance I had to begin with and sent me shuddering down the tunnels of introspection and cosmic-type thought that more or less paralyzed me for a decade; until I finally vomited up my wretched life and found myself no longer even an amateur writer but a bona-fide all-American- 1-out-of-16 psychotic.

That's Seymour Krim's testimony. This New York writer, editor, and man-about-magazines very candidly admits that he collapsed under pressure, but he is inclined to excuse himself and blame the pressure. This might seem on the face of it a chancy sort of special pleading, yet Krim pleads so very well in the long piece, "What's This Cat's Story?" from which I have quoted that he not only manages to exculpate himself, but by the time he has finished, he has also managed to make stick his indictment of oppressive hyperintellectuality on the community of New York critics. He makes a good case: "The phantom of great European-inspired ambition drove all of us in my group to the most miserable heights and voids of despair, like Hitlers in our own mad little Berchtesgadens; the reader shouldn't forget that the casual small talk of the people I greedily learned from was Kierkegaard, Kafka, Melville, Blake, Lawrence (Joyce was considered a misguided second-rater) and with such standards running wild and demonic in our lusting heads there can be little wonder that some of us cracked under the intense pressure we placed on ourselves. . . ."

And the essay in which he makes his case serves as introduction to a book that contains some remarkably frank self-revelations. *Views of a Nearsighted Cannoneer,* originally published in 1961, and then reissued in a second, expanded edition in 1968, is a sort of patchwork autobiography put together from pieces he wrote for magazines after he had managed to liberate himself from the tyranny he so ruthlessly describes. They are cast in the form of essays on such topics as homosexuality, suicide, masturbation, sexual relations between Negro and white, fame-hunger, and insanity, but in all of them he is so driven by the confessional impulse ("I am the man, I suffered, I was there") that even when and where he does not make explicit his personal experience of this sin or that folly, the expense of it all to him in raw, real pain can be sensed between the lines. It was in its own way quite an important book, because just at the time when Norman Mailer was beginning to make a game of self-revelation, Krim came along and gave it a hard push in the direction of art. Much of the

subjective and personally involved "gut journalism," which is the best journalism being written today, comes to us right out of *Views of a Nearsighted Cannoneer.*

These days Seymour Krim is understandably reluctant to talk much about that period in his life, for he feels that he has said about all he has to say about it in *Views of a Nearsighted Cannoneer* and in a couple of essays in his later collection, *Shake It for the World, Smartass.* "You get a reputation for repetition," he says, "and it's hard to live down."

However, he did loosen up one night and talked at length about the days when he turned that corner in his life, when he left the anxiety and joylessness of the rhetoricians and plunged into what, though not formally named, soon came to be known as the Beat movement. It was something in the nature of a liberation for him, and because that is how he remembers it, he gradually warmed to the subject as he talked about it and remembered. And as he talked, his cat prowled over the heaps of books and piles of papers that seemed to cover nearly every inch of his apartment on Tenth Street in the East Village. Scratchy jazz droned from the phonograph in the corner. Krim smoked on and told how it had been.

"When I got out of the nuthouse," he said, "I didn't return to my old haunts, where the crowd from the *Partisan Review* and *Commentary* hung out, but instead I began to go to the old Cedar Bar, which was then a hangout for abstract expressionist painters, for Beats, and Beat types. It was as simple as that. Just a change of scene made all the difference. Who was there? Well, everybody you might expect—Holmes, Ginsberg, Corso, and occasionally Kerouac and then others that might be thought of more as the Black Mountain crowd—Selby, Gilbert Sorrentino, and for a while Robert Creeley. People like that. But I'm making distinctions and groupings after the fact. It was just a bunch of people back then who came together evening after evening. And a change of bar meant a change of atmosphere for me. That was what was important for me—the change of atmosphere."

He explained that he was more comfortable there because he was feeling peculiarly vulnerable after having flipped out. "They were vulnerable, too," he said, "because they weren't so careful and always covering up so skillfully. In general, it was a more free-wheeling atmosphere. And that was what I wanted, God, what I *needed!* After all, my having flipped out was a revolt against all this tight carefulness. But I've already said this. I've spent myself in this area."

I asked if he felt that the Beat movement was entirely a catalytic thing. Was it just a matter of certain people—like the crowd at the Cedar—coming together and touching off the right sort of spark?

"Well, of course that has to be part of it, but I really think that the Beat thing that was an inevitable explosion of people with raw, primary instincts who simply refused to keep them dammed up any longer. They had been dammed up. I mean my own experience wasn't so unique in that way. After all, from about 1945 all the young writers were acolytes of the T. S. Eliot and Trilling legacy. These were the people in power. Well, the Beats changed all that. The domination of that whole critical thing has ended. We—the Beats—were just a sect back then, but now that sect has broadened into a whole society. And the younger generation that followed us is now so much in the saddle that older writers like myself are challenged and trying to sort out what they themselves really believe. I think it's reached an extreme point right now. But the total effect has undoubtedly been very, very good. Things are wide open now in a way they simply weren't before."

The Beat thing, according to Krim, was "like the law of gravity or the second law of thermodynamics or something"—and the nature of the movement can be appreciated if you remember that none of the people involved in it were critics. "They were poets, novelists, or whatever, but the real thing to remember is that they were people involved who had respect for their own experience and wanted to write from it. Why, the way it was before the Beat thing happened, there was absolutely no relation in the young writers of the time between their balls and their minds—and that's a *bad* situation."

This elitism that the critics practiced and tried to impose as rule of law—would he say that this was an aberration, a temporary detour that took American writing from its proper course?

52    "No," he said, "not quite. I don't think it can be disposed

of quite that easily. What this whole thing was, first of all—and this was the bad part—was an effort to impose European standards on American experience. And this was just playing on the old self-distrust of the articulate, educated American. He's always looking to Europe, see. And secondly—this was the good part—it was also thought of by many of the leaders among the critics as a genuine way to lift American experience and intellectual standards. The New Criticism in its beginnings was a scrupulous and worthy effort, but like so many such efforts, it became enslaved by its own criteria.

"The important thing, and ultimately the deadening thing, was that it didn't permit space for experimentation in the arts. It didn't permit errors. And errors are healthy. There can be more in the seeds of healthy errors than in the most careful art. So, on the whole, even though we may have gone to extremes in our efforts to slay the father, I really have no regrets, because the way I feel about it, the Beat thing was healthy, organic, and unstoppable. It had to happen."

We talked on a while longer, there in the warm gloom of that half-lit pad—had he seen Corso? how long until Krim himself would be leaving for Europe?—until at last I finished off my last can of beer and said goodnight. I went out onto Tenth Street and trudged over to nearby Second Avenue which was still swarming from a go at the Fillmore East that must have let out only a little while before. Here they were, a new generation making their own revolt, and they were slaying the father with remorseless equanimity. Was Krim right? Had the revolt of the young reached a point so extreme? Did the Beat veterans themselves feel now that the revolt had turned against them?

Allen Ginsberg arrived in San Francisco in 1953. It had been a destination for him, a sort of goal arrived at after a long year of travel that had taken him away from New York and out of the milieu that had supported him there. He had gone down to see Burroughs who by then was in Mexico, and went on to Cuba, fooled around Florida for a while, then headed west at last. It was a new start for him—that was how he felt about it, and that was what it proved to be. He carried with him a letter of introduction from his mentor, William Carlos Williams, to Kenneth Rexroth, one of the few poets of any stature in the West with whom Ginsberg felt any sense of kinship. Yet perhaps more than meeting Rexroth in San Francisco, his primary mission traveling west was to see Neal Cassady in San Jose.

Who was Neal Cassady? His is a name that recurs again and again in interviews and memoirs of the time. He is usually spoken of as the prototypal Beat, the guy who had been there first and showed them all the way. He is known to have been the original for Dean Moriarty in Kerouac's *On the Road*—and that portrait of him as the hipster hero is about as close as anyone is likely to come to getting down on paper the real Neal Cassady. Jack Kerouac had met him on one of his earlier California sojourns when both of them were working as brakemen on the Coast Division of the Southern Pacific Railway. Cassady, though mostly from Denver, had grown up in flophouses all over the West as he followed his father from job to job. By the time he had reached the age of twenty-five, when he met Kerouac, he had spent nearly as much time in jail as out, though most of it was on juvenile offender and pot convictions. And he was destined to spend more of his short life behind bars, too.

Just how important Neal Cassady was to Jack Kerouac and the writing of *On the Road* is perhaps not sufficiently appreciated. For not only was he the model for the novel's central character—the electric, charging, and dynamic Moriarty —but Cassady's wild adventures with Kerouac, as they rampaged from one end of the country to the other, provided the book with all in the way of plot and incident it has.

Just how important he was to Allen Ginsberg—and why Ginsberg should have pursued him out to the West Coast— should be apparent from these rather notorious remarks from the poet's *Paris Review* interview: "Mainly the thing was that I'd been making it with N. C., and finally I think I got this letter from him saying it was all off, no more, we shouldn't consider ourselves lovers any more on account of it just wouldn't work out. But previously we'd had an understanding that we—Neal Cassady, I said N. C. but I suppose you can use his name—we'd had a big tender lover's understanding. But I guess it got too much for him, partly because he was 3,000 miles away and he had 6,000 girl friends on the other side of the continent who were keeping him busy."

But it took Allen Ginsberg nearly a year to get to the West Coast, and by that time Neal Cassady was married to one of those 6,000 girl friends. Not one to be easily daunted by such an arrangement, Ginsberg sought Cassady out in San Jose where he was back working as a brakeman on the Southern Pacific, and moved in with him and his wife. Having arrived only a few dollars better than flat broke, he tried to get a job as a brakeman himself. Failing that, he hung on with them until Mrs. Cassady began objecting. And so, with regret, N. C. drove his friend up to San Francisco and left him there. It was a lucky thing for Ginsberg that he did.

Things were happening in San Francisco. The proper elements for a literary renaissance were at hand, and currents of talent and excitement had begun to coalesce around North Beach (where Ginsberg moved in), like the winter fog that swirls in from the ocean and blankets the area. He took a room at Broadway and Columbus, near the City Lights Book Shop, which was run then, just as it is today, by Lawrence Ferlinghetti, the poet.

Ferlinghetti, a New Yorker, had come to the city two years before "because it was the only place in the country where you could get decent wine cheap." Originally, he had become involved with Peter **Martin** (who subsequently returned to the East and started the New Yorker Bookshop on the Upper West Side of Manhattan) in a magazine called *City Lights,* à la Charlie Chaplin, a kind of broad cultural enterprise devoted to film, sociology, and politics. Their office was on the second floor of that building at Columbus and Broadway, and to get a break on the rent **Martin** had taken the first floor of the building as well. Not knowing quite what to do with the extra space, they decided to open a bookshop on the first floor, with Ferlinghetti in charge, just to pay the rent for the magazine office. "The magazine folded in a year," Ferlinghetti remembers, "but once we opened that book store we couldn't get the door closed from all the business. Well, it was understandable. There were absolutely no paperback stores in those days. As far as I know we were the first."

55       But there was more to it than that. The store became a sort

of social institution as well. City Lights was a place where writers—especially local poets—and a literate public might meet, talk, and argue. They bought lots of books, too, and thus Ferlinghetti managed not only to keep the store open, but to go on in 1956 to begin issuing his City Lights Books, one of the most important independent publishing ventures of the last twenty-five years.

All this is more crucial than perhaps you might suppose, for when there are places like City Lights where the barrier between the writer and the public comes down, then it is possible to get the sort of give and take between them, the fundamental dialogue that is one of the important preconditions if an independent literary culture is to begin to grow. A writer needs a primary audience, people with faces and names for him to address, people who can talk back.

"Two things, I think, are really necessary for poetry to take hold in any given time or place. First of all, you've got to have different people with different ideas of what a poem is. As it usually works out, they themselves are poets. They have strong opinions. From the exchange of such opinions comes controversy over the basic questions of what poetry is. And this is the sort of ground that new ideas grow in. "But second, and almost as important, you need not only a nucleus of poets, but an audience for them to speak to. That's where the enthusiasm comes in. And you need both—controversy and enthusiasm."

Robert Duncan speaking. The poet of *The Opening of the Field* was born and raised in the Bay area, had spent important years in the East during and after the war where he had become involved with the group at Black Mountain College, and then had returned to San Francisco—just in time for the renaissance. And he himself did a great deal to help bring it into being. At the time Allen Ginsberg arrived in the city, Duncan was teaching a poetry workshop at San Francisco State (where Michael McClure was one of his students), and he was also deeply involved with San Francisco's Poetry Center. Founded by Ruth Whit just after the war, the Center presented its first series of readings as early as 1947.

These provided the more formal occasions on which those
56  who met informally at City Lights and the North Beach coffee

houses might come together and feel a part of the greater world of letters. The readings were very well attended and attracted academics and some of the artier members of the establishment, as well. When poets came from outside the San Francisco area to read at the Center, they were invariably given a warm, courteous reception (Michael McClure recalls that he met Allen Ginsberg at a party given at the Poetry Center following a reading given there by W. H. Auden), and local poets were usually no less well received. There were always a lot of the latter to read and listen. In addition to those already named, there was another group made up of Jack Spicer, Robin Blaser, Thomas Parkinson, and a few others. There was an academic poet named Josephine Miles who taught at Berkeley and who, though unsympathetic to much of what was being done by other San Francisco poets, has remained active in the area for years. And among the Beats, ur-Beats, and Beats-to-be were Lew Welch, Philip Lamantia, William Everson (Brother Antoninus), and coming along a little later, Gary Snyder and Philip Whalen.

And over them all, if not quite a reigning monarch, then at least holding a highly favored position as elder statesman in the local republic of letters, was Kenneth Rexroth. Although not a native San Franciscan, Rexroth has been around as long as anyone could remember, and for years was the only poet— or writer of any sort—with a national reputation who lived and worked in San Francisco. He came to the city with his wife in the late 1920s, after he had already made for himself the beginnings of a literary reputation in Chicago. Why had he settled in San Francisco, as far removed as it then was from contact with the literary world? What did it have to offer that so appealed to him? In Kenneth Rexroth's *An Autobiographical Novel,* which concludes with his move west, this is as close as he comes to giving a reason for choosing to live where he did: "San Francisco was not just a wide-open town. It is the only city in the United States which was not settled overland by the westward-spreading puritan tradition, or by the Walter Scott fake-cavalier tradition of the South. It had been settled mostly, in spite of all the romances of the overland migration, by gamblers, prostitutes, rascals, and fortune seekers who came across the Isthmus and around the Horn. They had their faults, but they were not influenced by Cotton Mather." But this still leaves us wondering just what San Francisco had that made it for him and for others such fertile ground for literary cultivation—why the explosion of poetry that they were soon calling the San Francisco Renaissance took place when and where it did.

Because I thought Kenneth Rexroth would be more likely to know the answers to such questions than anyone else, I made it a point to look him up and ask him. Not point-blank. You don't ask him anything point-blank. You let him talk. And as he does, you resist the temptation to lean back and enjoy it, for the temptation is real enough. No, keep the pad out and the pencil working, for colorful, salty, and opinionated as they are, Rexroth's remarks are also always frank and well-informed. He has a way of saying just what he means. Just toss him a question now and again to keep him going, and you are sure to find out what you want to know. I did.

It seemed slightly anomalous to seek out Kenneth Rexroth in Santa Barbara in order to talk to him about San Francisco, the city with which he is so closely identified and where he has lived for so long. Lately, as it turns out, he has been living there only about a third of the year. The remainder he spends at Santa Barbara, teaching at the branch of the University of California there. Rexroth, as a teacher, is something to contemplate. You can get an idea of just how well he fits into the conventional academic environment by reading Mary McCarthy's *The Groves of Academe*, in which he puts in an appearance as the wild radical poet who messes things up so recklessly at that little eastern college during the latter part of the book. But Mary McCarthy never saw Kenneth Rexroth in action in UCSB.

There, in addition to the usual poetry workshop course, he teaches something called "Poetry and Song," a course that surely has no equivalent at any other American university. Kenneth Rexroth himself is quite pleased with it: "It was originally intended for 12 students, but 120 registered, so I said, 'What the hell, let them all in.' And so we run it just like a cabaret with songs and little spiels that end in songs. The kids write their poems, and then they sing them, and that's why it's so much fun. The point of it all is the community that comes out of it, the *agape*. In the beginning nobody knew anyone else. Now we're all face to face, I and thou with each other. That's what the arts should do, isn't it?"

He held forth in the library of the rented house in Montecito where he lives during the school year. It is a Santa Barbara suburb that is all shady pines and winding lanes. He lives there with his daughter, who is a student at the university, and his secretary. The university life seemed to suit him tolerably well. It had, in any case, not dulled the sharp bite of his wit.

I asked him first of all to expand on his reasons for choosing San Francisco when he moved west back in the 1920s. And he explained that going from the Chicago of that time to San Francisco was a very easy transition to make. "They had a lot in common," he said. "I left Chicago because it had started to change while I was there. Ben Hecht, Sherwood Anderson, Sam Putnam, Glen Wescott—they all got out. I was actually one of the last of that crowd to leave. And so the question— where to go? To New York? If I'd gone there to the marketplace, I would have been just another pig at the trough—and that's bad. The marketplace is always a bad place for artists to mature. If not an impossible one. No, it seemed the only place to go was farther west. I chose San Francisco because it seemed to have certain things in common with the Chicago I'd known during the Twenties. Both were far removed from the financial center of things—where all the money-changing was going on. But both, too, had had an intense regional development— literary, artistic, intellectual—that had all come about quite independently of the East. And just like Chicago, San Francisco was an old radical town."

I asked if he felt the western radical tradition was important to the development of the Beat thing and to the San Francisco Renaissance in poetry.

"Oh sure. No doubt about it. It goes back to Jack London and the I.W.W.—and the Wobblies were particularly strong in Oakland when I got out west. And all through the Thirties and early Forties you had Harry Bridges as a real power in town. He was ex-Wobbly and I am practically dead certain he wasn't a party member. Bridges was like Tito. He talked back too much to be a good Communist. He talked back to everybody!

"Yeah, there was a lot of native radical feeling out here—not Communist or even socialist necessarily, but a lot of it good old-fashioned anarchist-pacifist. For instance, I remember that a very big thing in San Francisco was the Randolph Bourne Council, which was founded right on the eve of war, or at the time of Munich, I guess. And the idea was to have a forum for the intellectuals to voice their opposition to the whole idea of war. As the war got hotter we sort of went underground or joined very respectable organizations like the War Resisters League or the Fellowship of Reconciliation. And all this led immediately after the war to the founding of the Anarchist Circle, a very important group while it lasted. Talk about your intellectual fellowship—well, you could really sense it in those meetings. Philip Lamantia was in it as just a precocious kid, and I guess I met Robert Duncan there in the Circle. He started going toward the end of the thing. What did we do there? Oh, it was no big, heavy thing. We just talked mostly, discussed things, our own ideas and so forth. The wonderful thing about it, though, was that you could say damned near anything there and not get sneered at or put down. It was all *open* in a way that real political discussion never is. This was *ideas*—beyond factions and politics."

I asked Kenneth Rexroth if the Anarchist Circle—which had brought Lamantia, Duncan, and himself together—might not perhaps have been the direct forerunner of the San Francisco Renaissance. Was it the essential factor from which everything else followed?

"Well," Rexroth said, "I don't know if you can say it was *the* essential factor. There were a lot of things happening back then, and they all contributed something—for instance, all the Conscientious Objectors who passed in and out of the city during the war. San Francisco was within hitchhiking distance of half the C.O. camps in America. They all came here—especially that bunch up in Waldport, Oregon. That was where they kept all the artists and special nuts. I don't know if William Everson—that's Brother Antoninus—came from there, but he came from one of the camps. And as soon as the war was over, and he was off the hook as a C.O., he settled down around San Francisco.

"But there were other things, too—an anthology they got up of San Francisco writing—they called it *The Ark*—and it gave all the contributors a special sense of identity. And there was a Communist magazine—or maybe it should be little-c communist—*Living Marxism,* that helped out a lot in the same way.

"All in all, I guess you could really say that the place was jumping from the end of the war to 1955. The development here was independent and counter to the dominant thing going on around the country then in poetry and art generally. So you see, when the Beats came here—mostly from New York, but McClure was from Kansas or wherever, and Whalen and Snyder were from the Northwest—they hit all this stuff that had been bubbling away in San Francisco, and it sort of exploded them. They never heard of anything like this."

And what about Ginsberg in particular? How did it all affect him?

"Well, it was the same with him, except that he seemed to react even more than the others. San Francisco really exploded him. You look at that early stuff he wrote. It was sort of *witty* William Carlos Williams—short lines and very epigrammatic and ironic. But when he got up at the Six Gallery that night and read that new thing of his, well, it just electrified everybody. It was different from anything he had done up until then—hell, it was different from what *anyone* had done until then."

But it took Allen Ginsberg quite some time to work up to that big moment at the Six. Most of it, of course, was time spent in San Francisco—though not, according to Kenneth Rexroth, quite all of it. "He seems to have gotten his personal history sort of mixed up. Ginsberg tells everybody he worked as a market researcher all this time in San Francisco. Well, that's great, but I don't think there was enough of that kind of work around then to support a market researcher in the town. Anyway, I remember that he began shipping out up to the Bering Sea on a regular run that was equipping the DEW line. Or maybe they were building it back then, I don't know. Anyway, he made a lot of money by shipping up there—but now he seems to want to forget about it. I guess that's because it wasn't exactly pacifist activity."

But whether it was after market-researching hours (for the San Francisco firm of Towne-Oller, as he has said) or between voyages to the Bering Sea, Allen Ginsberg became very well acquainted around the city—well known in places like City Lights, as a faithful attendant of the Poetry Center readings, and as a frequenter of all the right North Beach bars. The San Francisco arts community knew him not only as the local wild man, a reputation he seemed to carry with him wherever he went, but as a poet of ability and as William Carlos Williams' young protege from Paterson.

Most important, during this period Ginsberg was gaining in confidence and dedication for his vocation. There in San Francisco he was meeting other young poets like himself, who thought as he did about the fundamental questions and cared enough to argue out the rest. He was beginning, in other words, to sense and participate in the sort of fellowship of poets that Robert Duncan talked about. But in Ginsberg's case, the sense of fellowship he felt there was matched by his sense of belonging to the New York milieu as well. New York, San Francisco, all of it, he felt, was part of an even bigger thing, was part of that great cultural revolution that he and Jack Kerouac had talked about so often. Ginsberg wanted things to happen; he was impatient for the revolution to begin. And so he decided to do his bit to push it a little further along the way right there in San Francisco. He decided to organize a reading that would bring together all of the area's best young poets in one big evening of poetry. Kerouac was newly arrived in town on one of his visits from New York. The event was planned partly to introduce him to the scene and partly, too, because Ginsberg was convinced that the right moment had come for that big boom they had all been listening for so long. And with his usual good judgment for the proper move at the proper time (he had the keen instincts of a publicist), Ginsberg had sensed with perfect accuracy that the time was ripe for something big. For the result of his planning, of course, was the big reading at the Six Gallery that set everything in motion.

Ginsberg planned it. He handled publicity. He even mailed out postcards announcing the event. And here is what they said:

> Six poets at the Six Gallery. Kenneth Rexroth, M.C. Remarkable collection of angels all gathered at once in the same spot. Wine, music, dancing girls, serious poetry, free satori. Small collection for wine and postcards. Charming event.

The names of the six poets who were to participate were also listed—and for the record they were Michael McClure, Gary Snyder, Philip Lamantia, Phil Whalen, Lew Welch, and, of course, Allen Ginsberg himself.

Perhaps because he was there only as a member of the audience, Jack Kerouac was less inclined later to view the event as quite the earth-shaking occasion that it seemed to some of the others. When asked about it later, Kerouac put it all rather lightly: "The San Francisco Renaissance happened one night in 1955," he said. "We all went out and got drunk."

Kerouac, at least, was drunk at the Six Gallery the night of the reading: "Certainly he was," Kenneth Rexroth remembers. "By the time the second poet on the program started reading—that was Lamantia—Kerouac was already banging his big gallon jug of wine on the floor just to show his enthusiasm. Kerouac used to carry those gallons of port around the same way F. Scott Fitzgerald carried a flask."

But drunk or sober, the evening must finally have made quite an impression on him, for he talked of it often later on. And in *The Dharma Bums* he included an account which, though short on detail, is long on enthusiasm and does a lot to communicate the swinging jubilant mood of that night:

> Anyway I followed the whole gang of howling poets to the reading at Gallery Six that night, which was, among other important things, the night of the birth of the San Francisco Poetry Renaissance. Everyone was there. It was a mad night. And I was the one who got things jumping by going around collecting dimes and quarters from the rather stiff audience

standing around in the gallery and coming back with three huge gallon jugs of California Burgundy and getting them all piffed so that by eleven o' clock when Alvah Goldbrook was reading his poem "Wail" drunk with arms outspread everybody was yelling "Go! Go! Go!" (like a jam session) and old Rheinhold Cacoethes the father of the Frisco poetry scene was wiping his tears in gladness. . . .

Meanwhile scores of people stood around in the darkened gallery straining to hear every word of the amazing poetry reading as I wandered from group to group, facing them and facing away from the stage, urging them to glug a slug from the jug, or wandered back and sat on the right side of the stage giving out little wows and yesses of approval and even whole sentences of comment with nobody's invitation but in the general gaiety nobody's disapproval either. It was a great night. . . .

If the names seem unfamiliar and a little odd, they are simply Kerouacese for Ginsberg (Alvah Goldbrook) and Rexroth (Rheinhold Cacoethes). And as he tells us here, the climax of the evening came with Ginsberg's reading of "Howl" ("Wail"). On that all who were present seem to agree.

Allen Ginsberg had written "Howl" two weeks before the Six reading during a long weekend spent in his room under the influence of various drugs—peyote for visions, amphetamine to speed up, and dexedrine to keep going. He has said it was one of his earliest drug experiences and has implied it was also one of his most profound. In any case, that was how the poem was written, and once it was finished, Ginsberg knew that he had written not just a new poem, but a new *kind* of poem— one that came very close to communicating in an actual way the same charging, flowing electricity of emotion that he had felt in himself while he was writing it. He kept unusually quiet about what he had done and evidently read it to nobody until that night at the Six. When he read it, there he was himself half-drunk on wine, as Kerouac said, and he stood weaving, bobbing, and half dancing to the crazy inner rhythm of the poem as he chanted it. It was not just the poem, but Ginsberg's wild delivery of it that night that turned on the crowd and soon had them shouting encouragement to him.

64      And it was not only the audience Allen Ginsberg turned on,

but all the other poets present as well. Later, Michael McClure was to confess that his immediate reaction was a feeling of jealousy toward Ginsberg—but jealousy tempered by the realization that something was happening in this very room and that he was part of it. And Kenneth Rexroth: "All of a sudden Ginsberg read this thing that he had been keeping to himself all this while, and it just blew things up completely." Things would never be quite the same again for any of them.

*Howl and Other Poems* was published the following year by Lawrence Ferlinghetti's City Lights Books. It was one of the first titles in his Pocket Poets Series, in which many of the Beats first saw book publication. *Howl,* still in print, is even today Ferlinghetti's best and steadiest seller, apparently likely to keep going on forever. But in the beginning, there was some doubt whether it would be sold at all: publication of the book was blocked by an obscenity suit. It took no less than criminal lawyer "Jake" Ehrlich to win the case and get the book into distribution.

But once out, the book found an audience ready and eager for it. The notoriety brought to *Howl* by the trial had assured it wide distribution. This was the first national publicity of any sort given the Beats. It offered a foretaste of what was to come, and it gave clear indication that the only real interest of the press in Ginsberg's poetry was and always would be prurient. But in spite of the crude tone of the publicity, word had gotten out that *Howl* was something more than a collection of four-letter words arranged in loose syntax, and so there was some genuine excitement attending its publication. No reviews, of course, but a kind of underground murmur that preceded it, promising something different, something real.

The impact *Howl* had on its readers was nearly as strong as the impression the poem itself made on the audience at the Six that night when it was read by Ginsberg himself. Diane diPrima, in her scandalous, semipornographic little book, *Memoirs of a Beatnik,* tells how she felt one afternoon when someone handed her a copy of the Ginsberg poems in the middle of dinner:

65

I was too turned on to concern myself with the stew. I handed it over to Beatrice and, without even thanking Bradley, I walked out the front door with his new book. Walked the few blocks to the pier on Sixtieth Street, and sat down by the Hudson River to read, and come to terms with what was happening. The phrase "breaking ground" kept coming into my head. I knew that this Allen Ginsberg, whoever he was, had been breaking ground for all of us, though I had no idea yet what that meant, how far it would take us.

The poem put a certain heaviness in me, too. It followed that if there was one Allen, there must be more, other people writing what they heard, living, however obscurely and shamefully, what they knew, hiding out here and there—and now, suddenly about to speak out. For I sensed that Allen was only, could only be, the vanguard of a much larger thing. All the people who, like me, had hidden and skulked, writing down what they knew for a small handful of friends, waiting with only a slight bitterness for the thing to end, for man's era to draw to a close in a blaze of radiation—all these would now step forward and say their piece. Not many would near them, but they would, finally, hear each other. I was about to meet my brothers.

In point of fact, she did meet brother Allen Ginsberg and brother Jack Kerouac about a year later. And the night she spent on the same mattress with them and with two other boys provides the funniest sequence in a very wild book. It ends in yab-yum and lotus with Kerouac, as Ginsberg, otherwise engaged, recites Whitman.

This was back in New York, of course. The two had returned from San Francisco when at last it looked as if something might happen with *On the Road*. Kerouac had been trying to get it published for years and while it was at Viking Malcolm Cowley had taken a look at it. Cowley was impressed, if somewhat overwhelmed by it, and he went so far as to give favorable mention to "John Kerouac . . . and his unpublished long narrative, *On the Road*" in his own survey of postwar American writing, *The Literary Situation*, published in 1954. Cowley kept plugging the book to his publisher, and at last, after a few changes were made in the text (over Kerouac's half-dead body), and a standard punctuation job had been performed on it by the editors, *On the Road* was set for publication.

Just before it was brought out, *Evergreen Review* came along with its special issue on the San Francisco Renaissance. It included a good short piece by Kerouac, "October in the Railroad Earth," the full text of "Howl," and work by Lawrence Ferlinghetti, Michael McClure, Phil Whalen, Gary Snyder, Philip Lamantia, and a few others. More than anything else, that issue of *Evergreen* was probably responsible for popularizing a misconception that took some while to set right: that Ginsberg and Kerouac were native San Franciscans rather than "carpetbaggers" from the East.

The public was well primed for *On the Road* when at last it was published in the fall of 1957. Kerouac was already an underground celebrity, and now he surfaced with a vengeance.

PART II

CHAPTER 4

# The Avatar Repents

*On the Road* is the second novel by Jack Kerouac, and its
publication is a historic occasion in so far as the exposure of
an authentic work of art is of any great moment in an age in
which attention is fragmented and the sensibilities are
blunted by the superlatives of fashion (multiplied a million-
fold by the speed and pound of communications).

Thus resoundingly begins the review that ran in the *New
York Times* on Thursday, September 5, 1957. It was written
not by one of the *Times*'s regular daily reviewers, but by a
young writer, Gilbert Millstein, who was then working on the
Sunday magazine staff. Perhaps neither Orville Prescott nor
Charles Poore felt ready to deal with so unorthodox a novel.
Perhaps it was handed over to Millstein because of his known
partiality for avant-garde writing. In any case, the reviewer
had clearly had his ear to the ground, had caught the rum-
blings from San Francisco, and was well in tune with Kerouac's
paramount importance in the movement. He predicted that
just as *The Sun Also Rises* was the testament of the Lost Generation, *On the Road* would come to be accepted as that of the
Beat Generation. He was clearly writing to herald a new era
and to give recognition to Jack Kerouac as its "principal ava-
tar." Should there have been any doubt on just where Millstein
stood, it would have been erased by the short, solemn sentence
with which he concluded: *"On the Road* is a major novel."
The *New York Times* review did more than set the tone for
those that followed. It announced the ground swell that had

been building beneath the Beats as the word began to come from the West Coast, and as poems by Ginsberg, Corso, and others, as well as bits and pieces by Kerouac, began to appear in certain literary magazines. Gilbert Millstein's handling of the novel also assured that every other reviewer who wrote about it would at least have to take it seriously. However, by the time other reviews began to appear, popular response was so overwhelming and instantaneous that it hardly mattered what the critics thought of it. What caused all the excitement? Maybe it was the picture on the dust jacket that sold it— Kerouac tough-looking, brooding, unshorn, and unshaven with a silver crucifix around his neck that Gregory Corso had hung there a moment before the picture was taken. Perhaps it was only that the time had come at last for just such an explosion of interest and *On the Road* only supplied the necessary fuse. Or maybe this was the kind of book that spoke so directly and eloquently to the generation that was waiting for it that it needed only to be announced to be recognized. However we account for it, there can be no doubt that it was through Jack Kerouac and his book that the general public became instantly aware of the Beat Generation.

There was an immediate and impressive change in his fortunes. Magazines that had rejected him suddenly clamored to get back the very stories they had returned. Grove Press, which had actually bought Kerouac's novel, *The Subterraneans,* before Viking had accepted *On the Road* but had then delayed publication, announced plans to issue their book as soon as possible. Mike Wallace interviewed Kerouac on what was then television's most controversial and closely watched network talk show. Newspapers, radio, and television shows vied for places in the line that had formed just to talk to him.

A motion picture producer took an option on *On the Road.* Movie rights to *The Subterraneans* were sold outright for a good price. A television producer approached Kerouac on the possibility of a continuing series based on *On the Road,* the weekly adventures of Sal Paradise and Dean Moriarty. Jack didn't care much for the idea and declined. A season later the same producer came out with the very successful "Route 66" series, clearly imitation of *On the Road* and starring an actor named George Maharis, who bore a close physical resemblance to Kerouac.

Kerouac himself was somewhat bewildered by his spectacular success, for he remembered very well how hard it had been even to get the book published. In fact, somewhat to his embarrassment, he was always turning out to be a little older than people expected—thirty-five at the time *On the Road* was published—because the events covered in the novel had taken place nearly a decade earlier, and though he had written the book not long afterward, it had taken him over six years to see it in print.

The writing of it dated back to 1951. Jack Kerouac had said goodbye to Neal Cassady in California and returned to New York not long after the publication of his first novel, *The Town and the City*. Once back, he moved in with an old friend from the days around Columbia named Lucien Carr. At the time Carr was living in a loft apartment on West Twenty-first Street and was working for United Press. Kerouac had gotten hold of a typewriter and was about ready to start work on a book; he was eager to try an experiment in writing, a new technique influenced somewhat by the prosody of William Carlos Williams, and partly an imitation of the jazz soloist who blows chorus after chorus of purest invention right out of his head. In a later essay, he would dub the technique "Spontaneous Prose" and would urge:

> Not "selectivity" of expression but following free deviation (association) of mind into limitless blow-on-subject seas of thought, swimming in sea of English with no discipline other than rhythms of rhetorical exhalation and expostulated statement, like a fist coming down on a table with each complete utterance, bang! (the space dash)—Blow as deep as you want—write as deeply, fish as far down as you want, satisfy yourself first, then reader cannot fail to receive telepathic shock and meaning-excitement by same laws operating in his own human mind.

Kerouac even went so far as to urge writing "without consciousness" in the manner of Yeats's so-called trance writing.

In effect, however, what Kerouac planned to do was simply to write as fast as possible, never bothering to stop and think of the "proper" word, but concentrating only on the subject he held before him in his mind's eye. And if writing fast was the answer, he felt eminently well-qualified for the job—hadn't young Jean Louis Lebre de Kerouac once been speed-typing champion of the greater Boston area?

As he tried out his new technique on long letters and short stories, he found that the only thing that slowed him down was changing sheets of paper in the typewriter. It seemed that he no sooner had a sheet of eight by ten in the typewriter than he was down to the bottom of the page, reaching for another, shuffling it into the roller, perhaps tearing it in his haste to get on with the job. He tried using legal-size sheets, but the few extra lines they gave him really didn't help much. The problem was solved by Lucien Carr one night when he brought home a full roll of United Press teletype paper that he had lifted from the office. Kerouac was delighted. He saw that all he had to do was insert one end of the roll into his typewriter, and he could keep going for days and days.

How long did it take? Altogether, according to Kerouac, about three weeks. All that Lucien Carr remembers is that Jack worked at it practically nonstop. "Absolutely constantly," he declares. "I remember I was working days at the time. I'd get up in the morning to the sound of him at the typewriter, come in at night and he would still be at it, and when I went to bed he would be going strong. I suppose he must have stopped some times to eat and sleep, but you couldn't prove it by me."

Carr remembers that shortly after the manuscript was finished a little dog he had at the time attacked the roll and chewed up the last few feet of it. "It had perforce to be rewritten," he says, "but I know for a fact that that was the *only* part of *On the Road* that was rewritten."

And that, complained Robert Giroux (who was then Kerouac's editor at Harcourt, Brace), was just the trouble. Kerouac had felt quite close to Giroux, to whom he had originally been sent with the manuscript of his first novel, *The Town and the City* by his old Columbia teacher, Mark Van Doren. Robert

Giroux had also gone to Columbia some years earlier and was the son of a French Canadian father. That was enough for Kerouac: he dedicated his first novel "to R. G., Friend and Editor," and continued to hold him in high regard. That was why Kerouac was shocked and disappointed when his editor turned it down. "I couldn't imagine how he had gotten it on a roll of paper like that," says Robert Giroux. "Or *why* he should have wanted to. I remember I said to him, 'What about correctons? After all, the idea of separate sheets of paper is to make it easier to rewrite.' He said, 'I don't make any corrections. Everything's down there just the way I want it. That's the way it is. That's the way it will be.' " And he meant it. Although he had great respect for Giroux—and continued to have—Kerouac believed so deeply in his new Spontaneous Prose that he absolutely refused to change a word. "That was my first experience as an editor with this my-words-are-sacred attitude in a writer," Mr. Giroux says. "And I told him, 'Even Shakespeare, who, they say, didn't blot many words, blotted some, after all. And Jack, you ain't Shakespeare.' "

Later, when Kerouac told the story in an essay which he called "The Origins of the Beat Generation," there were curious discrepancies: "The manuscript of *Road* was turned down on the grounds that it would displease the sales manager of my publisher at that time, though the editor, a very intelligent man, said 'Jack this is just like Dostoevsky, but what can I do at this time?' It was too early." For his part, Robert Giroux is convinced—apparently mistakenly—that the roll manuscript that Kerouac showed him was not *On the Road,* or at any rate, was not the version that Viking finally published.

Sterling Lord, however, feels certain that it was. Jack was sent to him by Robert Giroux after the latter had turned the novel down. Mr. Lord was Kerouac's first and only literary agent. The two became fast friends. For his part, Lord was deeply impressed with Kerouac's talent and was convinced that *On the Road* was a truly important book that had to be published. Kerouac trusted him completely and came to value him as a literary advisor. The feelings that many writers lavish on their editors, he focused on his agent. He used to tell Lucien Carr, "The Lord is my agent. I will fear no evil." It was a favorite joke of his—but one that had some meaning for him all the same.

"*On the Road* was sent out again and again," Sterling Lord recalls. "So many editors saw it, realized immediately that it was like no other book they had ever seen, much less published, and would simply turn it down because of its strangeness." The story was a little different at Viking, though. An editor there, Keith Jennison, had an early look at the book and wanted to publish it, but was voted down. But this was years before it was actually accepted there.

It was sent out so often and seen by so many that the manuscript acquired a sort of legendary quality. Sterling Lord feels that what finally changed the minds of the Viking editors about the book was seeing pieces from it in print in literary magazines. He recalls that after one especially juicy bit had appeared in *The Paris Review,* he received a call from Viking's Keith Jennison, who declared, "Dammit! I always did like that novel. I think we ought to publish it before all of it has appeared in magazines. If I can get it past them here, will you take a $900 advance?"

Lord, seeing that at last it was really going to happen, sucked in his breath and said, "Let's make it a thousand, anyway, shall we?"

Jack Kerouac passed the six years that it took to get his second book published by writing no less than ten others. To this day, not all those written during this most prolific period have been published, and those that have been published are not all equally good. His nonstop method of composition—and he retained that, of course, from *On the Road* onward—practically assured a certain unevenness in the quality of his work.

He wrote everywhere and anywhere he could—from Neal Cassady's pad in San Francisco, where he had a cot in the attic and a typewriter next to it, to Mexico City where he wrote *Doctor Sax* "while I sat on Bill Burroughs' toilet bowl. I had no other place to write." Most of his writing, however, was done at his mother's place in Long Island. When he wasn't traveling, he was with her. He managed to pay the rent there most of the time with various odd jobs and unemployment checks, but she supported herself and his writing by working in a shoe factory.

And he kept on traveling, tirelessly and endlessly. The only job he held for any length of time during this period—that of brakeman on the Southern Pacific—was one that made it possible for him to stay on the move up and down the coast that he loved. And he not only wrote whenever he stopped to rest (on the typewriter, in pencil, and even with a tape recorder), he carried his manuscripts with him wherever he went. He told his bibliographer Ann Charters of a visit by the original Tristessa to his little hovel in Mexico City: "She came in the room and saw all my manuscripts on the clay floor and said, 'You've got millions of pesos on the floor.' I didn't have a cent but she said I had money on the floor. Turned out she was right. *Sax, Cody, On the Road.* I carried all that stuff with me in a duffle bag, my clothes and manuscripts and my canteen with water in it in case I got trapped in the desert."

Living on the run, writing in a rush wherever he paused to catch his breath, Kerouac passed six years in a kind of blur of raw experience in which time and place seem to merge. It is no wonder that the novels that came out of this period are written in the tumbled, explosive style they are. Had he not developed his rationale for Spontaneous Prose, circumstances of those years on the road would probably have forced him to write exactly as he did. He was fond of claiming a continuity for his novels, and once (1962) went so far as to say, "My work comprises one vast book like Proust's except that my remembrances are written on the run instead of afterwards in a sickbed." This may have been how he saw his work—and given the autobiographical nature of his writing, he could hardly see it any other way—but with the time that has passed and the subsequent novels that have appeared, it may help us to make better sense of his work if we look at it not as "one enormous comedy," as he called it, but as two.

There are the "road novels," first of all, those that in the manner of *On the Road* describe his travels and encounters with friends and fascinating strangers along the way and were written practically simultaneously with his experience of it all. And then, there are the "Lowell novels," the remembrances of his boyhood and youth that center, of course, in Lowell,

Massachusetts, where he grew up. There are no separate phases to describe in the writing of these novels. *Doctor Sax, Maggie Cassidy,* and *Visions of Gerard,* the three Lowell novels that were written during this six-year creation burst, were shuffled in among the rest, composed in the same hectic circumstances. Yet they are distinctly different in tone and quality from the road novels; the writing in them is softer, elegiac in tone and less precisely detailed than in the road novels. And in general, the Lowell novels are not nearly as good. They lack excitement, drive, intensity, focus—all the finest qualities of Kerouac's writing; by comparison they seem verbose, somewhat bombastic, and sentimental.

For any of us, things remembered from the distant past take on a shape and glow that are not so much unreal as super-real. Our memories of the good times we had or our fears and embarrassments during childhood are seldom, if ever, recalled in any sort of exact, objective context of detailed experience. What we remember is how *we* felt, and it is the subjective super-reality of such experience that the Lowell novels describe. Details—of the very specific that-chair, this-hand, who-said-what-and-how variety—are missing. And with Kerouac writing at his best, such details are all-important.

Details are the real strength of the road novels. In these books he is the open eye that sees it all, the memory that retains it all, the fingers that record it all with accuracy. Kerouac was a remarkable reporter, a recorder of things that happened just as they happened. And he seems to have retained the experience that went into the writing of these road novels only a relatively short time, in most cases no longer than a year. Some of them—*Tristessa* and the first part of *Desolation Angels,* for instance—were written practically from day to day as the events they described were happening. *The Subterraneans* ends with Mardou Fox telling Leo Percepied (Kerouac):

> "Baby it's up to you," is what she's actually saying, "about how many times you wanta see me and all that—but I want to be independent like I say."
> And I go home having lost her love.
> And write this book.

And that, quite literally, is what Jack Kerouac did. To him, however, "home" was *Memere,* as he always called his mother, and her place in Long Island. He traveled there clear across the country from San Francisco, where the action of the novel actually took place, and sat down at a typewriter in the basement to write the novel—admittedly only 111 pages in the published edition—in "three full moon nights of October" 1953.

Writing of this kind may belong less to the province of fiction than to journalism. It is not so much powerfully imagined as it is faithfully recorded. This is certainly not meant to detract from his work, but merely to place it. Kerouac himself often refused to call the books that followed *The Town and the City* novels; he called them, rather, "picaresque narratives." And while they are that, certainly, they also possess a quality that anticipates the personal journalism of, say, Tom Wolfe. For those critics who, in their enthusiasm for the kind of tell-it-all nonfiction that puts the narrator in the middle of the action he describes, are likely to forget where it came from and with whom it began. Although such personal journalism is often said to be the only significant literary development of the 1960s, it really goes back a little further than that. The true progenitor and first practitioner of the style was Jack Kerouac in this cycle that began with *On the Road* and ended with *Desolation Angels,* which I am calling the road novels.

Together, they form a fairly continuous narrative of Kerouac's life and travels between the years 1949 and 1957—or from some time before the publication of *The Town and the City* right through the publication of *On the Road.* They were not done consecutively. In writing them, he had a way of jumping forward and back over broad areas of experience, like a king across the checkerboard. Nor do their dates of publication give any firm indication of their true chronological order. Only reading them and rummaging their texts for biographical and historical details will do that.

Using that method, and adding a few details supplied by Ann Charters' *A Bibliography of Works by Jack Kerouac* and Sterling Lord, as well as by a few other sources, I have worked out a chronology that may not be absolutely accurate but should be helpful to anyone who wishes to read Kerouac's "enormous comedy" more or less as it happened. That, in my view, is how the novels should be read—as a diary of one man's times, or something larger, the chronicle of a generation.

*On the Road*, describes his early journeys with Neal Cassady (Dean Moriarty here) from 1947 to 1950. These include visits to William S. Burroughs (Bill Lee) in New Orleans and later in Mexico City. The theme that runs through the book, however, is Cassady's search for his drifter father through all the old haunts of the West.

*Visions of Cody*, at which Kerouac worked from the fall of 1951 to the spring of 1952, should be the longest of all his novels when and if it is published; only excerpts from the 502-page manuscript have ever seen print. It was held back, at least in the beginning, because it is the most frankly sexual of all his books. Again, it is about Cassady (Cody Pomeray), and it was begun in Long Island and finished while Kerouac was living with Cassady and his wife in San Francisco.

*The Subterraneans* tells of his 1953 affair with a black girl (Mardou Fox) in San Francisco. It ended unhappily for him; Gregory Corso (Yuri Gligoric) won her away.

*Tristessa* tells what happened during his third visit to Mexico City during the summer of 1955. Burroughs had left Mexico by this time and was in Tangier, so Kerouac moved into a little rooftop shack just above Burroughs' old fellow addict, the notorious Bill Gaines. Gaines was on opium. Kerouac picked it up every day for him from Tristessa, their connection. And that, he says, is how he got to know her. The two parts of this short novel were written at two separate sittings—the first as it was happening in summer, 1955, and the second in 1956.

*The Dharma Bums*, which was written just after the publication of *On the Road* at his mother's new place in Orlando, Florida, is his big San Francisco Renaissance book. It begins with his description of the reading at the Six Gallery in 1955, drops the action through a winter that he spent in the East, and then picks it up again with his return to the West Coast late in the spring of 1956. Gary Snyder (Japhy Ryder) is the central figure here, but all the San Francisco crew are on hand 80 and are easy to identify.

*Desolation Angels* picks up at just about the point *The Dharma Bums* left off. Kerouac returned to the West Coast in 1956 and spent a summer as a fire watcher atop Desolation Peak in Washington. And that is where *Desolation Angels* begins. A long meditation is followed by a run down from the mountain into Seattle for a wild visit to a burlesque show there, and then on to San Francisco, where he renews acquaintances and friendships. They are all there—Cassady (Cody), Corso (Raphael Urso), Ginsberg (Irwin Garden), and Peter Orlovsky (Simon Darlovsky)—and there is a vividness and zest to his description of their life and crazy times in the city by the Bay. All this, covered in Book One of the novel, was written while it was happening and just about as it happened. It would have served as an appropriate conclusion to the cycle. But no. Kerouac felt obliged to add a second book, "Passing Through," written in 1961 and covering the year 1957, including the publication of *On the Road*. And while it contains some fine episodes (the visit with Ginsberg to Paterson is very good indeed) it ranges far too wide—New York, Europe, Mexico City, and back to San Francisco—and attempts too much.

The only year unaccounted for here in this chronology is 1954. Interestingly enough, there is no indication that any of his published works—and this also includes his Lowell novels —were written during that year either. In his fine essay, "The Kerouac Legacy," Seymour Krim gives us the titles of two books besides *Visions of Cody* listed as unpublished—*San Francisco Blues* and *Wake Up*. They might have something to tell us about what happened then.

There is still another novel that might be added to these, one that could be appended to the road cycle as a kind of coda or epiloque. *Big Sur*, written in ten days of October 1961, describes what may well have been Kerouac's last trip to the West Coast, a journey undertaken in rather desperate circumstances during the summer of the year before. "One fast move or I'm gone," he declares here—and he meant it, for in 1960 Kerouac found himself slipping down, down into alcoholism and insanity. His trip to the West Coast that summer was an honest effort to break away from the social pattern in which he had been trapped there in New York every since the publication of *On the Road.*

He was living then with his mother in Northport, Long Island. As soon as *Road* was published and the great publicity machine began to grind away, he found his life was not his own. As he tells it in *Big Sur:* ". . . I've been driven mad for three years by endless telegrams, phonecalls, requests, mail, visitors, reporters, snoopers (a big voice saying in my basement window as I prepare to write a story:—ARE YOU BUSY?) or the time the reporter ran upstairs to my bedroom as I sat there in my pajamas trying to write down a dream—Teenagers jumping the six-foot fence I'd had built around my yard for privacy —Parties with bottles yelling at my study window "Come on out and get drunk, all work and no play makes Jack a dull boy!"

Yes, it was all this that he was running away from, but running away—he realized the irony of this—in grand style on a transcontinental train: "(all over America highschool and college kids thinking 'Jack Duluoz is 26 years old and on the road all the time hitch hiking' while there I am almost 40 years old, bored and jaded in a roomette bunk crashin across the Salt Flat)."

Could he break loose? His plan was to slip into San Francisco, quietly make contact with Lawrence Ferlinghetti (called Lorenzo Monsanto), and travel with him down to the poet's cabin in Big Sur, where Kerouac could hole up, dry out, and begin writing once more. But he makes a bad beginning, seeking out some old drinking buddies in North Beach, losing several days partying, and missing his ride to Big Sur. At last, however, he arrives at his destination, installs himself with a load of groceries and a typewriter, and in three weeks nearly goes mad from the solitude. It is touching to see him try to put himself back together again. Trying to write. Building a mill race with a careful, purposeful precision that recalls Nick Adams' self-therapy in Hemingway's "Big Two-Hearted River." Talking to the ocean, talking to a raccoon, talking to the open sky. At last he gives up in near despair and heads back to San Francisco, thinking that he may be able to recapture what he lost if he sees his old friends and visits the old places again.

But the great lesson of the book—and one that Kerouac, sadly, has learned very well by the end of it—is that nothing lost can be recaptured and no experience recreated. He tries hitchhiking to Monterey (the first time he has done it in years), can get nobody to pick him up, and ends up half-crippled from the blisters on his feet. He finds friends have changed; some of them, like Neal Cassady (Cody Pomeray again), are unable quite to deal with this new public Kerouac—and others all too willing to deal with him, that is, to take advantage, to see what they can squeeze out of him. It is all very sad, but very, very believable, too. When it all comes crashing down in a drunken breakdown, with Kerouac back in the wilds of Big Sur, we are struck only by the inevitable, inexorable, and sure movement he had been making toward this end from the very start of the book. It had to come just as it did.

The breakdown was real enough and sufficiently traumatic to put him out of circulation for nearly a year. "No, we never discussed it," says Sterling Lord, "but I've assumed that something just about like what he tells about in *Big Sur* actually took place. You'd call it a breakdown, I guess.

"Causes? Well, it's a thing that's happened before in American letters. I guess you might say he was kept from growing as a person and as an artist by his success, the adulation that followed. Of course he drank, but what you must remember on his drinking was this entirely new situation he was thrust into. Nothing in his life had prepared him to cope with this. He was actually a very shy person, you know, and the only way he could arm himself to deal with these strange situations was by drinking. He was an extraordinarily charming man when he was sober, though, and great fun to be with."

From the time of that California experience until his death nine years later, Jack Kerouac did what he could to shun the spotlight. He gave no more readings, made few public appearances, and became in all too short a time only a name remembered. The great roar of publicity that welcomed the Beat Generation in the late 1950s had diminished to a mere whisper as America moved optimistically into the Kennedy era. There were more exciting things to think about. Kerouac had managed so well to make himself inconspicuous in 1962, when

*Big Sur* was published, that Herbert Gold was moved to call for a Kerouac revival, pretending he had been out of sight for years.

Kerouac saw less and less of his old friends. Ginsberg was in India with Peter Orlovsky; Corso was traveling in Europe around the Mediterranean, and Burroughs was in London. Throughout this period Kerouac lived with his mother. When he was asked why he continued to stay with *Memere,* he would tell of a deathbed promise he had made to his father to take care of her, and would always remind the questioner rather pointedly that it was only because his mother supported him all those years with that factory job in Long Island that he was able to write those books in the first place. She was an old woman by this time and an invalid.

The breakdown Kerouac describes in *Big Sur* takes the form, more or less, of a religious conversion. There by the ocean he has a vision of the cross while he is being plagued by devils, a flying saucer, and a terrifying bat. It sounds like a classic case of delerium tremens—except for this vision of the cross. "I'm with you, Jesus, for always, thank you"—he thinks as he lies there sweating on the ground, studying the cross and regretting his dalliance with Buddhism. ("You old son of a bitch," his guru Gary Snyder had once told him, "you're going to end up asking for the Catholic rites on your death bed.") He feels a sense of repentence: "—My eyes fill with tears—'We'll all be saved—' "

No matter how traumatic the breakdown experience, he seems to have separated and retained from it all a true religious feeling that helped sustain him in those difficult years that followed when he felt himself more and more alone. Of course he was never very far from the old French Canadian Catholicism of his parents. Even while he was studying Buddhism he was keeping one eye on Saint Teresa. And if his ideas of Catholic mysticism, as expressed in *Visions of Gerard,* owe something to the religious calendars that used to hang in the kitchen back in Lowell, nevertheless, they were truly his and he held tightly to them until his death.

And the pattern of his behavior during that period was
very much that of a reformed sinner. He removed himself

from the "occasions of sin," avoiding his old friends and the places they used to meet. He stayed pretty close to home during those years—although to suit his mother he moved up and down from Florida a number of times with her—and from his sanctuary he watched the 1960s take shape with disapproval mixed with a sense of guilt for the part he had played in shaping it.

Jack Kerouac was politically a conservative. When he began to denounce Lawrence Ferlinghetti and Lawrence Lipton as Communists, many who knew him only slightly were astonished and chagrined. They said he had changed, that he had become a renegade reactionary. But no. Far from it. He was always conservative—or perhaps better put, libertarian—in his outlook. Michael McClure recalls that he shocked all his friends in San Francisco in 1956 by insisting that if he were voting that year he would vote for Eisenhower. "It just seemed a weird idea to us then," he said. "Not voting we could understand, but *wanting* to vote for Eisenhower!"

There is something a little too easy, perhaps, in associating the Beat protest with left radicalism, as so many have done. For a number of good reasons that was the direction that it took. But what the movement was, essentially, was apolitical —a last-ditch stand for individualism and against conformity. That, anyhow, was how Jack Kerouac saw it, and he was present at the creation. On the other hand, it would be a mistake to take Kerouac's political opinions very seriously, for they were compounded at least partly of old French Catholic conservatism, vague anti-Semitic feelings, and sentimental memories of the rabid anti-New Dealism of his father.

Allen Ginsberg saw Kerouac's withdrawal differently: "It seemed that he was so horrified by the police state he saw taking shape around us that he decided to stay as far away from it as possible. He practically went underground! So in a way he took it more seriously than any of us."

This was after Ginsberg had been very nearly thrown out bodily, trying to visit his old friend up in Lowell. Kerouac had married for the second time in 1966, an old girl friend of his, Stella Sampis whom he had known in high school. They lived for a while in Hyannis and then moved back up to Lowell.

When Ginsberg dropped in unannounced, he failed to find him but came face to face with *Memere.* She refused to tell him where her son was living, gave him a shove toward the stairs, and slammed the door on his face. And then she refused obstinately to open the door again or to provide any more information. Ginsberg left Lowell without seeing him.

It was no easy matter to see Jack Kerouac up in Lowell, Massachusetts. I found that out for myself when I went to visit him early in 1968, not long before the publication of his novel, *The Vanity of Duluoz,* the last in the Lowell cycle. I had tried unsuccessfully to reach him by telephone a couple of times and had been cut off once in mid-question. And yes, I had an address—but not, as it turned out, the *right* address.

Lowell is one of those old mill towns that blight the New England landscape, a depressed area in every way but the one that means people are unemployed. There seem to be plenty of jobs there—the textile mills are going full blast, the store windows are filled, and there are plenty of shoppers on the street. But what kind of a town is it, really? The kind that people come from. Not the kind they go back to.

I drove through the residential streets, surveying the houses that lined them, and found they were well cared-for, but there was a dreary sameness to them that bespoke a failure of nerve, a lack of imagination. I was looking for the address I had taken up there with me—it turned out to be the only Kerouac in the Lowell telephone directory, and the name was Herve Kerouac. I found it without too much difficulty, parked the car, and looked the house over—frame, nineteenth century from the look of it but in good shape, and up on a hill above the Merrimack River. I went up the stairs and rang the bell, not too long and not too hard, but politely.

The door opened wide, but the figure of a man blocked it completely. It was Herve Kerouac, a workingman, dressed in a flannel shirt and twill pants. He stood about five feet six or seven and weighed perhaps a little over 200 pounds, of which no more than five were fat. He smiled very tentatively, listened as I explain why I came to Lowell, but then he said that Jack Kerouac was nowhere around.

"But he does live in Lowell, doesn't he?"

"Well, yeah, but he doesn't live in this house. He lives a long way from here, and he doesn't want me giving out his address. Too many guys from New York come up here to see him. He doesn't like it. He wants to be left alone. You understand that?"

"Are you his brother?"

"No, I'm not his brother. His brother's dead a long time ago. I'm his cousin. Do him a favor. Go away."

Herve Kerouac is not the kind of man you argue with. I just nodded politely and left. I went down to the center of town and began asking about Jack Kerouac—first at a drug store. A kid behind the counter, barely twenty, laughed and shrugged when I asked him about Kerouac, said he was "crazy," and just shook his head when I asked if he knew where he lived. In a corner cigar store a customer over forty said, sure, he knew Kerouac, had gone to high school with him.

"What's he like?" I asked.

"He's just a guy, just like anybody else," he said, then added, almost as an afterthought: "But he was a pretty good football player, though."

Yes, sure, he knew he was a writer and all that, but he didn't know where he lived. "He hasn't been in town long, see." He had a pretty good idea where he might be right now, though, and he directed me to Nicky's Bar on Gorham Street.

And there was Jack Kerouac when I walked into the place. He was the guy sitting in back, talking across the bar to the bartender. There was no mistaking him. Of course, he looked older than he did ten years before when they took all those pictures. His hair—what I could see of it under the baseball cap he wore—looked about as black as it ever did. He was heavier, no doubt about that. Somehow, though, the face was the same.

The bartender with whom he is talking so intently turns out to be his brother-in-law, Nick, who owns the bar. Although he looks vaguely tough, he has a good reputation in Lowell, and he is proud of his sister's new husband. ("How did my sister meet him?" he echoes my query later on. "How should I know? Listen, this goes back a long way. The two of them, my sister and Jack, they've known each other all their lives. They

87

were high school sweethearts and all that. He's a good husband for her. He takes good care of her. I love him.")

I stood close by, waiting to be noticed. Eventually Kerouac threw an arm out in a bit of wild Canuck gesticulation, glanced in my direction, and said something like, "Oh, yeah, hey, hi."

I nodded politely and told him why I had come. I asked if he could talk to me for a little while. "Sort of an interview," I explained.

With that, Kerouac put two fingers in his mouth and whistled shrilly. The old heads at the bar turn in our direction, and Nicky, the bartender, walks away. *"Interview!"* Kerouac shouts, "interview! New York is here, America is listening!" Light laughter, fading to smiles—but they know this routine and soon they are back drinking their beer, talking their old-guy talk to one another.

I asked him then if he thought he and his writings had changed much in the last ten years.

He didn't seem to think much of the question. "Maybe. Or sure, I don't know." He shrugged. "But listen, that whole Beat scene is dead. And if you want my opinion, if anything, my writing has improved, because *I've* improved. Let me tell you, a true writer should be an observer and not go around *being* observed, like Mailer and Ginsberg. Observing—that's the duty and oath of a writer. Here in Lowell, I just sit around and take in the scene. It's great. But you'll be able to judge for yourself. My new novel was written right up here. I think it's better than anything I've done for quite a while. Read it, and you can decide for yourself."

I asked about his politics and told him that some who said they were old friends of his were claiming that he had changed his position recently.

He bridled at that. "How? *How?* Listen, my politics haven't changed, and *I* haven't changed! I'm solidly behind Bill Buckley, if you want to know. Nothing I wrote in my books—*nothing*—could be seen as basically in disagreement with this. Everybody just assumed I thought the way *they* wanted me to think. What really bothered me a lot, though, was the way a certain cadre of leftists among the so-called Beats took over my mantle and twisted my thoughts to suit their own purpose."

"Just what kind of relationship do you—"

"Hey," he said, looking at me oddly, "aren't you going to have anything to drink? Hey, Nicky, come on and give this guy something to drink."

I ordered and Kerouac called for another glass of wine. It was thick and dark. It looked like port.

"I was going to ask if you thought the hippies came out of the Beat movement."

He batted this one around for a long while and made a number of starts and stops before he really said anything. For the first time I really noticed that he was beginning to show his drinking. The hippies bothered him. He didn't want to claim them. But Kerouac persisted, and after a moment's pause in which Nicky put our drinks down in front of us: "Of course the hippies followed us in certain ways, so yeah, I guess you could say they are the descendants of the Beat Generation. Maybe what separates us from them is not so much age as acid. I tried LSD once, and I couldn't write and I couldn't paint the way I wanted to while I was having this trip. All I could do was have these visions of heaven. I wrote it all down afterward, but it didn't really seem so great to me by that time."

"Would you say that—"

"Listen," he interrupted, "I don't know if you've thought about this much at all, or maybe you already had your mind made up about me before you even came to talk to me. But anyhow, one thing I wanted to say—I want to make this very clear. I mean, here I am, a guy who was a railroad brakeman, and a cowboy, and a football player—just a lot of things ordinary guys do. And I wasn't trying to create any kind of new consciousness or anything like that. We didn't have a whole lot of heavy abstract thoughts. We were just a bunch of guys who were out trying to get laid."

"What about all the rest of those guys, though? Do you see them much anymore? What about Allen Ginsberg?"

"Well . . ." Kerouac shrugs, making a play of indifference. "You probably heard the story about Allen and what happened when he came up here six months ago. He wasn't allowed to come and see me by my mother. I can't say I blame her, though. He scared hell out of her with his beard and his bald head. He bothers me, too. If you ask me, he's got sort of an evil format to his program—in the poetry racket and the youth racket the way he is. I meet him on the street in New York, and he says, 'Give me your riches!' I say to him, 'What riches? I don't have any riches.' And I don't. I'm just an ordinary guy who's trying to do his job, and my job happens to be that I'm a writer."

Was he working on another book then? "There's always another book. If I live long enough, I'll write my Hollywood book next. How will I do it? I'll just sit down, and let it flow out of me, like I did all the rest of them since *On the Road*. It's a spontaneous flow that comes, and nobody could understand what I was talking about when I said you should just open up and let it come out. It's the Holy Ghost that comes through you. You don't have to be a Catholic to know what I mean, and you don't have to be a Catholic for the Holy Ghost to speak through you."

He had nothing more to say to me after that. He talked a while longer, but he said nothing more.

# Beatniks and Hipsters

Since the Beat Generation was so often said to be no more than a creation of the Luce publications, it might be surprising to learn how little, really, *Time* or *Life* had to say about them. The Weekly Newsmagazine reviewed their books, commented now and again on their readings around the country, but ran no cover story on the Beats. It was left to *Life* to do an in-depth treatment of the phenomenon—and that came fairly late in the game, toward the end of 1959. A long, carefully researched, and fairly comprehensive piece by Paul O'Neil appeared then, which described the Beat Generation as "a cult of the Pariah," and said that its real significance lay in the fact that it was the only rebellion around. (Remember, this was 1959.) More interesting, however, was the way he characterized its spokesmen, the Beat writers whose work we are talking about here. He called them "the most curious men of influence the 20th Century has yet produced," and he went on to say: "The poets, almost to a man, are individualistic and antisocial to the point of neuroticism. They are dissidents so enthralled with their own egos and so intent on bitter personal complaint that they would be incapable of organizing juvenile delinquents in a reform school. But the Beat Generation is their baby for all that, and the country's current Beat-consciousness is their doing." That is fairly consistent with the tone of the entire piece. The tactic followed, a familiar one in such treatments, was to ridicule the Beats in all particulars, yet to take them seriously in general—as a trend, an indication of something greater taking shape beneath the surface. And while that may have proved, in the longest possible run, to be fairly accurate as prophecy, such an interpretation in not nearly as sympathetic as one would expect from the article that was supposed to have "made" the Beats. No, by and large, the treatment given them in the big circulation magazines and the major newspapers reflected, as it generally does in most cultural matters even today, the going opinions in the mandarin intellectual press. It may have mattered only to a comparative few what Diana Trilling thought of Allen Ginsberg, but among that few were certainly the staff members of the *New York Times Book Review* and those who wrote on the arts for *Time, Life,* and *Newsweek.*

But the sudden, spontaneous, and enormously wide appeal of the Beats could not easily be dismissed. It vexed the *Partisan Review* people and caused interest and concern among the editors of the mass media—as well, in both instances, it should have. It was the first truly popular literary movment to take hold among the American young since the Lost Generation of the 1920s. And at its height, interest in Kerouac, Ginsberg, Corso, et al., reached down further in society than it had with Hemingway and Fitzgerald thirty-five years before. And to older Americans and those of the young who were of more conservative disposition, the Beats were at least an interesting disruption in what even they had come to regard as an all too placid period. Thus the "Beat" coffee shops that opened in nearly every American city over a 100,000; thus the spate of Beatnik jokes that celebrated the casual perversity of their attitudes in the old-fashioned jive talk—lots of "cool" and "crazy"—that was the popular version of Beat jargon; and thus, too, the butchered movie version of Jack Kerouac's *The Subterraneans* and an even worse film titled, *The Beat Generation;* and thus finally the Beatnik characters that showed up in *The Romance of Helen Trent* and *Popeye,* and the rent-a-Beatnik fad that ran its course in the classified columns of the *Village Voice.*

Interestingly enough, after that first year following the publication of *On the Road,* during which Kerouac and Ginsberg did all the readings and appearances on radio and television they were ever going to do together, the individual who took over as front man for the revolution was one who had met none of its protagonists until recently, who had little or nothing by way of experience in common with them, and whose commitment to the Beats was essentially intellectual. Nevertheless, as a theorist and as the Beats' celebrity-in-residence, Norman Mailer made quite a contribution.

He was intellectually respectable, according to those who kept charts on such matters, and, of course, none of the Beats were. A New York intellectual, a veteran of the Progressive party's Henry Wallace campaign, and the author of the only novel worth remembering to come out of World War II, *The Naked and the Dead,* Mailer was skilled in the old thrust-and-parry dialectic that passes for rational discourse among that crowd, and a writer whose great potential even more than his past performance made him impossible to dismiss. He had lately, however, been having some problems. His career had begun to drift dangerously after the savaging of *Barbary Shore* (1951) and the relative failure of *The Deer Park* (1955). He had vague plans for a vast work, a cycle of novels of which he had actually committed only a little to paper. There were starts and stops, a column that ran for a while in the *Village Voice,* and a short novel, "The Man Who Studied Yoga," that many said showed he was rounding back into form as a writer of fiction. But as it turned out, the most important single work by Mailer during this period was an essay, which he published in *Dissent* in 1957, called "The White Negro."

In it, he set forth the philosophy of hip. He presented it as a kind of gut existentialism, an ethic based on the pattern of behavior that had been forced on the black man: "Any Negro who wishes to live must live with danger from his first day, and no experience can ever be casual to him, no Negro can saunter down a street with any real certainty that violence will not visit him on his walk." Mailer's hipsters are "a new breed of adventurers, urban adventurers who drifted out at night looking for action with a black man's code to fit their facts." They seek danger for the possibilities it affords; they bet everything on the main chance; they are connoisseurs of violence and sexuality. The hipsters are, finally, in a phrase of Mailer's that is chilling in its implications, "philosophical psychopaths."

Critics and public alike quite rightly associated Mailer's
93  hipster and his ethic of existential expedience with the Beats.

The term, and even more certainly the ideas behind it, recur in the work of John Clellon Holmes, Corso, Burroughs, and all the rest. In "Howl," Ginsberg speaks of "angel-headed hipsters," and might well have had Neal Cassady in mind when he wrote it, for Cassady was considered by them to be the hipster par excellence.

All of the Beats, however, probably got their ideas of who and what a hipster was from Burroughs, Herbert Huncke, and their circle. The etymology of the word takes us well back into the jazz and drug world in which they moved then. Hip derives directly from "hep," which musicians were using even before the war to describe an intuitive quality of instant understanding, as early as 1945 or so there was a jazz singer and pianist operating around New York who called himself Harry "the Hipster" Gibson. Huncke was a hipster. In fact—and this is a point that must be made at Mailer's expense—almost any narcotics addict was a hipster by virtue of his addiction. "The White Negro" describes a pattern of behavior that was certainly well established by the time the essay was written, but it was one that could be most properly identified with one group—and that was the drug addicts. They had no choice. The sort of reckless gambling with life that Mailer describes (and by implication, urges) was forced on the junkie because of the marginal quality of his existence, the constant threat of arrest under which he lived, and the way that all his concerns were really reduced to a single purpose, getting his next fix. Did Mailer know all this and decide not to tell? He must have. It is all a little like those wanted descriptions that used to appear in the newspapers in which the information that the suspect was black was coyly withheld. Obviously, sociologist Ned Polsky was trying to set the record straight three years later in *Dissent* in his own essay describing "The Village Beat Scene: Summer 1960." In it, he made clear that the mores and code of conduct of these hipsters had been determined largely by the fact of their addiction.

Because Mailer felt that in the public mind his hipsters had been coopted by the Beat Generation, he kept right on making distinctions and pointing up differences between the hip and 94 the Beat as long as anyone would listen. What seemed to attract him most to the hipster culture was the violence he saw in it. And true enough, if the two groups did exist as in any true sense separate, the difference between them lay in their attitude to violence. Think of the hipsters as the Beat Generation's right wing, Mailer said: they are charged by the threat of physical danger, turned on by it; it is not merely that they have not renounced violence, as have most of the Beats, but that violence gives the hipster his sense of identity, his purest sensation of reality in this most unreal world.

This was the message that Norman Mailer preached during the period when he became so closely associated, at least in the media, with the Beat Generation. He seemed out to evangelize the world in the name of "healthy" violence. It was largely because of this that a certain aura of brutality and aggressive hostility became attached to the entire Beat movement, one that was a little difficult to reconcile with the drop-out doctrine of disaffiliation to which the Beats officially subscribed. It may have been easy enough to read into the extreme language of "Howl" a kind of glorification of violence, to see it as a kind of antiprayer for force and power to wreak vengeance on society; but in this way "Howl" represents a kind of outer limit reached by Ginsberg and was not characteristic of his work as a whole, even at the time. As for Kerouac, it is difficult to detect anything approaching Mailer's version of the hipster in his portrait of Dean Moriarty. It is remarkable, in fact, how little violence of any kind there is to be found in Kerouac's novels. No, it was Mailer who introduced this element into the Beat ethos, although Burroughs subsequently did a lot to reinforce the association with cruelty and violence.

That said, it should be added that Norman Mailer proved a good friend to the Beats. An articulate and energetic defender of the faith, he appeared often on television talk shows and usually made a point of identifying himself with Kerouac, Ginsberg, and Burroughs and promoting their work. It was in such a context that Truman Capote's notorious put-down of Jack Kerouac was delivered. Mailer's version of the story is interesting because it adds a certain dimension to an anecdote that has now become almost legendary. "It was on a sort of panel discussion show on the Beats," Mailer remembers. "I was coming on long and hard for Kerouac—really talking too much, it's a habit of mine. At intermission, Truman turns to me and says, 'Damn you, Nawmin, youah *so* articulate.' He pots at you that way. He's a deceptively slight little guy, but under that swishy exterior, he's tough and hard. Well, I went on about Kerouac's rapid writing, how I think he's the best *rapid* writer in America today. And when I stopped just long enough to catch my breath, Truman comes in with 'Writing! That's not writing, it's just . . . *typing!'* Now this is a great put-down. And New York is a town for the one-line put-down. But Truman took it very hard when it was quoted all over, practically apologized. He said to me later, 'I shouldn't even have been on that show. I've got this *small* talent for ridicule.' "

This came out in the course of an interview I had with Mailer at about the time he was most vocal in the Beats' behalf. He made a kind of declaration of his purpose as a writer at this time that I think bears repeating here: "I think we've got to get a new view of man. To do this, you've got to break through all the layers of cultural junk that have accumulated over your consciousness. And you've got to be very tough. I don't know if I'm tough enough to do it, but that's what I'm trying to do. William Burroughs is one writer who *is* doing it, I think." This is interesting in the way that Mailer puts himself in a position junior to Burroughs. As few as four years later, he would certainly not have deferred to him in this way.

When I asked him then why he felt the Beats were uninterested in involving themselves politically or, in the narrow sense, socially, Mailer answered, "Well, I feel there are . . . reasons why the Beats haven't been involved. One of them is not really to their credit. . . . It goes back to what we were saying earlier on self-censorship. There is a sort of instinctive sense in them that they should stay away from politics— or make their remarks on politics surrealistic. For example, when Kerouac says, 'I like Eisenhower. I think he's a great man. I think he's our greatest president since Abraham Lincoln.' Well, you know that's not a serious political remark at all. I don't think he even believed it, except, perhaps, when he said it. It's a surrealistic remark. He's mixing two ideas that have absolutely no relation to each other—one of them is greatness and the other is Eisenhower."

And finally this, for it gives us a sense of the indignation that Mailer felt on the Beats' behalf and an indication of just why he stepped forward as their defender: "One of the most frightening things about the whole business was the enormous antipathy the Beats aroused in the more vested centers of literary power. It was remarkable. There were people who made a career out of attacking the Beats. Even without being at all political they were attacked crudely and unfairly. To a degree, they asked for it, but it had nothing to do with the way they got it."

As time went on, Norman Mailer seemed to become obsessed by violence. In the journalism that he undertook for *Esquire* magazine, and even more flagrantly in remarks he made in interviews, his pronouncements on the subject seemed intended to outrage liberal sentiment. In one interview published in *Mademoiselle* magazine his remarks sound as though they had been ghosted by the Marquis de Sade in collaboration with Julius Streicher. He urged, for instance, "If you're going to grind your heel into the face of a dying man . . . let the act finally be authentic." Mailer declared that "in the act of killing, in this terribly private moment, the brute feels a moment of tenderness for the first time perhaps in all of his existence." Even if this were empty rhetoric, such talk would seem dangerously extreme, but Mailer certainly wanted these ideas on the redemptive nature of violence to be taken seriously.

His hipster passion for violence, together with a kind of Manicheistic personal theology he had been developing along the way, finally found expression in a novel, *An American Dream,* which was published in 1965 after having been serialized in *Esquire* through the previous year. It is a maddening book, one so filled with occultism, Dostoyevskyan vapors, and plain looniness that it is easy to overlook what is good about it. His intellectual hipster, Stephen Rojack, commits amoral murder, and in each new chapter meets and passes a new test to emerge scarred but triumphant at book's end, having revealed nothing less than the shape and texture of the heroic fantasies of the author. It is not Rojack we see but Norman Mailer, naked before us, the hair on his chest beginning to gray, his gut sagging a bit, a little heavier all the way around than we had expected. There he is, showing us all and daring us to look. His friends turned away in dismay (*An American Dream* caused deep consternation among the members of the New York intellectual community who viewed it as the final outrage in Mailer's program of literary exhibitionism), but those who were less personally involved with him were able to take in the view somewhat more dispassionately and were more kindly disposed toward what they saw. For after all, if Mailer was wearing his fantasies like the emperor's new clothes, you had to admire the style of the man who was revealed underneath them. To have such heroic dreams as these, and to reveal them with grace and apparently without embarrassment seems in itself an act of purest heroism in such an age as ours.

For better or for worse, the Mailer we know today is a self-creation dating from that period in his life when he emulated the hipsters and defended the Beats. Whatever the source of the energy he received from them, it eventually proved enough for him to remake himself into a very different writer. He has created a great personal myth from the elements he found around him then. He is his own greatest work.

Norman Mailer was in Chicago to do a benefit reading for *Big Table* when I spoke with him in 1960. He was just one of a number of such efforts made by writers associated with the Beat Generation to keep alive this magazine, the chief organ of the movement. Born out of a censorship squabble at the University of Chicago, the first issue of the journal was brought out under the editorship of Irving Rosenthal and then subsequently handed over to the care of the poet Paul Carroll. Carroll had to scrape so for money through the issues that followed that it is remarkable that he was able to produce a magazine of such high quality. Under his editorship, *Big Table* published a fairly wide range of writing that included work by Beats, Black Mountain poets, and others of compatible style and sympathies, such as John Logan, Edward Dahlberg, and

98    John Rechy. But eventually Carroll exhausted all possible

means to support the magazine and had to try the impossible kind: "I had to turn, finally, after three issues had been published and printer's bills paid, to the great American foundations for support. Despite the fact that *Big Table* had a circulation of 10,000 and had demonstrated that it was trying to do its best to provide an outlet for some of the new, experimental work being done by American writers, and despite the fact that none of the editors received salary and worked at night and on weekends to publish the magazine, not one of the foundations—Ford, Rockefeller, several smaller ones—exhibited a suspicion of interest beyond mailing complicated forms to be filled out and informing me that no funds were available for such a purpose." *Big Table* staggered on a year longer, however, and finally fell of its own weight in 1961. Paul Carroll suggests that the literary phase of the movement ended then with the collapse of the magazine.

It was one of a number of publications that was started in that rush of enthusiasm that came with the appearance of the Beats on the scene. All of them featured creative over critical writing (reversing the formula that was well-established by then in the university quarterlies) and were open to work by the Beats and their fellow travelers. The *San Francisco Review* and *Contact* came out of the Bay area; John Logan's *Choice* was issued in Chicago; and in New York there was LeRoi Jones' *Yugen,* and a number of (very) little magazines whose function it was to publish the work of the New York poets. Eventually all of them succumbed (although *Choice* has since been revived), leaving it up to the *Evergreen Review* and *Nugget,* the girlie magazine which was edited honorably from 1961 to 1965 by Seymour Krim, to carry the load.

Krim's stand at *Nugget* had especially interesting results. It was not just because of the writers he published—although these included Gregory Corso, John Clellon Holmes, Jack Gelber, Kenneth Rexroth, and John Rechy, among others—but because of the kind of work they produced for him. He got these and others to try their hand at the kind of writing—part reporting, part commentary, part confession—that he does so well himself; in this way, as an editor, he gave a big boost to the style of personal journalism.

About the *Evergreen Review* there is not much to say, except that it was and still is the steadiest and most frequent publisher of writing that might be described as Beat in style or substance. Both the format and the contents of the magazine have changed a good deal since *Evergreen* came out with its San Francisco Scene issue in the middle of 1957, which set the stage for the big drama that followed. Yet somehow it remains curiously the same, frozen in an attitude of revolt that seemed spontaneous enough a decade ago, yet now seems static and predictable. Accretions of bile and hostility seem to have swollen it so that it now almost resembles the ponderous monoliths of American life that are attacked with such mechanical regularity in its pages: it is the revolution institutionalized.

If such a complaint seems gratuitous and somewhat overstated, I suppose I am railing against a development that was predictable, even inevitable, as the Beat protest lost the characteristics of a literary movement and became broader in shape and more political in direction. As greater numbers were consumed by the flame of revolt the Beats had sparked, the protest became diffused and generalized to the point that it has also become a mass movement with established positions and official organs such as *Evergreen* and *Ramparts.* This is ironic, of course, for the passion that seemed to unite them all a decade or more ago was the antipathy toward mass movements of all kinds—left, right, or center. It was the price the Beats paid for succeeding as they did.

While this sure development from literary to social has kept several, such as Norman Mailer and Allen Ginsberg, in the spotlight, it has also taken its toll on many who were on the scene at the beginning. It was not just the specifically literary magazines that were casualties of the shift, but along with them the more specifically literary writers as well. Fish or cut bait in the service of the revolution—that was the message that came through sooner or later to all those who were involved in the early Beat protest. Many of those who wished to remain just what they were simply opted out—and Kerouac was not the only one who did this. One or two drifted off to the Orient, a few others to Europe. Some have moved to other cities and submerged themselves in urban American anonymity. A couple have dropped out via the drug route. Has the revolution devoured its own? No, worse luck, it has spit them out and left them in corners to decay.

# CHAPTER 6

# Son of Naomi

The central fact that one must come to grips with in understanding Allen Ginsberg and his present importance as a prophet and teacher (and only incidentally as a poet) is that he is now very different from that intense, wrathful young man who first exploded onto the scene, snarling out his "Howl" to the world. "He began with the muse of hatred," wrote Alan Harrington of a character readily identifiable as Ginsberg in his novel, *The Secret Swinger:* "Having reviled his times and been honored for it, the poet had raged out of his dark strangeness and become attractive." And while other portraits of the younger Ginsberg may vary somewhat in emphasis, they all seem to agree that he was a chronically angry and reckless experimenter with life, his own and others'.

And today? Today he is much different: certainly one of the most completely open and altogether decent people you are likely to meet among the great public personalities of our age. And yes, you *are* likely to meet him, for all that really takes is the courage to thrust out your hand to him and introduce yourself.

He has a most disarming manner. People who approach him with specific ideas about who or what he is are most likely to find that their preconception of him has changed within the space of a few minutes conversation. His biographer Jane Kramer is a case in point. In her Introduction to *Allen Ginsberg in America* she describes her first meeting with him, a meeting to which she carried an idea of him as "a worn beatnik, whose poetry was affecting but whose style of life was bound to be ridiculous." And true enough, there is much in his style of life that is ridiculous—Ginsberg, I think, would be the first to concede that—but as Miss Kramer discovered, none of it mattered much when once she got to know him.

I'll confess to a certain uneasiness of my own when I first met him, which just goes to show how tightly we hold onto first impressions. For my earliest exposure to Allen Ginsberg dated back to 1958, and I had immediately perceived the hostility in him that then always bubbled near the surface. There were stories of shouting matches, angry denunciations of whole audiences, and that classic anecdote from an early reading in Los Angeles. He was asked rather skeptically by a member of the audience just what he thought he was trying to prove with his poetry. To which Ginsberg replied simply, "Nakedness." Unsatisfied, the questioner persisted, "What do you mean by that?" Whereupon Ginsberg took off all his clothes and showed him. Well, I'm not sure what I expected when I actually met him some years later, but I wasn't quite prepared for the directness and easy cordiality I got from him then. Sure he'd see me, of course. He was going out of town on a lecture tour—as a matter of fact, he was catching a jet out of Kennedy in an hour—but after that, certainly. "I'm the Allen Ginsberg in the phone book," he added. "Call me."

Eventually, I did, marveling that he still kept a listed number. What must that cost him in interruptions? I asked myself. I'm not sure that he really remembered me from our brief earlier meeting, but we made a date and I showed up at the appointed hour, notebook in hand and full of questions and apprehensions. He disposed of the latter very quickly. There was a sort of pause before we began, in which he did what he could to put me at my ease, asking general questions about what I was interested in, trying to get *me* to open up. By the time I was ready to start asking him questions, I found that he had been answering them a while already.

"Yes, sure, there are many elements of continuity from the Beats to the present." This was volunteered and not in answer to a direct question. "Just look around you, and then look back and you can see where it all began. Drugs? The first serious experimentation with altered states of consciousness came with the Beats using pot and peyote. Indigenous music? You can see the movement from jazz and rhythm and blues in *On the Road* to rock today. You could say we had a preoccupation with the Thoreauvian and Whitmanic tradition and so we were very responsive to this whole rediscovery of the Body of the Land. And the Eastern elements that interest young people today—well, look at Gary Snyder. Look at the Buddhist stuff in *Mexico City Blues.*"

"Look at yourself," I put in.

"Yes," he said. "Look."

Just then I could hardly have done otherwise, for as Allen Ginsberg began to warm to the subject, he began talking *at* me in the way he often does. His face was close to mine, and though we are about the same height, I found he was peering up at me, for he had dropped down into a crouch as he went on. The thick beard he wears obscures the lower portion of his face almost completely, so that attention naturally is drawn to his eyes, which flicker and move intently, rather than stare.

I asked him how he might sum up the Beat movement as an idea. What was at the heart of it intellectually?

"Well, there was the return to nature and the revolt against the machine, and I think this was very important, for you can see all this in the reduplication of the cycle today. The fact that the basic human proportion has not been lost owes something, I think, to these beginnings. Because we can still talk to one another in these human ways, you see—you and me together —means that art is still possible."

Ginsberg hesitated a moment as though grasping back for the thread, and then plunged on: "It's all been in the gnostic tradition, the underground mystical tradition of the West. Not that we originated it, just carried it on a little here in America. Yes, here, *here* it's a problem. Because it's only by getting out from under the American flag and marching to a different drummer in the Thoreauvian sense that one can find one's own self here. And you have to do it, too. It's either that or take that mass-produced self they keep trying to shove down your throat with their cigarette advertisements and so on. . . .

"But look," he concluded suddenly, "I'll bet you want to talk about more practical matters, don't you?"

"Well, I . . ."

"Addresses? You want addresses? You said you would be

going out to the West Coast, didn't you? Here, let me get my book, and maybe I can help you decide who to see out there." This, as sudden as the shifting of gears, was a new Allen Ginsberg, one that I had heard talked about often but never seen in action. In a sour moment Gregory Corso is supposed to have called him "a Jewish businessman." And, perhaps curiously, there is certainly that quality in him: he gets things done. That apartment in the East Village which he shared with Peter Orlovsky served for years as a kind of command post for the Beat movement and the cultural revolution that evolved from it. Out of it, Ginsberg wrote letters and made phone calls, urging editors to publish the work of this young novelist or that poet, rallying support for causes of all kinds. And Allen Ginsberg's address book, which he carries with him wherever and whenever he moves, is fabled as a kind of international who's who of the revolution. If you want to get in touch with an old Wobbly poet in Seattle, Ginsberg has his address and the phone number of the next-door neighbor who takes his calls. Who sells the best hash in Kabul? It's in Ginsberg's book.

The addresses I needed were the ones you might have expected, a few poets on the West Coast, Burroughs' address in London, and a few others in Europe. And so on. Ginsberg was free with suggestions: "Oh, you really must see so-and-so!" or "What about such-and-such? He's been buried down there for years and he'd be delighted if someone came and interviewed him." That kind of thing. All in all, most helpful—and when we had at last exhausted the resources of the pages of that thick book of his, he urged me to get in touch with him if there was someone I wanted to see whom we hadn't discussed. "If I don't have a phone number, I can always get it." In Hollywood it would have sounded like the most shameful vainglory; coming from Allen Ginsberg, it was simple fact.

One of the San Francisco addresses given me by Ginsberg was poet Michael McClure's. During a long evening's conversation with McClure some time later, I remember that I talked a little about Allen Ginsberg and said he turned out to be much different from what I expected.

"How?" asked McClure. "What did you expect him to be like?"

"Oh, I don't know. Maybe it's that he's more relaxed than I thought he would be—though he's still pretty intense, isn't he? I guess he's just nicer than I expected."

"Well," he said, "we're all nicer now. Allen certainly is, but everybody else is, too—including me." Then McClure added with a wry smile, "But Allen's been nice for five years and I've only been nice for two."

I laughed, of course, but later I found that with regard to Ginsberg, at least, what McClure had said was absolutely accurate. For that "five-year" estimate, which I thought had been tossed off merely as a joke, fixed the time of the very perceptible change in Ginsberg as his return to America from an Indian sojourn of nearly two years.

For nearly half his lifetime Allen Ginsberg had looked forward to visiting the Orient. Very early on, his interest had been fixed in what he called the "gnostic tradition," and it was following this tradition that led him there. As early as his Columbia years he was having visions of sorts: one, a kind of beatific perception of a great consciousness shared among all those present one afternoon in the Columbia bookshop; and another, an "apparitional voice," which he assumed to be that of the poet, William Blake, reciting "Ah, Sunflower" and illuminating him in its wisdom. These experiences merely made him hungry for more.

And it was this search for experience that made him so restlessly explorative during those early New York years. He thought of it as a sort of holy search whose subject was wisdom and thus must have felt empowered to be a little ruthless with himself and others. And although, when his misadventures with Huncke and a couple of his criminal friends landed him in the Columbia Psychiatric Institute, he came upon Carl Solomon there and introduced himself as Prince Myshkin, Ginsberg probably thought of himself far more often then as Raskolnikov.

This straining after experience, which became so much the pattern of his life through the late 1940s and early 1950s, had 106 included a certain amount of drug-taking. This culminated in the heavy drug session during which he produced "Howl" in a single weekend in San Francisco. All that peyote, benzedrine, and amphetamine must have had a liberating effect on him, for as he began writing, he later said, he thought not to write a poem but simply to put down in lines the things he held back in poems past for fear of embarrassing his father: ". . . let my imagination go, open secrecy, and scribble magic lines from my real mind—sum up my life—something I wouldn't be able to show anybody. . . ."

Thus it poured forth, and the results were impressive even to Allen Ginsberg. It was a breakthrough that had been achieved, at least in part (as he saw it) through the taking of drugs. The way was clear to him then—more drugs, more visions, striving for direct, mystical experience of the greater reality, and then recording these higher states, these super-realities in poetry directly as perceived. And this is roughly what he did. The results? You can study them for yourself in the final pages of *Kaddish and Other Poems 1958–1960*. Beginning with "Laughing Gas," the poems seem to take a leap far out into a kind of void, an enormous endless space which he occupies as a skydiver, moving prettily but endlessly falling. There is a desperate earnestness to these poems that demands answers to the largest questions he can put. If there are visions they are of a rather frightening sort:

> It is a multiple million eyed monster
> it is hidden in all its elephants and selves
> it hummeth in the electric typewriter
> it is electricity connected to itself, if it hath wires
> it is a vast Spiderweb
> and I am on the last millionth infinite tentacle of the
> spiderweb, a worrier
> lost, separated, a worm, a thought, a self
> one of the millions of skeletons of China. . . .
> ["Lysergic Acid"]

And if there is wisdom, it is of the arcane kind which, though delivered by Ginsberg at the top of his voice, seems neither to illuminate nor satisfy him.

No refuge in Myself, which is on fire
        or in the World which is His also to bomb & Devour!
            Recognise His might! Loose hold
        of my hands—my frightened skull
                —for I had chose self-love—
    my eyes, my nose, my face, my cock, my soul—and now
            the faceless Destroyer!
        A billion doors to the same new Being!
    The universe turns inside out to devour me!
    and the mighty burst of music comes from out the inhuman
                                    door—
                                    ["The Reply"]

All very unclear, of course, meaning much and signifying little.
What does come through loudly and unmistakably, however,
is a growing feeling of self-loathing:

Yes, I should be good, I should get married
find out what it's all about
but I can't stand these women all over me
smell of Naomi
erk, I'm stuck with this familiar rotting ginsberg
can't stand boys even anymore
can't stand
can't stand
and who wants to get fucked up the ass, really?
Immense seas passing over
the flow of time
and who wants to be famous and sign autographs like a movie
        star. . . .                              ["Mescaline"]

There is a growing determination to get beyond "this familiar
rotting ginsberg," no matter how and no matter what the
price. As he puts it in a terse note to the reader at the end of
the collection, "The message is: Widen the area of consciousness." He is so programmatic about all this, so *determined* to
succeed ("Yet the experiments must continue!") that we see
that of course he was bound to fail. And fail he did, quite
spectacularly. Or, as he himself put it later on, "Well, the Asian
experience got me out of a corner I painted myself in with
drugs." And yet the choice of the Orient, and of India in particular, seemed to be dictated at least partly by the ready availa-

108

bility there of certain drugs—or one drug, opium—that were difficult to procure in the United States; so he intended no immediate break with the drug pattern and there was none. For the most part, however, Ginsberg's passage to India was undertaken as a kind of pilgrimage, a holy journey to a land that he honestly believed to be one of the world's places of wisdom. It was in search of wisdom that he went and also as a kind of penitential act, renouncing fame and whatever wealth had come his way: "At least I'm down in possessions to Peter & a knapsack. I still am loaded with Karma of many letters & unfinished correspondence. I wanted to be a saint. But suffer for what? Illusions?"

Clearly, what he had in mind was divesting himself of nonessentials, peeling off layer after layer of personality until he had gotten down to some quintessential, hidden self. That being the case, his record of those years in India, fascinating though it may be to read, is a rather sad one. Allen Ginsberg's *Indian Journals* details in page after page the continuing frustration of this fruitless effort. An example, one of many:

> Why am I afraid to go back into that Creation? Afraid it is a 3-D delusion I'll enter & never get out of.
> Because I am still clinging to my human known me, Allen Ginsberg—and to enter this thing means final, complete abandonment of all I know of my *I am* except for this outer-seeming otherness which requires my disappearance.

And only a few pages further on, he bemoans the fact that as his spiritual development "seems blocked so also does my 'creative' activity." And he concludes, "I really don't know what I'm doing now. Begin a new page."

And on and on so, one new page begun, and then another and another. Month after month of it, and all the while listening to the screams of the beggars in the streets, examining their sores and their leprosy-stumped hands, and smelling the vomit market. India was around him, enclosing him in its poverty, inescapable in the constant closeness of its physical presence—and Ginsberg trying ever harder to withdraw from it, from himself, to lose himself in the vast, unknowable pool that

109

he was sure was there within himself, within all of us. Yet always unsuccessfully. By the end of his stay he is utterly exhausted spiritually, hating India, hating Peter Orlovsky, but most of all hating himself:

> All month since I came back from Bodh Gaya Peter unwelcoming & silent & determined on his separate music & untouchable energies—slow drift to we silent & curt answers, neither raising voice in my sadness or he in his irritation and no long talk except on Morphine he telling me I'm washed up & sold out to go teach in Vancouver broken poetry vow he judged—I had nothing to say, being washed up desolate on the Ganges bank. . . .

And then this bleak note: "Now all personal relations cold exhausted." Had something similar been offered in confession by some young acolyte, scholar, or poet in medieval times, the father confessor would have diagnosed the spiritual malady as acedia: spiritual apathy, exhaustion, dryness. Ginsberg was utterly spent spiritually, and was without the comfort of a God to pray to.

But help was on its way. That subconscious of his, which he had prodded and poked with experiences of all sorts, and shocked and abused with everything from LSD to opium, was now preparing a shock of its own for him. Bubbling along below the surface were all the elements he needed for a really first-class satori. They had been coalescing, eddying, and simmering away for nearly two years. It had been that long since Ginsberg visited the Jewish theologian Martin Buber in Jerusalem on his way to India. "Buber said that he was interested in man-to-man relationships," Ginsberg later recalled in his *Paris Review* interview, "human-to-human—that he thought it was a human universe that we were destined to inhabit. And so therefore human relationships rather than relations between the human and the non-human." And again, later, as he recalled, there was the visit to Swami Shivananda in Rishikish to whom Ginsberg went for spiritual advice. And what was he told by him? The swami said, "Your own heart is your guru." This message, practically delphic in import, was not the one he expected to hear in India, but he kept getting it there again

110

and again from different sources: ". . . a whole series of India holy men pointed back to the body—getting *in* the body rather than getting out of the human form."

A little more than a month after he left India, all this boiled over in a sudden illumination that he experienced while traveling across Japan on the Kyoto-Tokyo express—what more appropriate place for a satori? He renounced drugs ("I suddenly didn't want to be *dominated* by that nonhuman any more, or even be dominated by the moral obligation to enlarge my consciousness any more"); he forgave himself ("I was suddenly free to love myself again, and therefore love the people around me in the form they already were"); and he managed to stop hating his body ("I was completely in my body and had no more mysterious obligations. And nothing more to fulfill, except to be willing to die when I am dying, whenever that be. And be willing to live as a human in this form now"). Even in Ginsberg's own words the revelation, which worked such a real and permanent change in him, may seem somewhat disappointing. Was he merely making his peace with expedience? Accepting necessity? No, something greater, I think. To come to terms with one's mortality is no small thing. To see in it a basis for a feeling of solidarity and love for those around you is the kind of death-defying existential leap that Camus urged in *The Stranger.* It would certainly have satisfied Martin Buber, those Indian holy men, or even that father confessor I posited a paragraph or two back. More important, it satisfied Allen Ginsberg.

That experience on the Kyoto-Tokyo express, though never very successfully articulated by Ginsberg in any interview or conversation (such experiences never are), became the basis for one of his finest poems, "The Change." All the conflict that he had felt in himself between body and spirit is brought into focus in the poem's dominant image: that of human birth.

> Who would deny his own shape's
> loveliness in his
> dream moment of bed

Who sees his desire to be
horrible instead of Him

Who is, who cringes, perishes,
is reborn a red Screaming
baby? Who cringes before
that meaty shape in
Fear?

Yet not some vague *symbolic* rebirth, merely, but as is characteristic in so much of Ginsberg's writing, the image is made compellingly real. And in this case, right from the start in a graphic description of the poet's passage in rebirth:

Come home: the pink meat image
black yellow image with
ten fingers and two eyes
is gigantic already: the black
curly pubic hair, the
blind hollow stomach,
the silent soft open vagina
rare womb of new birth
cock lone and happy to be home
again
touched by hands by mouths,
by hairy lips—

"The Change" is one of the most physical of Ginsberg's poems —yet quite properly so, considering that it expresses an affirmation by Ginsberg of his own physicality, the inescapable reality of his own mortal body. Yet not quite so obviously or inevitably, it is also one of Ginsberg's most *female* poems. Breast images are repeated. Births and bellies recur in stanza after stanza.

Not to probe too deeply or ingeniously here, but I think it should be recognized that the excluded middle in this syllogism at the heart of "The Change" is that physicality equals female. Curious that this should be so, coming from a homosexual male, for who could be more physical in his awareness of the sexual potential of his own body? Who more keenly aware of nuance and suggestion conveyed by the bodies of
others?

Yet if, within the limits of "The Change," we be allowed to read this—physicality equals female—as an implicit statement, we need not look too far for the why and wherefore supporting it. Look at "Kaddish." For after all, whether we consider Ginsberg as artist or as human being it is impossible to ignore this poem, an elegy written in 1959 in memory of his mother, Naomi Ginsberg, who had died three years earlier. It is not only his longest work, it is his best. It is not only Allen Ginsberg's best, it is the finest single literary work to come out of the Beat movement. And finally, for all its excesses, grotesqueries, and rawness, I hold it to be the most powerful, the most significant, or simply put, the *best* poem by an American written since the war.

If you are unfamiliar with "Kaddish," don't dismiss it out of hand because of the oozing sentiment potential in its subject —an elegy for Mama. It does sound like the sort of thing Sam Levenson might have bled forth some Passover night, remembering the last time the whole family sat down together at his mother's table. But "Kaddish" is utterly unsentimental, ruthless in its frank revelations of events, details, and feelings. And it is so not just for the obvious reason that Allen Ginsberg is no Sam Levenson, but also because Naomi Ginsberg was nobody's Yiddishe Mama.

Born in Russia, she emigrated with her parents to the United States as a child, became involved in radical politics and eventually a member of the Communist party. As a schoolteacher and a campaigner for radical causes, she overworked terribly, fell to tension and paranoia, and had a nervous breakdown, the first of many, in 1919. She married Louis Ginsberg and moved with him to Paterson, New Jersey, where their two sons, Eugene and Allen, were born. As the boys grew up, they watched her deteriorate before their eyes. One breakdown followed another, put her in and out of hospitals, and left her in a more or less permanent state of paranoia:

'Allen, you don't understand—it's—ever since those 3 big sticks up my back—they did something to me in Hospital, they poisoned me, they want to see me dead—3 big sticks, 3 big sticks—

Her feelings of persecution were tied in the most twisted knots to her background in radical politics. Nothing was clear-cut. Everyone was against her:

> The enemies approach—what poisons? Tape recorders? FBI? Zhdanov hiding behind the counter? Trotsky mixing rat bacteria in the back of the store? Uncle Sam in Newark, plotting deathly perfumes in the Negro district? Uncle Ephraim, drunk with murder in the politician's bar, scheming of Hague? Aunt Rose passing water thru needles of the Spanish Civil War?

"Kaddish," in its long first two sections, is a great, untidy parcel of those awful memories one would best forget: Naomi strapped into a stretcher, screaming and vomiting as they take her off to the state hospital; visits to her with glimpses of "old catatonic ladies" and "wrinkled hags acreep, accusing—begging my 13-year-old mercy."

And then, returning from her longest stay in the hospital, another attack, and she runs away from Louis and her two sons to her sister in the Bronx. Perhaps—though this is not made explicit in the text—she felt that her husband was also plotting against her. And so she stayed in New York, eventually getting a job and striking a precarious balance in life. Her two sons each stayed with her for separate extended periods. Allen's memories of her at this time, his adolescence, are of his mother's gross carnal reality—of dresses hitched to the hips, pubic hair exposed, the smells of the body. Yes, always the body, her body. In the end her madness, her delusions of political persecution, were subordinate, perhaps attached in Ginsberg's mind, to the overwhelming corporeal reality of the woman, his mother.

In "Kaddish," woman is the mindless, body principle dominating each line, each prose stanza in a great, uncouth, spreading sprawl. Revulsion is the key emotion, yet it is put forth so frankly that his belief is clear here that revulsion articulated is revulsion mastered. Is his belief justified? What resolution has the poem? None, really. Naomi dies, he assembles incidental memories into a kind of hymn, and then in the last section of the poem, he shrieks out a chant in sudden abstract anger, whirling his scorn about him like a whip, lashing out almost indiscriminately:

O mother
what have I left out
O mother
what have I forgotten
O mother
farewell
with a long black shoe
farewell
with Communist Party and a broken stocking
farewell
with six dark hairs on the wen of your breast
farewell
with your old dress and a long black beard around the vagina
farewell
with your sagging belly
with your fear of Hitler
with your mouth of bad short stories
with your finger of rotten mandolines
with your arms of fat Paterson porches
with your belly of strikes and smokestacks
with your chin of Trotsky and the Spanish War. . . .

And on and on so for many more lines. I do not read in this the forgiveness—the asking and giving of it—that some claim to see. Agony and outrage are there, certainly, and an emotional intensity of such a level that the reader feels himself nearly deafened by the voice of the poet haranguing him. But forgiveness? No. Resolution? None. It makes a shambles of the classic elegiac form with its apostrophe of uplift. Understanding, forgiveness, and overcoming revulsion for the body principle, all these came eventually—but not for a few years.

And these were specifically the years that he spent in such desperate, headlong flight from his physical self and into that nonhuman otherness that he was seeking through drugs. This was the period that ended in that experience on the Kyoto-Tokyo express, the illumination that he expressed in personal, poetic terms in his poem, "The Change." Coming to terms with the body meant coming to terms with the body principle, woman. This, by image and metaphor, is what Ginsberg tells

115

us in that poem. And thus "The Change" may—and should—be read as the missing final movement of "Kaddish." Resolution: To forgive the body that Naomi had made him hate was to forgive the body principle, woman, Naomi herself.

At last he was empowered to love, to accept, and to embrace. This was the devious and complicated scheme of the change that was worked in Allen Ginsberg. He has been able to live with himself, with others, ever since.

CHAPTER 7

# Poets in the Open Field

There are plenty who would dismiss the Beats' social influence over the past decade and would attribute the very real changes in attitude and style that have taken place purely to vague social forces or to the estrangement of the young due to the war in Vietnam. Even if—for the sake of argument—we accommodate such a view, it does little to diminish the real importance of the Beats, for the question of their literary influence remains to be dealt with. It has been considerable and must surely be apparent even to those who deplore it.

Here it is tempting to claim a little too much. A case could be made, for example, for the Beat mode in prose fiction—the charged, confessional manner of Kerouac, Burroughs, and Mailer in his hipster phase—as the dominant one in the American novel today. It probably is. But the confessional mode has been so well established for so long that whatever direct influence the Beats may have had on this young writer or that comes from further back than any of us would care to remember. The beats may have pushed things along a bit, adding muscle to a form whose general outline was already clearly defined, but they did nothing to alter a course that had, after all, been set long before.

In poetry, however, that is just what they did. What a change they worked—and in how short a time! Take 1955, for instance, the year of the big reading at the Six Gallery in San Francisco, the one that kicked things off so emphatically there. What sort of poems were the "right" journals and quarterlies publishing then? You remember them? Crabbed, pinched, elliptical, and oblique things, often rhymed and metered and in exotic forms such as the ballade or the sestina. It was academic poetry, not merely in fact, for it was written almost without exception by ill-paid assistant professors or instructors in creative writing, staying up until all hours in their quonset huts—but academic by intention, too. It was the kind that was written for other assistant professors and instructors, not merely to be read, but to be deciphered. "Difficulty," preferably of the learned, pedantic kind, was quite generally considered a most desirable virtue among academic poets.

Today all that has changed radically. We find passionately raw confessional poetry, just as intense and graphic as anything the Beats wrote, now being churned out by some of the very poets—now well up the academic ladder—who held them to ridicule just a decade ago. The very conception of the poet has changed. The man who once understood his mission as sitting in solitude, uttering precise and cryptic truths into the dark, now conceives of himself as a seer, a prophet who tumbles forth words to inspire the multitude to direct action. How are we to account for this change? Not, surely, as any sort of direct development from the poetry deemed acceptable fifteen years ago. No, there has truly been a turning. American poetry now follows a much different course. Follow the stream back to its source—and who do we find sitting astride the watershed but those canny old masters, Ezra Pound and William Carlos Williams?

Of the two, the influence of Dr. Williams has been far more direct and pervasive—perhaps only because he was always the more physically and intellectually accessible. We recall, of course, just how profoundly he contributed to Allen Ginsberg's early poetic development: we remember their friendship and the younger poet's letter contributions to Book Five of *Paterson*. Ginsberg's earliest published poetry, *The Empty Mirror,* is written in clear imitation of Williams' terse, short-line, free-verse style. He would often quote to young poets that key dictum of Williams' "No ideas but in things," urging them always to be specific and concrete. And even when he had moved into the later, Whitmanesque phase of *Howl,* Ginsberg still supported the idea of the one-breath line, but he insisted he was now writing in the long lines only because longer breaths

118  "are more natural to me than Williams's short simple talks."

For the most part, Ezra Pound's early enthusiasms and his statements on poetics coincide remarkably with Williams's. The latter's "No ideas but in things," for instance, finds its direct equivalent in Pound's "Any tendency to abstract general statement is a greased slide." Poets could and generally did draw the same conclusions from reading Pound's earlier poetry that they did from Dr. Williams's. Yet the writing of the later *Cantos* represented for Pound a radical break with his past, almost a denial of the earlier mode. Erudite to the point of pedantry, opaque, and generally incomprehensible except to the most dedicated literary archaeologists, the later *Cantos* kept away many who would have come to him quite naturally as a teacher. And so, of course, did the U.S. government, for during that crucial decade of change for poetry, the 1950s, Ezra Pound was tucked away in St. Elizabeth's Hospital, a prisoner for his wartime follies. A few took the trouble to visit him, but he could leave the hospital to see no one.

Yet it may well have been more than Pound's inaccessibility that diminished his influence with the new generation of poets that was then struggling to be born. In a more devious way, it was probably because Ezra Pound, with his secure niche in the literary history of the modern movement, was more academically respectable that his impact was less than Dr. Williams's. For make no mistake, those (Beats and others) who have brought about the changes we see around us in poetry today are by conviction, intention, and precedent antiacademic. Some of them, it is true, now teach in colleges and universities themselves, but it is also true that many of these same poets did a lot to alter the situation and style of the university writer. It's not they but the academy that has changed.

So dedicated in their antiacademicism were these poets that a number of them made their headquarters a sort of antiacademy—Black Mountain College in North Carolina, which was founded just after the war to give greater emphasis to creative arts in a less rigid college structure. And although Black Mountain (now defunct) never succeeded in getting proper academic accreditation for itself, it certainly managed to attract a distinguished faculty. Heading its music department was composer John Cage, painter-in-residence was Robert Rauschenberg, and for the dance there was Merce Cunningham. Not only was this a richly creative group, it was also a mutually influential one. They traded viewpoints and principles, and they developed an approach to the arts which, though hardly unified, was at least consistent in many of its most important points. It was fundamentally organic: the Black Mountain artists believed in creating from the materials at hand, whatever they were. They also believed in breaking down the barrier between artist and audience or at least radically altering the relationship between them. And they believed that both the artist and the audience were rightly more interested in the artistic process than in the product, thus their emphasis on spontaneity in the aesthetic gesture and the artistic act.

Charles Olson was the poet who was earliest associated with Black Mountain College, and he was certainly one of the most influential members of its faculty. He came there shortly after the 1947 publication of *Call Me Ishmael,* a singular study of Melville which he had written on a Guggenheim grant. At that time he had already some reputation as a poet of the Williams-Pound school. His fame increased as his influence grew among those poets (Ginsberg among them) who have gradually brought poetry to its present state. At the time of his death, on January 1, 1970, Charles Olson was one of the most important figures in American poetry.

Next to his excellent, somewhat oracular poetry, Olson's great influence rests on his formulation of the process of "projective" or "open" verse. This provided a new and very usable system of prosody to a whole generation of poets, who may well have felt that a development of some sort was needed from the poetics of Pound and Williams, yet sought something in the same context of freedom. Some took projective verse directly as their own; many more shaped and adapted Olson's theories to their own ends. But what is remarkable is the number of poets—and eventually critics, as well—who were finally deeply affected by this enthusiastic and somewhat eccentric man. Charles Olson mattered greatly. He changed their

minds.

If we take a moment to look at his rules of projective verse, I think we will be able to appreciate just how profound and widespread his influence on younger poets really was. (Just see, for instance, how neatly Olson theory ties to San Francisco practice!) His debt to William Carlos Williams and Ezra Pound should also be clear from what follows:

First, some simplicities that a man learns, if he works in OPEN, or what can be called COMPOSITION BY FIELD, as opposed to inherited line, stanza, over-all form, what is the "old" base of the nonprojective.

(1) the *kinetics* of the thing. A poem is energy transferred from where the poet got it (he will have some several causations), by way of the poem itself to, all the way over to, the reader. Okay. Then the poem itself must, at all points, be a high energy-construct and, at all points, an energy-discharge. So: how is the poet to accomplish same energy, how is he, what is the process by which a poet gets in, at all points energy at least the equivalent of the energy which propelled him in the first place, yet an energy which is peculiar to verse alone and which will be, obviously, also different from the energy which the reader, because he is a third term, will take away?

This is the problem which any poet who departs from closed form is specially confronted by. And it involves a whole series of new recognitions. From the moment he ventures into FIELD COMPOSITION—puts himself in the open— he can go by no track other than the one the poem under hand declares, for itself. Thus he has to behave, and be, instant by instant, aware of some several forces just now beginning to be examined. (It is much more, for example, this push, than simply such a one as Pound put, so wisely, to get us started: "the musical phrase," go by it, boys, rather than by, the metronome.)

(2) is the *principle,* the law which presides conspicuously over such composition, and, when obeyed, is the reason why a projective poem can come into being. It is this: FORM IS NEVER MORE THAN AN EXTENSION OF CONTENT. (Or so it got phrased by one, R. Creeley, and it makes absolute sense to me, with this possible corollary, that right form, in any given poem, is the only and exclusively possible extension of content under hand.) There it is, brothers, sitting there, for USE.

Now (3) the *process* of the thing, how the principle can be made so to shape the energies that the form is accomplished. And I think it can be boiled down to one statement (first pounded into my head by Edward Dahlberg): ONE PERCEPTION MUST IMMEDIATELY AND DIRECTLY LEAD TO A FURTHER PERCEPTION. It means exactly what it says, is a matter of, at *all* points (even, I should say, of our management of daily reality as of the daily work) get on with it, keep moving, keep in, speed, the nerves, their speed, the perceptions, theirs, the acts, the split second acts, the whole business, keep it moving as fast as you can, citizen. And if you also set up as a poet, USE USE USE the process at all points, in any given poem always, always one perception must must must MOVE, INSTANTER, ON ANOTHER!

It should also be fairly evident that Olson's projective verse ideas are in close harmony with the general artistic principles of the Black Mountain group—the emphasis on the organic ("A poem is energy transferred from where the poet got it") and on the process and act of poetry. One is haunted by the notion that if Rauschenberg had been the composer, Cage the poet, and Olson the painter, it might all have come out the same.

Charles Olson's most ardent apostle was Robert Creeley (the R. Creeley mentioned above, of course), a poet who is almost as closely associated with Black Mountain poetry as Olson himself. Creeley quit Harvard a semester short of graduation and went off to a chicken farm in New Hampshire to write. Through Cid Corman, the editor of a little magazine called *Origin,* he came to know Olson, who greatly admired Creeley's poetry and sensed the similarity in their approach. As for Creeley, his admiration for the older poet was unbounded. Eventually (1954) he was invited down by Olson to teach writing at Black Mountain, and while there he edited the *Black Mountain Review.* It was one of two publications—the other was *Origin*—that in the early 1950s was open to the new poetry in the Williams-Pound tradition. Through these publications, by correspondence and visits, these writers came to know one another. A single issue of the *Black Mountain Review* (Number 7), for example, contained work by Ginsberg, Corso, Kerouac, Burroughs, Gary Snyder, Robert Duncan, Philip Whalen, Philip Lamantia, Louis Zukofsky, Hubert

Selby, Jr., and Denise Levertov. There grew among these people a sense of community and singleness of purpose. They certainly did not divide themselves among beats, members of the San Francisco school, and Black Mountain poets. No, if they thought of themselves as anything at all, it was simply as writers who were sympathetic to one another, whose approach was fundamentally similar.

It was here, however, among the poets that the idea of a *literary* generation began to gain some currency. When Kerouac first spoke of his as a Beat generation, he meant the whole of it, a *social* unit. It was left to the poets to define themselves in literary terms, to see their mission as one of opposition, writing the kind of work that would *not* be deemed acceptable by the going standards of the poetry establishment. Creeley spoke for most of them when he complained that "what confronted us in 1950 was a closed system indeed, poems patterned upon exterior and traditionally acceptable models. The New Criticism of that period was dominant and would not admit the possibility of verse considered as an 'open field' " (echoing Olson in that last phrase, of course). Defining themselves negatively as they did had its disadvantages, however. It simply did not allow for positive critical standards of even the most general sort. It made it possible, even necessary, to accept nonpoets such as Peter Orlovsky just as long as they showed the right spirit.

Because they had thought so about this question of generation, many of these poets were quite willing to be called or call themselves Beats when the term came into vogue. If that was the name of their generation, then all right, let's get on with the work—that seemed to be the attitude. And if some, such as Denise Levertov, Paul Blackburn, Joel Oppenheimer, and Creeley were not directly identified with the Beats they nevertheless felt a sense of solidarity with them. They shared a feeling that they were all part of the same generation, the same larger movement.

Because the movement in poetry was not built, as most movements are, around a set of rigid rules or standards or around a critical dogma, some little difficulty was experienced 123 even by those who took part in determining just who they were and what they were about. And for that reason, too, a number tried. Paul Carroll, for example, was most eclectic in his essay, "Faire, Foul and Full of Variations: the Generation of 1962," and seemed willing to settle for definition by chronology and not much else. Here is how he came up with 1962:

> I want to thank Robert Bly for having suggested the arithmetic by which this date was found. Bly says that a good way to find the year with which to identify our generation would be to begin with the obvious date of 1917 for the Eliot-Pound-Williams generation and then to add 15 years for each succeeding generation. It works out well. In 1932 Hart Crane committed suicide—perhaps the most important single event in the Crane-Tate-Warren generation. (How startling to realize that if Crane had chosen to live he'd be 70 today.) In 1947 Lowell's *Lord Weary's Castle* won the Pulitzer Prize —still the best book of the Berryman-Lowell-Shapiro generation. And in 1962 Allen Ginsberg was in India learning from gurus; and such important volumes as John Ashbery's *The Tennis Court Oath* and James Wright's *The Branch Will Not Break* were published.

This is interesting, I think, because Paul Carroll never really succeeds in defining his own generation in the rest of the essay (in which he talks mostly about the variety of their writing and attitudes) as well as he does here by contrasting his to the generations that preceded it.

In the end most of them settled for definition by anthology. Not, by any means, so abject a fate in this case, for the anthology that did the job was a most comprehensive and intelligently assembled one, *The New American Poetry*, edited by Donald M. Allen. No less than forty-four poets are represented in it, and while one might quibble with a few he selected and others he neglected, nobody really essential has been omitted. He divides his poets into five separate groups: the Black Mountain poets; the San Francisco Renaissance poets; the Beats; the New York poets; and younger poets, including Gary Snyder, Philip Whalen, and Michael McClure, who were—or should have been—considered Beat Generation poets. Nearly all the poets included in the Allen anthology were pleased by it; there was a feeling of kinship among them, of having been a part of something big.

It helped, of course, that *none* of those included in *The New American Poetry* had appeared in *The New Poets of England and America*, an anthology published three years earlier that was edited by Donald Hall, Robert Pack, and Louis Simpson. It provided a list of those younger poets who were approved by the academic poetry establishment. These were the poets-in-residence and grant-getters, writers of familiar themes in traditional modes. Combining the work of both English and American poets of about the same age in a single volume was in itself a quiet vote for the single tradition in English and American letters on which the academic critics and poets (who were usually one and the same) insisted. Reading at random in *The New Poets* and *The New American Poetry*, it should be immediately apparent just how drastically different were the two approaches they represented. With no duplication whatever in the two tables of contents, this developed as a real battle of the anthologies. These were clearly two quite separate and, as it developed, mutually hostile groups. The academic poets were on top and meant to stay there, and those who followed the Williams-Pound tradition meant to unseat them.

There can be no question who won the battle. Take a turn through *The New Poets*, and you will be surprised at the number of American poets represented in it who have dropped out of sight completely. Nearly all those who did not have altered their style and approach to poetry in the direction of the Williams-Pound tradition. Some, notably Robert Bly and Louis Wright, were in the process even at the time of publication. Others, like John Hollander, eventually came around. Even the star of the anthology, Robert Lowell (who hardly qualified as a *new* poet, even in 1957), writes in a much different, freer, and more open style than ever before. He has noted the change himself and gives credit for it in part to an early encounter with the new poetry. The poem in question here is the last one in his volume, *Life Studies*, a piece which critics agree marked a definite break with his earlier manner.

"Skunk Hour" was begun in mid-August . . . and finished about a month later. In March of the same year [1957], I had been giving readings on the West Coast. . . . I was in San Francisco, the era and setting of Allen Ginsberg, and all about very modest poets were waking up prophets. I became sorely aware of how few poems I had written, and that these few had been finished at the latest three or four years earlier. Their style seemed distant, symbol-ridden and willfully diffi- cult. . . . I felt my old poems hid what they were really about, and many times offered a stiff humorless, and even impene- trable surface. I am no convert to the "beats." I know well too that the best poems are not necessarily poems that read aloud. Many of the greatest poems can only be read to one's self, for inspiration is no substitute for humor, shock, narra- tive, and a hypnotic voice, the four musts for oral perfor- mance. Still, my own poems seemed like prehistoric monsters dragged down into the bog and death by their ponderous armor. I was reciting what I no longer felt. What influenced me more than San Francisco and reading aloud was that for some time I had been writing prose. I felt that the best style for poetry was none of the many poetic styles in English, but something like the prose of Chekhov or Flaubert.

There is an interesting sidelight to the change in Robert Low- ell. The poetry he wrote at Harvard during his first year in college, none of which was published, was free verse some- what in the manner of William Carlos Williams. He transferred to Kenyon College, however, and came under the tutelage and influence of John Crowe Ransom; and he began there to de- velop the dense style for which he was first known. Thus there is some reason to regard Lowell's present style less as a radical break with his poetic past than as a return to an earlier, more natural mode. Such a journey may well be symbolic of the course followed by American poetry during the last fifty years.

No poet today is more frequently—or for that matter, more justly—identified with what I have been calling the Williams- Pound tradition than Robert Duncan. He has moved from group to group, influencing and being influenced in turn, act- ing as a sort of poet-catalyst whose personal chemistry is the sort that is just right for making things happen. And, though

126

not a great originator nor a leader of movements, he has made them happen in the subtle ways of a gentle, generous man.

Robert Duncan was born in 1919 and grew up in the San Francisco Bay area, the adopted son of a prominent architect. He was closely identified with the early San Francisco group that included Jack Spicer and Robin Blaser, but was well acquainted with all the city's poets, including Philip Lamatia, Kenneth Rexroth, and the other members of the old Anarchist Circle. Reading *Origin* he came under the influence of Charles Olson and his theory of projective verse. He corresponded with Olson, became a contributor to *Origin* and *Black Mountain Review,* and was himself invited out to teach at Black Mountain. The title of Duncan's best-known book, *The Opening of the Field,* is meant as a tribute to Olson and an acknowledgment of his debt to him. Thus Robert Duncan was at once a member in good standing of the San Francisco Renaissance and one of the foremost of the Black Mountain poets. And in addition, once he returned to San Francisco, he was made a kind of honorary Beat, one who was always included in the anthologies and special issues yet seemed a little out of place. It was not just that he was older than most (for there were always Brother Antoninus' lined visage and Kenneth Rexroth's rheumy gaze there on the page next to Duncan's much younger-looking face), but there also seemed something fundamental that separated his work from the rest—a certain elegance, a love of beauty for beauty's sake, a gentleness that was at variance with the popular conception of Beat.

This quality of separateness, not to say detachment, characterizes the style of Robert Duncan's life. For a man who has been identified with so many different groups and factions, Robert Duncan leads a rather retiring existence. Most of his communication with other poets and literary friends is carried on by mail. Although he remains in San Francisco, he does not regularly see the prominent members of the literary community there. This is partly by choice (he allows that he has not talked to Kenneth Rexroth since Rexroth called Marianne Moore a fascist on the air), and partly due to the fact that he resides in the city's somewhat remote Mission District.

127     So there Robert Duncan stays, living with his "constant

companion in life," the painter Jess Collins, in a slightly ramshackle nineteenth-century house on a sidestreet in a Mexican slum. There is a heavy-wire grate cage around the door and mesh protecting the windows. I rang the bell, and after being given a brief inspection, I was buzzed in by Jess. Brushes in hand, paint on his shirt, he looked as though he had just stepped away from the easel. I explained my visit, assured him I was expected, and was invited into the living room to wait. It was a funny, comfortable old room in just that sort of house. Furniture was of the massive, overstuffed variety and of no particular style. A large canvas of a hill against a yellow sky bore the inscription, "This painting is dedicated to Jess." There were potted plants about and many books arranged neatly in old-fashioned glass-door bookcases. I was, I'll confess, inspecting the titles—a terrible habit of mine—when Robert Duncan emerged from the rear of the house and came to meet me. He is a man of medium height with a handsome face and jet black hair. His manner is somewhat strained, but he was friendly and made me feel welcome. Although I cannot really say he relaxed appreciably during our morning-long talk, he seemed to enjoy it truly enough and talked on with no hint of reticence.

For openers I remarked on the books on the shelves. There were art books there, which didn't surprise me, but many or most of the rest seemed to deal with anthropology and various aspects of religion. I asked him about this.

"Oh yes," he said with a genial wave of his hand, "I ransack religion all the time and know I'm not really religious. I'm like Pound and Williams in that. The difference between our attitude and some others would be that we consider poetry a real and substantial way of thinking in itself, in fact one of the primary ways of thought. This doesn't mean it is a substitute for science or for religion, but that as a way of thinking it is coequal with them."

"Does this make you a formalist?" I asked.

"Yes, you might say that. We believe that form and content are, or should be, identical. This is probably not the case with Allen—Allen Ginsberg, I mean. His idea is that poetry should be the vehicle for some higher message. But my ideas haven't shifted much. I'm very retrograde, you see."

"Where does the content come in? What is the content?"

"My poetry is the imagination of what man is. That may make it sound a bit more impersonal than it really is. For you see, I get to be in it because the subject is man, and I'm my own best source data. That, in a way, is how it's always been with all poets. Any study of world drama, for instance, would be a study of what man thought he was. But poetry written today, at just this moment of time, brings us back to what man feels like he is."

With a wave toward the books on the shelf, I observed that this sounded like a rather anthropological approach to poetry.

Then, with a smile: "No, I don't *think* anthropology. I *ransack* anthropology."

I asked about Duncan's development as a poet. And telling it as a tale, he went back to his student days as a young anarchist at the University of California. "My politics," he said, "were antiwar. I was radical in that sense. For this was also, you see, the period of the Moscow trials and the Spanish Civil War, and I had developed a fairly fanatic anticommunism from the period. I saw myself as an anarchist of the native American sort, in the tradition of Thoreau and Emerson—that is, essentially without politics. My only politics then were antiwar, and I would have gone to jail for them, but I didn't have to. I wasn't finally draftable because I'm homosexual."

He spent the war years—1939 to 1945—in New York and found his friends among painters there. This was the time when the abstract expressionist movement was just beginning to take shape, and Duncan gained from it and from frequent trips to galleries a sense of painting that showed up in time in his poetry: "I often tend to treat a poem architecturally. Long poems tend to be blocked out in this way, composed in areas, as though there were the living room, the dining room, the bathroom, and so forth. It's natural, I suppose, to surround yourself with walls. The in-dwelling artist indwells in his thought."

Then back to San Francisco in 1946—the Anarchist Circle, Philip Lamantia, Kenneth Rexroth. . . . "Rexroth?" Duncan echoes my query. "A very strong directive force. It's remarkable how much he anticipates the conjunctions of the American traditions. Always on top of things." In 1947 Robert Duncan's first book of poetry, *Heavenly City, Earthly City,* was published, and shortly after that he met and, he says, came under the influence of Jack Spicer, six years his junior, "a wizardly poet who committed alcoholic suicide." He, Robin Blaser, and Spicer would get together every day to discuss poetry and more: to read one another's work, criticize it, tear it apart. Important event of the period? "For all of us—and I mean that 'us' in a very broad way to include poets I knew then and others I was to know later on—the real decision came in 1946 and 1948 with the publication of *The Pisan Cantos* and *Paterson.* The division lines were drawn with these. There were those, to put it simply, who looked on the publication of these two books as real poetic events, and those who did not."

"Those who did," I suggested, "would, of course, have included the Black Mountain poets?"

"Of course. But it would be a mistake, you know, to think of that one as a group in a strict sense. There was a college there. There was the *Black Mountain Review.* And there were poets, some of whom—Olson, Creeley, and myself—who thought very much alike. Others associated with the college or the *Review* thought somewhat differently. Denise Levertov, for example. There were complications with her.

"Yes, you know, that has been the tendency—to lump us all together, to ignore or wipe out the differences between us. By 'us' in this case I suppose I mean the poets who appeared in Don Allen's anthology. We were defined by that anthology, but perhaps defined in terms that were too general. Actually, there were a great many different kinds of poets represented there. We had among us poets who worked in the three major traditions of poetry."

"Which are?"

"The bardic tradition—the Dylan Thomas sort of poet whose work is not redeemed by content as he delivers it. He simply sings it out like a bard. Jack Spicer, you could say, was in the bardic tradition. The prophetic tradition—Whitman, of course, and the best recent example would be Ginsberg in his

Jeremiah mode. And finally, the tradition of the poet as maker

—the poet who sees the world itself as creation. We—I should say poets who work in this tradition—feel closer to science than others and are more comfortable with it."

"And you ransack it?"

"Yes"—delighted—"we ransack it."

I asked just how the university poets fit into all this. "Are they in the maker tradition?" That didn't seem quite right.

"Ah, the old poetry establishment with its bewildering little ententes and all. That is—or was—something a little different. Their idea of poetry was purely literary and based on a tradition from Dryden that real poetry—or literature—was the consensus of taste of reasonable men. This was why the past was so central to their idea of writing. For as soon as they produced anything they knew it had to go up against the consensus of taste of reasonable men over the past several hundred years. They know, too, they don't fit into any of the three major traditions, and they are very disturbed by this. But they can't really do anything about it, because that would mean dropping these nineteenth-century ideas of Literature and starting to write instead, and so they just turn off their hearing aids and continue as they have been doing. I mean the real old prehistoric monsters among them. Some real poets have managed to strike a bargain with all this, however—Randall Jarrell and Richard Wilbur, for instance. Look at Richard Wilbur's first book some time. It's a real poet's book.

"And you see a funny twist on this with Gary Snyder, too. He doesn't quite fit into the three traditions, either. He's not a maker. His poetry is based on his own conception of the taste of a reasonable man. But the funny thing is that Gary's idea of what is reasonable is based on Buddhist tradition. His idea of the right way of thinking lies outside the realm of poetry."

He had referred to the university poets as the "establishment" a moment before. I asked if that was indeed how he thought of them.

"No, I don't think of them as a powerful establishment anymore. They have a tradition of sorts, but young people don't know what it is. Whatever power they have or had is based on their power in the universities—on Tate and Ransom preparing more and more New Critics, who in their turn prepared more still. This is the way that universities tend to perpetuate themselves. That's one reason why they are blowing up today—the kind of dull smugness that sort of self-perpetuation breeds. We were university renegades. To a man. I know a little about these university people, you know, and that is why I was so appalled to see all this develop as it did, the New Criticism and all. Tate, for one, has only read literary criticism. I was so shocked at the ignorance of the man outside his own little specialty. And Ransom—a monument of ignorance! He didn't know what went on in the intellectual world. And his idea of proper-mindedness. Really, it got to be so narrow."

I asked Robert Duncan, leading him a bit, if perhaps Tate, Ransom, and all the poets who derived from them did not perhaps represent some sort of mutation from the native strain. If the true American tradition did not perhaps lie closer to the work of the poets represented in the Allen anthology.

But no. He refused to swallow that.

"Tate is authentically American. All these professors are. I'm afraid you have a particular kind of America in mind. Well, all right, fine. So have they another particular kind in their minds. We must all remember that America is a mixed bag at least."

He echoed it then, underlining for emphasis: "Yes, at least a big and very mixed bag."

# CHAPTER 8

# An Urchin Shelley

Time takes me by the hand
born March 26 1930 I am 100 mph o'er the vast market
    of choice
what to choose? what to choose?

For Gregory Corso, the simple act of choosing has always provided profound difficulties. It is a theme that runs through his poetry—decision-making or, alternatively, refusing to decide—and it can be read even more plainly in the record of his life. Corso is that young man described by John Dos Passos in the prologue to *U.S.A.* who "walks by himself, fast but not fast enough, far but not far enough . . . he must catch the last subway, the streetcar, the bus, run up the gangplanks of all the steamboats, register at all the hotels, work in the cities, answer the wantads, learn the trades, take up the jobs, live in all the boarding-houses, sleep in all the beds. One bed is not enough, one job is not enough, one life is not enough."

Corso is Saul Bellow's Eugene Henderson, running through the frozen fields of Newfoundland, chanting *"I want, I want, I want"* to himself. But what is it that Gregory Corso wants? What does he thirst for so insatiably?

I want no song Power
I want no dream Power
I want no driven-car Power
I want I want I want Power!

He wants, in other words, what life has denied him, a sense of mastery, a feeling of achievement to match the hungry, restless desire within him. His has been a hunger of expectation, peculiarly American in its restless, all-devouring, urgent desire. Corso, the poet, is self-invented, a fantasy projection of his own John Garfield self, the slum kid who wants all, takes all, only to feel it trickle through his fingers as he grasps it tight in his hands.

The son of Italian immigrants, Gregory Corso was born in New York and grew up on Bleeker Street. His mother died when he was quite young, and his father remains a hazy figure even, apparently, to Corso. He was a street kid. He claims never to have attended high school; at thirteen, according to Carolyn Gaiser,* he spent some time in the children's observation ward at Bellevue. At sixteen—again according to Miss Gaiser—he and two of his friends devised a fantastic and complicated master plan for robbery, involving the use of walkie-talkie radios on which Corso was to give orders to the other two. Evidently they put the plan into operation at least once, for what is certain is that Corso was arrested and at sixteen was sentenced to a term in Clinton Prison, Dannemora, New York, for robbery.

Far from embittering him, his prison years seem to be remembered by Corso almost as an enriching experience. He has remarked on the maturing effect that it had on him and went so far as to dedicate his second book, *Gasoline,* to "the angels of Clinton Prison who, in my 17th year, handed me, from all the cells surrounding me, books of illumination." He began to read in prison and even started in a rather tentative way to write.

Upon his release, he met Allen Ginsberg and started on the course that in less than ten years brought him national prominence. Perhaps, even probably, his life would not have taken the turn that it did had it not been for Ginsberg. Corso was young—only nineteen, he says—impressionable and eager; yet without knowing quite what he wanted nor what he was eager for. Ginsberg set him straight on that.

Through him, Corso was introduced to the whole New York Beat scene. He met Kerouac, John Clellon Holmes, and

*In her article "Gregory Corso: A Poet the Beat Way" in Thomas Parkinson, ed., *A Casebook on the Beat.*

134

eventually William S. Burroughs as well. But at least as important to his development as a poet was his meeting with Mark Van Doren, also arranged by Ginsberg. The great Columbia teacher was the first writer with an established reputation that Corso had encountered until then. He was also a man of academic standing, and to Corso, who had none whatever, this was quite impressive, perhaps disproportionately so. Van Doren looked at Corso's jail poems, commented on them as tactfully and in about the same way he would to any of his students, and encouraged Corso to write more. Corso visited him a number of times and speaks of Van Doren as an important personal influence.

After hanging around New York and soaking all this in for something better than a year, he wandered off to the West Coast and lived for a while in Los Angeles. Returning east, he went to sea, shipping out through 1952 and 1953 on Norwegian vessels on cross-Atlantic runs. And then he settled down for a while without quite intending to, accepting an invitation to visit Cambridge, Massachusetts. He had wanted to see Harvard, and he had been told that it would be all right for him to read there in the library. He liked it. What he intended to be just a visit lasted the better part of two years:

> In spite of voices—
> Cambridge and all its regions
> Its horned churches with fawns' feet
> Its white-haired young
> and ashfoot legions—
> I decided to spend the night
>
> But that hipster-tone of my vision agent
> Decided to reconcile his sound with the sea
> leaving me flat
> North of the Charles
> So now I'm stuck here—
> a subterranean
> lashed to a pinnacle. . . .

But no, his testimony here notwithstanding, Corso wasn't left flat. He put his time to good use there, reading regularly and according to a plan he had worked out, writing his first successful poems, and making friends among the Harvard students and university hangers-on. He managed to get a few of these Cambridge poems published in periodicals of one kind or another, attracted some attention with them, and when his Harvard friends offered to publish a collection of them, Corso was delighted. Pledges were made, subscriptions taken, and in 1955 *The Vestal Lady on Brattle* was published.

The poems in the book, which include "In the Tunnel Bone of Cambridge," whose first stanza I quoted, are an uneven lot —not surprising for a first book, of course. But it is not only that the quality of the individual pieces is rather up and down, but that the forms and the diction of his poems vary markedly as well. He will jump from rhymed and metered short lines on one page to sprawling Whitmanesque free-verse stanzas on the next. Short lines predominate, however; and these are more or less in the William Carlos Williams mode of the early Allen Ginsberg (see *Empty Mirror*). The diction of the poems is what is most original in them—sometimes awkward, occasionally leaden, even once or twice simply in error—but usually the words and the voice that speaks them are distinctive and recognizably Corso's own. He does, on a few occasions, however, indulge in a few flashing flights of language that ill suit the subject matter of his poems. The influence here would seem to be Shelley, whose ardent fan and loyal reader Corso had become.

Following the publication of *The Vestal Lady on Brattle*, which failed to attract any review attention to speak of, Corso began traveling again. He went to Mexico in 1956 and then out to the West Coast with Ginsberg and was there in San Francisco as Raphael Urso through the crazy scenes described by Jack Kerouac in *Desolation Angels*. But it wasn't long before Corso was wandering once more—to Europe this time where he kept on writing and sending the poems back to Ginsberg who was conscientious in getting them published. A few were brought out in various literary magazines, but the real triumph came when Ginsberg arranged for book publication.

*Gasoline*, as his second collection was called, is the eighth book in Lawrence Ferlinghetti's Pocket Poets Series and the only one for which Allen Ginsberg has written an Introduction.

In it, he eulogizes appropriately enough, though he seems unwilling to consider Corso's work at any level but its surface of language: "But what is he *saying?* Who cares?! It's said!" Corso is a poet with a limited number of themes which he tends to repeat with variations over and over again. The best of the *Gasoline* poems—or at any rate, the most successful— are the shorter pieces, most of them made up of bits of nostalgia and simple, though very precise, description. Sometimes, however, Corso's memories are of a darker sort—as in "Italian Extravaganza":

> Mrs. Lombardi's month-old son is dead.
> I saw it in Rizzo's funeral parlor,
> A small purplish wrinkled head.
>
> They've just finished having high mass for it;
> They're coming out now
> . . . wow, such a small coffin!
> And ten black cadillacs to haul it in.

Corso shows an uncanny ability in some of these shorter poems to touch reality directly with language. In the descriptive section of his poem for trumpeter Miles Davis, "For Miles," he comes about as close as any poet has to recreating in words the feeling created by music in the listener:

> Your sound is faultless
> pure & round
> holy
> almost profound
>
> Your sound is your sound
> true & from within
> a confession
> soulful & lovely. . . .

Yet this one dithers off predictably into an I-remember-one-night bit of irrelevance that only detracts from the passage that precedes it. There are very few wholly good poems in Corso's first two books. Even in "Italian Extravaganza," which I like

137

very much, there is the willful discord of "... wow, such a small coffin!" It is there, of course, just as Corso intended it to be, as a fingernail scraped across the blackboard, a fail-safe device against the sentimentality lurking in its subject matter. And yet ... and yet ... Perhaps something a little less conventionally conversational would have worked better.

And while there are few wholly good poems in *Gasoline*, there is one that seems wholly bad, and that is "Ode to Coit Tower," a bombastically affirmative jumble of mock-Shelley set out in the Whitman-style long lines that Allen Ginsberg had then lately adapted to his own purposes. There is a counterfeit quality, more or less apparent, in all the long poems in this collection. They are enthusiastic, energetic, and positive—and in this they are genuine enough—but the voice behind the words seems to be not quite Corso's own. Or perhaps it is Corso pulling ventriloquist's tricks, trying different voices from that vast market of choice. Refusing, ultimately, to choose his own.

Gregory Corso came back from Europe in 1957 for the publication of *Gasoline* and was on the scene at just the moment that the Beat Generation thing was beginning to explode. He completed the trio that posed for the photos and talked to reporters. In the beginning, at least, he gloried in the role of the bad boy. He made sure everyone knew he had served time at Dannermora, muttered non sequiturs and putons whenever he was interviewed, and told *Life* magazine's Paul O'Neil that he had never combed his hair, "although I guess I'd get the bugs out of it if I did." Yet quite unexpectedly, he began to attract some real critical interest at the poetry readings he gave with Allen Ginsberg with a poem called "Marriage." It is a long, 111-line work with no narrative thread to sustain it—only the dialectic of a rambling and delightful debate on the pros and cons of the matrimonial state. Quite fittingly—because it answers so few of them—"Marriage" begins by asking questions:

> Should I get married? Should I be good?
> Astound the girl next door with my velvet suit and
> faustus hood?

And as the poem progresses, he asks more questions, examines all the possibilities, and imagines all the situations. Yet he does so in perfect comic detail and with genuine sympathy for all concerned:

> O how terrible it must be for a young man
> seated before a family and the family thinking
> We never saw him before! He wants our Mary Lou! . . .
>
> And the priest! he looking at me as if I masturbated
> asking me Do you take this woman for your lawful wedded
> wife?
> And I trembling what to say say Pie Glue!

He fantasizes on the honeymoon horrors of Niagara ("The whistling elevator man he knowing/The winking bellboy knowing") and threatens to foil them all by becoming "the Mad Honeymooner/devising ways to break marriages, a scourge of bigamy/a saint of divorce—"

Yet as funny and entertaining as all this certainly is, it is not merely that, for in its zany way "Marriage" offers serious criticism of what is phony about a sacred American institution. That it was done with good humor and a sense of comedy throughout does not dull its sharp cutting edge in the slightest, for genuine wit and Corso's finest, most casually precise, use of language save the day. With what beautiful fluency it seems to pour forth! It is one of the best-sustained performances in the conversational style to come from any American poet of the post-World War II generation. And it is easily one of the two or three most important poems to come from the Beats.

Yet in it, characteristically, Corso manages to hedge. A poem pondering a choice—"Should I get married? Should I be good?"—concludes with no choice made. Ultimately, he seems to lack the courage of his convictions. Without really rejecting marriage, he manages to accept it only as an abstract notion, a possibility:

> Ah, yet well I know that were a woman possible as I am possible
> then marriage would be possible—

Like SHE in her alien gaud waiting her Egyptian lover
so I wait—bereft of 2,000 years and the bath of life.

Not to quibble, however, for in the writing of "Marriage,"
Corso did make a choice, his most important, for the matter
and form of it are distinctly his own. It was the first long poem
entirely and successfully in his own voice.

It would be good to be able to say that all the other poems
in the collection *The Happy Birthday of Death,* in which
"Marriage" eventually appeared, were just as distinctive, just
as certainly his. But reading through its pages will show you
they are not. Some are, of course; the delightful "Hair"
is certainly one of these. Yet in so many of the others he per-
sists in straining after Ginsberg and Shelley, dropping classical allusions, and attacking subjects that do not suit his
talents.

And the same might be said of Corso's next collection,
*Long Live Man,* published two years later. There is an uneven
quality to this one, too—yet with a few differences. The fren-
etic manner of "Power," "Army," and "Police" of the previous
collection, which I would attribute to Allen Ginsberg's strong
and persistent influence, is largely absent from *Long Live
Man.* For the most part, it is quieter, more restrained, and alas,
generally less interesting than the earlier Corso; somehow a bit
of the zip is gone from his work. Yet, finally, a new quality is
there. Gregory Corso, zipless though he be, has something
more to offer:

> I am 32 years old
> and finally I look my age, if not more.
> Is it a good face what's no more a boy's face?
> It seems fatter And my hair,
> it's stopped being curly. Is my nose big?
> The lips are the same.
> And the eyes, ah the eyes get better all the time.
> 32 and no wife, no baby; no baby hurts,
>       but there's lots of time.
> I don't act silly any more.
> And because of it I have to hear from so-called friends:
> "You've changed. You used to be so crazy so great."
> They are not comfortable with me when I'm serious. . . .

The mood is valedictory. This poem, "Writ on the Eve of My 32nd Birthday," which is the last in the collection, is in the nature of a careful kind of summing-up, an inventory of his youth. There is an absence of bravado, an utter honesty to the poem that does more than charm: it invites our admiration.

> I think I had a pretty weird 32 years.
> And it weren't up to me, none of it.
> No choice of two roads; if there were,
> I don't doubt I'd have chosen both.

It ends in a reaffirmation of his vocation as poet and offers—no, not wisdom, but the promise of wisdom to come. He carefully refrained from publishing anything anywhere until a number of years had elapsed.

And a marriage, too. In 1963 Corso met and married Sally November, then twenty-five, a schoolteacher from Shaker Heights, Ohio. Yes, as it turned out, she had heard of the Beat Generation and all that, but never of Gregory Corso until she met him, and he liked her all the better for it. When a reporter from *Newsweek* tracked down the couple on their honeymoon and chided Corso with the sentiments the poet himself has expressed in "Marriage," Corso replied quite coolly, "Getting married means having a child. I have never denied life. One falls in love. Is that conforming?"

That first summer they were to spend counseling at a summer camp in upstate New York. And after that, well, he was working on a sort of travel book which would contain all that he had seen and experienced over the last several years. Yet somehow, that book never got written and money got to be a problem. Because of his jailbird background and his lack of formal education, and because of the unconventional, hand-to-mouth poet's life he had led until getting married, Corso soon found it difficult to earn a living in the straight world. He tried, all right, but somehow it seemed he was always unqualified or uninterested. Finally, after a couple of false starts, he agreed to go back to Cleveland to work in his father-in-law's florist shop. At that, too, he failed rather spectacularly. "He was honestly eager to make good," a friend of Corso's told me, "but

141

working for her father was a disaster right from the start. It was very, very sad for him, but at the same time very funny in its particulars. Gregory would get carried away and give away flowers, fail to ring up sales, and in general just failed to do the things a clerk in a flower shop was required to do."

In what he may well have considered his final performance as breadwinner, Corso accepted an offer to come to the State University of New York at Buffalo as a teacher. He had hoped for years to find some sort of teaching job and now he was delighted at being given the opportunity at last. Not only was this a way to earn money in the present, it also offered the possibility of a rosy future of straight jobs. All that stood between him and a productive life in the straight world was the Feinberg certificate.

He knew about it when he took the job, all right—but somehow he supposed they would make an exception for him. After all, weren't there already five cases being pressed to test the constitutionality of the state law requiring the signing of the certificate? Didn't everyone agree it would never stand up in court?

The Feinberg certificate (named after the state legislator who had introduced the measure) was a written declaration to the effect that the signer was not then a Communist, and that if he ever had been, he had so informed the proper authorities. In this case the proper authority was understood to be the head of the university, for signing was required of all state university teachers in New York.

Gregory Corso came to the State University at Buffalo in January 1965 and began teaching a course in Shelley—his old favorite—two nights a week. But he delayed signing the certificate, and then—on principle—refused outright. He was dismissed on March 8. Students were outraged, rallied to Corso's cause, and began picketing the university. But somehow nothing ever came of it. Afterward, the students blamed the faculty for failing to come out openly in his support; if they had, students said, the administration might have backed down.

And yes, it was only a short time—before the Feinberg certificate was withdrawn. State university teachers no longer have to sign it. But that, of course, did Gregory Corso no good.

142

By then, he had left America on his longest ramble, his marriage now broken beyond repair. He stayed away for over two years, shifting his scenery at will, but favoring the eastern Mediterranean, the Aegean islands, and Greece. He felt closer to something important there. He had started writing again.

In the fall of 1967, when I met and talked with Gregory Corso, he had only been back to America a short time. He was living in the West Village then, far west, on Greenwich Street, a block of warehouses with a single corner tenement not too far from Sheridan Square. Corso was there on the ground floor of that tenement. "Ring the unmarked bell," Peter Orlovsky had told me. "I'll tell him you're coming and when. He'll be expecting you." I later heard that there was a little tension at the time between Corso and the members of the Ginsberg household, due to the fact that he was then financially semidependent on Ginsberg's Foundation for Poetry, Incorporated. I would never have guessed it, however, from the easy greeting I got from Corso and the warmth with which he spoke of Ginsberg.

It was a bare, makeshift sort of place with pillows, a sleeping bag, and a mattress for furniture. No pictures on the wall. No decorations of any sort. It occurred to me that Corso could have packed and left the apartment in five minutes flat. Still, there was a peculiar charm to it, especially when he showed me out the back way to a little overgrown garden. We sat there on deck chairs and talked at length in the autumn sun. There were cats around, two or three of them, as I recall. They wound their way in and out around our feet, coming and going indolently through the door into Corso's apartment. From time to time, he would pick up one of the cats and hold it in his lap, stroking it comfortably as he talked on. It was F. Scott Fitzgerald, I think, who suggested that all the world might be divided between those who were fundamentally canine and those who were feline. Gregory Corso, I discovered to my surprise, was pure cat.

Talk turned early to his teaching experience at Buffalo. He brought it up, wanted to talk about it, and betrayed no bitterness as he recalled what it meant to him. "Buffalo was a great experience for me. It really was. You knew I was fired? About the Feinberg loyalty oath and all?"

"Yes," I said, "I heard something about it but I'd like to hear it from you."

"Well, I was teaching a course in Shelley. Imagine that. Of all the people who wouldn't sign a loyalty oath it's Shelley! And of course the way I left was lousy, but the actual teaching I enjoyed. I was very socratic in my approach. I just kept asking questions and let the kids answer them and that way we managed to pick up all the major themes in his work. And so I was learning, too—from their answers. If you can have real rapport with twenty people in a class like that, well, it's just great. I'd say I approached that with them."

Did he see a future for himself in teaching as he was doing there at Buffalo?

"I guess I must have thought so for a while," Corso said. "Here were these great people like Charles Olson and Fiedler who were there, and sure, of course I wanted to be a part of that. Who wouldn't? But now that I'm away from it, I honestly doubt that I could do this as a regular pattern."

He talked a little about his own self-education—his stretch at Clinton State Prison, his two years at Harvard ("It was a great ball. My friends would get me into classes or the library by day and I would write by night"), and his endless travels. "As for myself," he said, "I've always had this great enthusiasm for things. Maybe too much. I don't know. I get excited by places I go, people I meet, things I read. And when I get excited, that's when I start to think and learn."

From whom had he learned? From what? "The thing that hit me hard when I was starting out to learn was where you go to look for wisdom. And then the answer, who can a poet go to but to another poet?" He broke off, laughing, then added almost as an afterthought, "not to that Catholic God anymore! One man I read a lot and learned from was Randall Jarrell. He made me see things around me—fat ladies at the supermarket. Look at that, he says. What? you say, because you don't see anything great about them. But then suddenly you do! He illuminated me this way, got me to see.

144    "And of course you learn from experience. I've had a weird

thirty-seven years, let me tell you. I could write a real potboiler about all the things that happened to me. I won't, but I might write a play."

I asked about the sources of his poetry. What influence had his reading had on it? His experience? "Oh, well, it all plays a part. You know." He shrugged. "As a poet, of course, I'm stuck with getting at it through language. That's the prime interest with some poets. Though some people would say I'm crazy on this I think that's McClure's prime interest—language. So sure, of course, I'm into that, but I'm also stuck with myself, with everything I was and am at the moment I write. So in that way, see, I've always written for myself. But poets who always inject themselves into their poetry usually have a lousy Yin." Said at his own expense and in the manner of an embarrassed confession, although he did not bother to make his meaning explicit. (The idea was that the feminine, passive side of his personality was underdeveloped.)

"Today," he continued, "if you can make it perfect here" —he tapped at his chest above his heart—"then it will be perfect on the page. But it's hard, you know? Death, life, and society are always pushing into your thoughts. Sometimes you can't clear them out of your head and take up the routine of writing. It takes certainty to really do it. That's the thing. Some pretend to have it. I don't. My friend Allen [Ginsberg] really had it, and I envy him. He knows where he's at, where he is all the time. I certainly don't." Corso made a vague gesture of helplessness, and added as though to himself, "Does a bag of water have to go through all this?"

I was puzzled. "A bag of water?" I asked, having no idea, really, what he meant.

He shrugs, "Oh, that's what Burroughs says. He says we're all just bodies, just bags of water, so why worry about anything." Corso suddenly assumed an attitude and began speaking in a nasal drawl that I realized must be an imitation of Burroughs: "You're on a sinking ship, man, you've got to have it now. Let havoc happen. Why worry about wars? They happen." Then, suddenly, he was Corso again, pressing the point eagerly. "But myself, I question the idea that I'm just a bag of water. My body may be, but I'm not yet convinced that I am.

I think I'm a reality greater than that. I remember once I was with Timothy Leary, and Burroughs, and Francis Bacon in Tangier, and I was trying to show Burroughs what I meant. And so I told them that I could get rid of them all with a single bullet, if I wanted to. Like this—" He made a finger-and-thumb pistol and raised it to his temple in demonstration—"Bang! They're gone, see, but I'd still be there."

He had just brought up Burroughs and had mentioned Ginsberg a couple of times already, and so just touching base, I asked him about Kerouac.

"Jack? I'm occasionally in contact with him. I guess I saw him last about two years ago. He's a sweet soul. Really, he is. You know, he married a Greek woman, a childhood love of his —married her in his forty-third year. See? He's getting on. So am I. I'm thirty-seven years old now. None of us are young in the way we were when the mass media 'discovered' us."

"When you became the Beat Generation?"

"That's right." He leaned back and squinted up for a moment into the sunny September sky. "All it was was four people. I don't know if that's a generation. Can you call that a generation? That's more of a Madison Avenue thing. It was like here we were, speaking in our own voices, and the mass media couldn't control us, so they did the next best thing, they 'discovered' us."

"But something did come of it all, didn't it?" I asked. "Didn't a kind of revolution take place?"

"Okay," he waggled his hand indifferently, "maybe a *kind* of revolution, but a revolution without one drop of blood spilled, mostly a revolution in poetry. I'll grant you the hippie business, these kids you see today down on St. Mark's Place, that's right from us, out of our little bag of tricks. Did we influence them? Well, they don't write, so you can't tell that way, but just go down there and look around. The hippies are acting out what the Beats wrote. The whole thing worked out with us like a Madison Avenue ad campaign or something— you know, how they say something's going to happen, and suddenly it *is* there, maybe just because it was predicted."

146    I asked Corso about the writing he had been doing. I had

seen nothing for some time. "Maybe I just didn't look in the right places?"

"No," he said with an emphatic shake of the head. "I haven't had anything published in the last four years."

"Why not?" I asked. "You haven't stopped writing, have you?"

"Oh no, no. Come here. Let me show you." He got up and led the way back into the apartment and over to the sleeping bag. From a kind of rucksack in one corner behind it, he pulled a thick sheaf of papers. "See these?" he said. "This is four years right here—or more than four years because some of these poems I held back from before to make sure they were right. There's a lot of work here, but I have to be sure in my own heart that it's right, see. I really feel like I have to be able to stand on these poems. There's too much written and too much said today. I have to be sure these poems matter at least to me for me to publish them.

"See, that's why I've been doing all this traveling. I've spent four years thinking, trying to get right back to the source of things. I had this scary feeling that all I know about is writing and poetry, and so I made up my mind to learn. I stayed in Europe—in Greece and Crete—and I read the oldest books— *Gilgamesh*, the Bible, the *Book of the Dead*, all the Greek literature—just trying to put it together for myself.

"That's what's in these poems." He shook the sheaf at me. "And that's why I've got to be sure about them."

In the next few months I looked for his new book of poems, but none appeared. I tried to reach him once again in New York, just to talk, but heard that he had just left for the West Coast. How could I reach him out there? Well, he was acting funny, I was told, wasn't talking to people much. If I felt like I had to get in touch with him, I could probably write in care of Ferlinghetti at City Lights. When a trip to San Francisco was imminent, I did write to him there, but I received no reply. When I met Lawrence Ferlinghetti, I asked him about Corso, and he just shrugged. "He's sort of bitter now," he said. Did he get the letter I sent? "Sure," said Ferlinghetti. "I saw him read it myself. He just shook his head and walked away."

Years elapsed before the sheaf of poems he showed me that afternoon in the Village appeared as a book. When at last it did, I found myself smiling frequently in recognition of ideas, phrases, and bits of personal data that had come up in our conversation. I could have made out a travel itinerary from the place names mentioned in the poems that would have matched up fairly well with the one he outlined for me. And yes, there was evidence of his scholarship in "Geometric Poem," the odd, long, hieroglyph-festooned work whose source is clearly the *Book of the Dead*. And in "Eleven Times a Poem": "I think of Gilgamesh . . . Gil/astride on the redcedar bronze ramp-ed ziggurat/Of all those White Bull of Heaven energies. . . ." Names are named, particular anecdotes recounted. It is a book that looks back on a decade and sighs.

The tone is elegiac, and this is underlined by the title: *Elegiac Feelings American,* after the book's long first poem, a kind of requiem in verse "for the dear memory of John Kerouac." That one is an outstanding piece, a solemn poem for a solemn occasion which I would judge to be Gregory Corso's finest. The real accomplishment of the poem lies in the dualism of its subject. He has written a poem that is at once an elegy for a dead friend and also a memorial to a dying America:

> Yours the eyes that saw, the heart that felt, the voice that
> sang and cried; and as long as America shall
> live, though ye old Kerouac body hath died,
> yet shall you live. . . .

Kerouac's vision of America, his love of the country—how does Corso square these with the American reality?

> The prophet affects the state, and the state affects the
> prophet—What happened to you, O friend,
> happened to America, and we know what
> happened to America—the stain . . . the stains.
> O and yet when it's asked of you "What happened to him?"
> I say "What happened to America has happened
> him—the two were inseparable" Like the wind
> to the sky is the voice to the word. . . .

And again, it is also a deeply personal poem, one that bespeaks a certain sense of mission and a solidarity with the other Beat protagonists that he would never admit to in conversation:

> We came to announce the human spirit in the name of
>     beauty and truth; and now this spirit cries out in
>     nature's sake the horrendous imbalance of all
>     things natural . . . elusive nature caught! like a
>     bird in hand, harnessed and engineered in the
>     unevolutional ways of experiment and technique

These things it does and a good deal more, for it is a very long and complex work. I have quoted enough of it, I think, to indicate the beautifully sustained high seriousness of its diction. There is nothing of the bombast or facetiousness of his early work. "Elegiac Feelings American" is a poem of great maturity and (something never before felt in Corso's work) power. It is the work of a man who has at last made a fundamental choice, an artist.

CHAPTER 9

# One Big Happy Movement

When I was still busy bringing together the material for
this book, I happened to mention to an official of the United
States Information Agency in Washington, D.C., that I was
planning to write something on the Beats. He was most interested. "You mean Kerouac and Ginsberg and that crew?" he
asked. "You know, you really can't imagine how widespread
the interest in them is. I've met writers and teachers in places
like Beirut and Karachi, or even Helsinki, where they may
never have heard of any American writers *except* Ginsberg
and Kerouac. It's remarkable. You can forget about Herman
Melville, Mark Twain, or Henry James. All they know about
American literature is the Beat Generation—and that's all they
need to know. They love it."

That is the kind of impression they made on people in even
the most distant corners of the world. It wasn't just that they
were young, for other American writers—Hemingway and
Fitzgerald are good examples here—were much younger
when they first became known and symbolized youth and
vigor in a way the Beats never really did. And yet none were
known to so many, none inspired so much honest enthusiasm
all over the world as did Kerouac, Ginsberg, Corso, & Co. The
worldwide movement brought forth by them—whether you
call it Beat, hip, or underground—was the first ever to origi-
nate in America. By 1965 it was so prevalent that when *Commentary's* Marion Magid went out on assignment for *Esquire*
to survey Europe for an article misleadingly titled "The Death
of Hip," she found, frankly to her surprise, that hip was anything but dead. After about 10,000 words of diligent country-
hopping, she summarized: "We found them first in London

150

thinking we had stumbled on an accidental enclave only to discover as we proceeded on, that these enclaves were to be found in every city, headquarters of what could be called the marijuana culture, with institutions, an ideology, and an ethic of its own." And today, of course, with the hippie subculture manifesting itself in nearly every country in the West (and a few outside it as well), it simply cannot be seriously disputed that what began years ago as a literary movement in America is now a social movement of international dimension.

Why? What had they that caught the imagination of so many? What did the Beats mean to the growing army of followers who themselves represented so many different cultures and national styles?

First and fundamentally, I think, the Beats' appeal was due to the fact that they were American. Remember, they emerged at the end of the 1950s, and surely no decade ever belonged to any nation in quite the way that the 1950s belonged to America. In the eyes of the world, the United States was then still living comfortably off the moral capital it had gained by defeating Nazi Germany in World War II. And if the conquest of Japan had been marred somewhat by the nuclear destruction of Hiroshima and Nagasaki, nevertheless, the enormous technological capability that the development of the bomb represented was in itself truly awe-inspiring. Some, too, made much of the fact that when America had had the nuclear means to bend the Soviet Union (or any other nation) to her will, she had refused to do so. The two superpowers had settled into a stalemate. That distressing postwar drift, when it seemed that one nation after another was falling under Communist domination, had apparently ended with America standing her ground and fighting a limited war in Korea. It was a golden time. We were the richest, strongest, freest, most generous and virtuous nation on earth, and our people were the strongest, smartest, and best. Or so the myth ran, anyway.

But by decade's end, this image was beginning to fade a little, the gilt was starting to flake. There had been a number of specific embarrassments, such as Sputnik, the U-2 incident, as well as our belated discovery that we had a "Negro problem." More important, however, the people of the world had begun to grow a little tired of us. We had oversold ourselves shamefully. No matter how grand a pose we may have struck in public, we admitted to ourselves in private that America was neither as strong a nation nor as perfect a society as we had pretended. It only needed someone to come along and say all this out loud.

Some several did. They were the Beats. And what they symbolized to a world grown dyspeptic from swallowing too much of the American myth was the relief of regurgitation. The Beats rejected. They vomited up the American dream and left the mess quivering on the floor for the world to walk around. They said they didn't want the sort of material success that everyone else in America was working so hard to achieve. And if a chance to hit the jackpot was all a culture could offer, then, they declared, that wasn't much, was it? The reputation they soon acquired as nay-sayers helped the Beats create a myth of their own. Theirs was a sort of antimyth, one that turned the idea of America inside out. Instead of American cleanliness, the Beats offered dirt; for industry, sloth; and in place of the official, fundamentally Protestant American ethic, they presented their own, a morality with principles but no rules. This was how the Beats looked to the world at large. Accepting them, it was possible to reject some aspects of American culture, and still retain affection for those qualities of the national character that have always been most appealing —informality, enthusiasm, openness to adventure, and a kind of bold, plain-spoken honesty.

Of all the Beat Generation protagonists, Allen Ginsberg most perfectly incarnated these virtues, and of them all he became best known. They were an itinerant lot. Following the example of Jack Kerouac and Neal Cassady, they had made a pastime of crisscrossing the North American continent, had soon pursued Bill Burroughs to Mexico City and points south, and given the opportunity and boatfare, they had found their way around Europe and the Mediterranean with no difficulty. But Ginsberg traveled farthest. He journeyed as a kind of missionary, spreading the Beat gospel wherever he went with all the zeal and fervor of a true believer.

152      He might pop up just anywhere. Traveling nearly always

in the company of Peter Orlovsky, sometimes with Gregory Corso and others as well, Allen Ginsberg went on a drug expedition to Peru, put in an appearance in England at about the time the first word on the Beats had begun to spread, then traveled down to visit Burroughs in Tangier (where, as apocrypha has it, he collated the random pages that the addict-author had been dashing off between fixes and came away with *Naked Lunch*). For nearly two years, in what amounted to a pilgrimmage, he was in India, talking with the Sadhus and learning from the gurus, developing the idiosyncratic brand of Hindu philosophy that has sustained him ever since. Back from India in 1963, he "rested" for something over a year, and hit the road again, showing up first in Cuba, from which he was expelled for speaking disrespectfully of the revolution. He then traveled to Russia, and next to Czechoslovakia, where he was first crowned King of the May and then unceremoniously kicked out for alleged homosexual activities.

What sort of impact did Allen Ginsberg have on the places he visited? Liverpool poet Adrian Henri is quoted in *The Liverpool Scene*, an anthology of work from the distinctive "pop poetry" school, on the occasion they all remember on Merseyside: "Ginsberg has so much bloody personality that you can't ignore him: the man stands up and talks to you and you sit there and listen. He had a fantastic effect on Liverpool. He was very different in London—he was very tied-up there. The great thing here was that nobody knew who he was—you take him to the pub and all you get is these guys saying, 'Who's that funny fellow with you, the fellow with the long hair?' And Allen would just stand there and talk to you for five minutes and just wander away and you'd see him talking to somebody and then he'd wander off and talk to somebody else. And hundreds of people kept coming here for weeks afterwards, saying 'Hey, that American bloke with the long hair who was with you—he's gear, isn't he?' You know, all sorts and conditions of funny people whom you wouldn't expect to were terribly impressed by him. And the musicians, you know—we took him to The Cavern, and he went up to the Cavern office afterwards and got into a discussion with two drummers from beat groups, and brought out his finger-cymbals and was playing all these Tibetan rhythms and they thought this was great."

And for that matter, the feeling was mutual. Ginsberg had come to the gray, brawling Lancashire port city at the height of the Mersey Beat craze to find out just what it was in the polluted air of the place that had produced the Beatles and those other big beat groups. He came away saying that Liverpool "is at the present moment the center of the consciousness of the human universe. They're resurrecting the human form divine there—all those beautiful youths with long, golden archangelic hair."

The Beat influence had preceded him to Liverpool, however. Another of the pop poets, Roger McGough, recalls that when Allen's *New American Poetry* anthology found its way to the city, everybody in town who was interested in writing seemed to have a copy of it, and they were shouting poems out of it to one another across crowded pubs. "Adrian Henri was very much Ginsberg," he recalls. "For me it was Corso and Ferlinghetti. It was great, totally new to us. They were writing about what was there all around them, and that seemed the way to do it, so we started to try to do it exactly their way. In the beginning it was funny. We were just imitating. Everybody here was writing poems here with Yellow Cabs in them, which of course in Liverpool we haven't got. But eventually, through the Beats, I discovered Liverpool, and I started writing about what I saw around me right here. That was the big lesson we learned from them."

And that was the big lesson that writers all over Great Britain, all over Europe, were learning from them. Certainly, as their works became available in translation, the Beats began to acquire imitators and disciples even in non-English speaking countries. The noisiest, most energetic of all these was Holland's Jan Cremer, whose autobiographical fantasy *I Jan Cremer* was a best-seller in his own country in 1964. In a way, his writing owes about as much to Mickey Spillane and Henry Kane as it does to Jack Kerouac, for the chicks that he lays always have bulging buttocks and colossal tits (for further information consult *My Gun Is Quick* et al.); he treats them rough and is tough to his male antagonists, too. But the formless spontaneous drive of that first book and his second, *Jan*

*Cremer Writes Again,* is pure Beat, as is the manic, swinging quality of life it extolls. Jan Cremer seems to be caught at what Roger McGough would call the Yellow-Cab level of Beat expression. "I've been a fanatic Americanophile ever since I was a kid," he proclaims at one point in his second book—and believe me, it shows. In setting a scene he usually gives us a radio in the corner of the room blaring out Fats Domino and Elvis Presley or puts on Art Blakey record on the phonograph. He begins one chapter, "In the morning mist her skin had a Max Factor glow." In fact, he keeps up such a steady barrage of Americanisms and indulges so shamelessly in Yankeeolatry that it is necessary to remind oneself from time to time that this was originally written in Dutch.

"I knew I'd go to America sometime. Had to. That was my Paradise. My Valhalla. I'd come through over there. Hard work for hard money." This is a refrain that is repeated again and again in his work. And when Marion Magid ran into him in Amsterdam during the course of her survey of the international Beat scene for *Esquire,* he told her, "I'm going to the United States. I'm too much for Europe." Eventually he made it to his Paradise, his Valhalla. He came over about the time *I Jan Cremer* appeared in its American edition. The Beat critic-confessionalist Seymour Krim generously contributed an Introduction to the book, which he began by declaring that Cremer "can rank unashamedly as the crazy sixties' brilliant illegitimate son of such giants of imaginative autobiography as Louis-Ferdinand Céline, Henry Miller, Jean Genet and Maxim Gorki," but ended by betraying a certain uneasiness at Cremer's ruthless and unashamed passion for self-promotion. And afterward, Krim recalled, "He would like to be a fantasy figure, 'a world idol' as he puts it looking you right in the eye without a smile, a rough combination of Bobby Kennedy and Yevtushenko and Cassius Clay. . . ." I would point out that he hasn't yet achieved that ambition.

But if there were Dutch Beats, Turkish Beats, French Beats, and German Beats (and there were), there was nowhere that the movement had greater or more lasting impact than it did on England. There were a number of good reasons for this, and most of them had to do with the ascendance of the United

States to the position of uncontested leadership in the English-speaking world. As has happened so often, political, economic, and military leadership have brought cultural domination as well. Or perhaps in the case of America, which has had a very strong and distinctive national culture since the beginning of this century, the reverse was true. Perhaps cultural penetration came first and made all the rest possible. In any case, the cultural leadership of America today is fact, and anyone who doubts it just hasn't read this week's *New Statesman.* I mean this as generally true—at all levels from top to bottom, that is —but it is most apparently so in the area of pop culture. More and more, with groups and supergroups trading back and forth across the Atlantic, with television so nearly the same in both England and America, and with the near total domination of the English motion picture industry by American capital, what the English young people saw, thought, and heard during the last twelve or fifteen years has been very largely determined by going trends in America. Below university level, the English young are far more directly influenced by American pop culture than by their own high culture.

It is in a sense embraced by them as the antithesis of their own official culture. Thus the Beats as outsiders made a strong direct appeal to working-class youth, or to those who, for social reasons or as a matter of taste, were hostile to the English university culture. To the extent that the Beats represented American pop culture and to the extent that they drew the disapproval and derision of the English cultural mandarins (which was considerable in both cases), the Beats found acceptance among the great mass of English youth.

And acceptance came early. As early as 1961, a young writer with a foot firmly in the pop music world, Ray Gosling, gave a patois description of England's young takeover generation: "It's De Beat generation all Europeanized with Banning the Bomb and Jazz and De popular arts. And the point is that down in the beer and piana bars and in the jazz rooms they really are mixing."

That quotation was lifted from an interesting book on the development of the English underground, *Bomb Culture,* by one Jeff Nuttall, poet, painter, and one-time jazz trumpeter. In it, he emphasizes quite rightly the more political quality of the movement in England. Indeed, in Europe as well, wherever the Beat style was adopted, it was usually by those (the Provos, for example, in Holland and Rudi Dutschke's SDS in Germany) who were far more political in their orientation than were the original American Beats. In the development of the underground, Nuttall gives about equal weight to the English ban-the-bomb movement, the passion for pop music, and the American influence in the arts, particularly that of the Beats. And he indicates, too, that the focal event for the anti- or "Bomb" culture in England was the famous Albert Hall poetry reading held June 11, 1965. All the right elements were brought together that night. On this everyone seems to agree.

It was a spur-of-the-moment affair. Organized in about a week, the reading was billed as the first International Poetry Incarnation and along with a number of fine British poets, it featured Allen Ginsberg, Gregory Corso, Lawrence Ferlinghetti, and the Russian poet, Andre Voznesensky. It was a benchmark event for the movement in England. Certainly it was a success; there was no trouble filling the huge London auditorium. But there was a special pride for those who planned and appeared at the reading that the British underground movement had come so far and was now so very visible. There was an almost apocalyptic optimism in the invocation to the first International Poetry Incarnation which was read at a press conference a week before. It begins:

England! awake! awake! awake!
Jerusalem thy Sister calls!

And it continues in a litany of friendly publishers, publications, and institutions:

Now! Sigmatic New Departures Residu of Better
Books & Moving Times in obscenely New Directions!
Soul revolution City Lights Olympian lamb-blast!

And it concludes, directly addressing those in sympathy with the movement who may have felt themselves isolated, suffering alone in silence in Coventry or Manchester:

157

> You are not alone!
> Miraculous assumption! O Sacred Heart invisible
> insurrection! Albion! awake! awake! awake! O
> shameless bandwagon! Self evident for real naked
> come the Words! Global synthesis habitual for this
> Eternity! Nobody's Crazy Immortals Forever!

That was the kind of evening it was. There was electricity in the air and ecstasy in the hearts of those who had come, some of them a great distance (Coventry and Manchester were there) just to be present. The crowd was spirited, noisy, but ultimately respectful. To them, proper conduct seemed a matter of not merely sitting and listening in docile silence, but really taking part in what seemed to them a miraculous event. As Allen Ginsberg read, for example, one girl rose to her feet and began moving slowly in a weird twisting dance, a marvelous moment. This vignette and others that characterized the whole, crazy joyous atmosphere that prevailed that night have been caught on film in Peter Whitehead's *Wholly Communion,* a documentary of the Albert Hall reading that in intention and feeling prefigures *Monterey Pop* and *Woodstock.*

None of the British poets who read that night, except perhaps Christopher Logue and George Macbeth, would have passed muster at the universities. They were by the stringent standards of the poetry establishment, a rather scruffy lot—grammar school lads almost to a man, who had worked in and out of factories and the trades before becoming involved in the movement. One of them, Adrian Mitchell, who brought down the house that night with his reading of "You Get Used to It," later described the enormous significance that evening had for them all: "Ginsberg and Ferlinghetti and Yevtushenko opened the gates and out we rushed, blinking and drinking in the light. In the past five, six, seven years more and more British poets have been stomping the island giving adrenaline transfusions in cellars, town halls, schools, clubs, pubs, theaters, anywhere. Whenever enough people knew that poetry was around they came, grabbed it and started chewing. So it's no surprise that 6,000 plus came to the Albert Hall feast. It wasn't the beginning of anything, it was public proof that something had been accelerating for years."*

It was evidence, then, of the healthy existence of a movement that Mitchell is sure will eventually overcome: "I want poetry to bust down all the walls of its museum tomb and learn to survive in the corrosive real world. The walls are thick but a hundred Joshuas are on the job." Feelings such as these found expression in the same sort of writing that came directly out of the Beat movement. Quite naturally so, for both were protests against stifling restrictions of official culture and national spirit. In many ways the British underground and the American Beats were bucking what were fundamentally the same restrictions. And in just as many ways the two were merely separate divisions in the one big movement that had started at a poetry reading in San Francisco in 1955 and was now sweeping the world.

There is good reason to consider it so. There is a striking continuity here, not just of style, feeling, and ideas, but of specific personalities who carry through from time to time and place to place. Again and again the same people seem to emerge, submerge, only to re-emerge at another time and place, saying just about the same things and influencing new people in just about the same way as before.

A case in point is Alexander Trocchi. This Scotsman with the Italian name was there onstage that night at Albert Hall. He was the only one present to read a work of prose, but what a work of prose *Cain's Book* is—compelling, brutal, yet casually beautiful in its honesty. As a testament of the addict's life, it ranks close to William S. Burroughs' much different *Naked Lunch*. It is a confession delivered in unsynchronized fragments, bits and pieces of a hell so real that it survives the rude dislocations of time and space that we are put through reading it. The difficulties are his as well. He remarks on them in the course of *Cain's Book:*

*Quoted from Michael Horovitz, ed., *Children of Albion: Poetry of the Underground in Britain* (Harmondsworth: Penguin, 1969).

When I write I have trouble with my tenses. Where I *was* tomorrow *is* where I *am* today, where I *would be* yesterday. I have a horror of committing fraud. It is all very difficult, the past even more than the future, for the latter is at least probable, calculable, while the former is beyond the range of experiment. The past is always a lie; clung to by an odour of ancestors. It is important from the beginning to treat such things lightly. As the ghosts rise upwards over the grave wall, I recoffin them neatly, and bury them.

The above, I would say, is about one part a statement of his philosophical position, and an equal part a description of the peculiar problems faced by the writing addict. ("It was just really a whole sheaf of notes," says Trocchi. "I just went on and on, and the end of the thing was originally at the beginning. Then Dick Seaver helped put some of it together.") But finally, it must stand also as a kind of hands-in-the-air admission of befuddlement at the direction his life has taken and the speed with which it has been moving. Tenses have begun to blur for him just a little.

You get a little of that when you meet him—a kind of tight-lipped wonder at the world about him, a sense that he made a vow some time ago not to show surprise at anything. And a lot of surprising things have happened to him, too. In 1950, hardly more than a boy, he went off to Paris to prove he was a poet, and wound up editing a little magazine called *Merlin* that had a short but distinguished life from 1952 to 1955. In 1952 he also wrote his first novel, *Young Adam,* which he says was done in reaction to Camus' novel *The Stranger.* ("It seemed to me that cod Meuersault resigned himself a bit too easily.") Survival is what *Young Adam* is all about, and survival was soon enough the story of Trocchi's own life. In 1956 he left Paris for New York and there became a heroin addict. His life as a bargeman up and down the docks of New York and New Jersey, unpromising as it would have seemed to a get-ahead type, was just the thing for keeping an addict alive. A minimum of effort was required; most of the time just being there was enough. As long as he could make it into the Village from time to time to make his connection, then he was home free. This is what *Cain's Book* is all about: nights spent schlepping on a barge through New York harbor with the rain blowing in his face; days passed in the bunk after scoring; and weekends spent huddled with other addicts in the darkest corners of the Village. Although these may not have seemed the materials for a conventional novel the immediacy and reality of the writing made it a book that once read cannot be forgotten.

That it was written at all is both a tribute to Trocchi's vocation as a writer and to the friends who sustained him through this rough period of his life. Dick Seaver, of course: he had helped out on *Merlin* and was now working as an editor at Grove Press, the publisher that eventually brought out *Cain's Book.* Allen Ginsberg and Peter Orlovsky were also contacts that he had made through *Merlin.* Through Ginsberg, of course, he got to know a great many people—and most important of these, he feels, was Irving Rosenthal (cofounder with Paul Carroll of *Big Table* and the author of the scabrous *Sheeper*). "They were a big influence, Rosenthal and his group. This whole *Musee Imaginaire* they had going anticipated Kesey and the Merry Pranksters. That psychedelic bus trip of theirs was like a continuation of everything that had been discussed and projected as part of the *Musee Imaginaire.*"

After a brief stint in the Beat colony in Venice, California, he pulled up stakes and in 1963 returned, with his American wife and American-born son, to Great Britain. He had his drug problem under control and was then sporting some reputation as the author of *Cain's Book.* His first stop, as a matter of fact, was at Edinburgh, where he sat in distinguished company as a panelist at the International Writers Conference that had been organized by the British publisher John Calder. With him there was William S. Burroughs, whom Trocchi had met only two years before. The two decided at the Edinburgh conference to move down to London.

Once there, Trocchi soon became a key figure in the English underground movement. He brought with him a certain prestige and the international contacts that the movement badly needed just then. In his own odd, furtive way, he is a natural leader, a real *macher* of the revolution. It was not long before he had his own thing going, Project Sigma, through which he has proposed an "invisible insurrection" by means of a so-called *coup du monde,* a cultural revolt that "must seize the grids of expression and the powerhouses of the mind." The object: the establishment of "spontaneous universities" in which men of genius and good will can devise plans to rescue the world from the "brink of disaster."

Alexander Trocchi was busy on Sigma matters the afternoon I looked in on him at his apartment in London's Notting Hill Gate section. A number of people were meeting there to discuss the tense local racial situation in which white "skinhead" toughs had begun harassing London colored people of all shades. Marianne Faithfull, the pop singer, was there, as well as Michael X, the black nationalist who has become such a thorn in the side of official Britain. Trocchi stepped out of the meeting, tall, stooping, and cadaverous, and suggested that under the circumstances the best place for us to do our talking might be the pub around the corner.

As we went, he asked me, apparently only half joking, just how he knew I was who I said I was. "You could be with the CIA, taking notes on all of us."

"I could, I suppose, but I'm not."

He shrugged. Evidently that convinced him—though it wouldn't have convinced me—and he indicated the entrance of the pub just ahead. Once we were settled inside, I asked just what influence he thought the Beats had had here in England.

He thought a moment and said that he wasn't very comfortable with labels like that. "People, yes. Certain people have had a lot to say to me and to others here. But as for groups and movements, it's all been very linked up, practically one. For me, you see, this movement, whatever it is, has been continuous from 1950 on. In different places, with different people involved, but all fundamentally the same go."

Have there been changes? Has he seen results?

"Yes, but it took a while. It wasn't until 1960 that I saw young people were really going to do it. Changes? Of course there've been changes—even in dress. Just look around you. They're doing things now we couldn't have done before.

"No, I see it all as a very unified battle. I think it's going to continue in more or less the same direction. The underground will become more and more powerful. Burroughs has a much blacker picture. In one way or another he sees everything falling apart—maybe Nixon will die and Agnew will take over. But not me. That's not the way I see it. I think that the underground's getting so powerful that in another few years the Marines will be led by the underground. Then they won't be able to impose a solution in their terms."

I asked to be brought up to date on his writing, and he explained that he had been so absorbed with Project Sigma, writing articles for it and so forth, that he hadn't really done much of *that* kind of writing (meaning fiction, confession, whatever, terms fail). "But you know about my Francis Lengel books don't you?" He explained that these were good books "of their kind" that he had done a long time ago in Paris for Olympia Press. He ticked off a few titles—*Helen and Desire, White Thighs, Thongs.* "They've all been pirated, so Maurice Girodias is reissuing them under my own name. Bob Creeley has even agreed to do an introduction to *Thongs.*"

We spent some moments checking chronology, dates, facts. Did he know this person? Had he been in contact with that one?

"Look," he said then. "What you must realize is that all these people are in contact. What we've got going now is a very solid underground. Many are unknown to the outside world. Many are quite successful—a funny word to use under the circumstances. But all of them are staying in touch and in a general way working together, you might say. These are all kinds of different people—Burroughs, R. D. Laing, Michael X, old Provos in Holland, Situationists in Paris, and the people you might expect here and in the States. Oh, there've been some petty breaches. Nevertheless the spirit behind it all is moving toward something big like the free universities, the Sigma idea."

I asked Trocchi about his particular role in all this. "In a way it's because I'm in contact with everyone that I'm trying to direct efforts toward the free university. But as for me personally, I've always remained underground. This is how I see my life. Fortunately my books are now making money. But any conceivable future would be more or less anonymous in the underground."

At about this point he leaped to his feet and began apologizing for having to cut the talk short. He really did have to get back to the meeting at his place, though. "You don't get people like these together every day," he explained. "You're planning to see Burroughs, aren't you?"

I said I was.

"I'm involved with him on many different levels. He'll have a lot to tell you, I'm sure. But right now I've really got to be on. Sorry."

And in a moment Alexander Trocchi was gone, trailing in his wake a calendar of appointments, high hopes for the cultural revolution, and a broken career as a writer.

CHAPTER 10

# The Holy Monster

William S. Burroughs, I'm sure, would argue against his inclusion here. For one thing he has iterated and reiterated in all his interviews, literary and otherwise, is that he does not wish to be considered a Beat writer. By now it seems to come from him almost in the once familiar rote style of congressional committee testimony: I am not now, nor have I ever been, a member of the Beat Generation. The accused pleads not guilty.

Here, for instance, is how he put it to the French writer Daniel Odier in *The Job,* a book-length series of Burroughs interviews conducted over a period of months. At a point early in their sessions, M. Odier asked him about his relation to the Beat movement, and Burroughs replied: "I don't associate myself with it at all, and never have, either with their objectives or their literary style. I have some close personal friends among the Beat movement: Jack Kerouac and Allen Ginsberg and Gregory Corso are all close personal friends of many years standing, but were not doing at all the same thing either in writing or in outlook. You couldn't really find four writers more different, more distinctive. It's simply a matter of juxtaposition rather than any actual association of literary styles or overall objectives. . . ."

He has a point, of course. All the Beats were to some extent different from one another. They had to be. They were writers, after all, and as such they were bound to emphasize what was individual and unique in themselves. Indeed, many of those we have talked about here have very little in common. It could certainly be argued that any movement that could contain writers as fundamentally unlike as Gary Snyder and Seymour Krim lacked definition. And true enough, it did. This should remind us once again that one reason the purely literary phase of the movement was so short-lived was that it failed to develop specific principles and identifiable forms to which true believers would have to adhere. (And, of course, they lacked the critical mafia necessary to make such rules stick.) The reason for this is that it was precisely because they were against such rigid principles, inflexible forms, and enforced conformity that the Beats got together in the first place. It was about all they had in common. The situation made for a bit of bandwagoning by young and/or unrecognized writers who wished to associate themselves with the happening thing. It also made for a bit of confusion among many of the Beats themselves as to just who they were, what they wanted, and where they were going. A few, as I have tried to indicate, did know and had their answers ready. But for the most part, the Beat Generation as a literary movement lacked unifying principles; it had in their place only certain shared characteristics and attitudes. The Beats knew what they were against; it was trying to decide what, if anything, they were for that confounded many of them.

But the Beats certainly—and probably most importantly—were also a social movement. William S. Burroughs knew that. (In fact, he goes on to say as much to M. Odier.) And to the extent that the Beats have wielded social influence, Burroughs should be considered one of them. He was, of course, popularly associated with them, particularly in Great Britain and Europe. Distinctions in style and literary intent that may have meant a great deal to him have been, for the most part, lost on his readers. If they did perceive the intellectual differences that separated him from Ginsberg, Kerouac, Corso, et al., they saw even more clearly that he shared with the others the reckless antagonism to the postwar American scene that seemed to activate the whole Beat movement. And of them all, his rejection was the most categorical and emphatic, the most contemptuous, his rage the most eloquent. Those who responded to this, whose attitudes toward authority and the star-spangled status quo, were soon radically changed, saw Burroughs simply as one of "their" writers, no more or less Beat than the rest.

166

It may seem here that I am trying to minimize the literary importance of Burrough's work and simply consider him from the point of view of his effect on his audience. But that would be a mistake, of course, for he is a very considerable prose artist —intellectually accomplished, technically innovative, the sort of absolute writer who, given different subject matter, would have enormous appeal to academic critics. Even so, some seem to see him as a kind of John Barth of the drug culture. There is a general willingness to accept Burroughs—or to accept *Naked Lunch,* anyhow—by many critics who dismiss the work of the Beats out of hand.

Mary McCarthy for one. Her article on Burroughs in *The New York Review of Books,* which appeared not long after the publication of *Naked Lunch,* probably did more than any other single piece to establish him with "serious" readers. Her imprimatur, seldom given without some reluctance to living Americans, has been bestowed on Burroughs, she declares, in order to set the record straight. She complains at having been misquoted by the English press in her comments on *Naked Lunch* delivered at the International Writers' Conference at Edinburgh in 1962: ". . . I said that in thinking over the novels of the last few years, I was struck by the fact that the only ones that had not simply given me pleasure but interested me had been those of Burroughs and Nabokov." This modest praise was inflated beyond all measure, she says, and so she must tell now what she really thinks of Burroughs and *Naked Lunch.*

None of her thoughts on the subject turn out to be very original. She compares him, for example, to Jonathan Swift, just as a number of others have done, including Jack Kerouac. Then with a flourish, Miss McCarthy reveals Burroughs as a humorous writer. This is a little like unmasking Charles de Gaulle as a Frenchman. Of course, Burroughs is humorous. He is the rawest, most brutally funny American writer since Ambrose Bierce. But let it pass, let it pass, for she does a fair job analyzing the source and style of his humor and comes up with appropriate examples. And after all, readers of *The New York Review of Books* probably need to be told that it is all right to laugh at Burroughs' vicious humor and not merely scrutinize the text with the usual serious frown and treat the jokes as symptoms of serious social disorder.

Norman Mailer sat on that same panel with Miss McCarthy in Edinburgh, and he spoke somewhat more enthusiastically of the book and its author. Earlier, on the strength of excerpts of *Naked Lunch* he had read in *Big Table,* he had called Burroughs "the only American novelist living today who may conceivably be possessed by genius." At Edinburgh, he came on just as strong, saying that he thought that Burroughs' novel was the most important one by a contemporary in America. The effect of having two eminents like Mary McCarthy and Norman Mailer endorse a writer whose published work was then available only in an Olympia Press edition in Paris had just about the effect of tying him to a skyrocket and lighting the fuse. He took off. The Grove Press edition of the book was out a short time later and was widely reviewed, enthusiastically praised, and generally accepted as a work of major importance.

The obscenity suits helped, of course. Proceedings against *Naked Lunch* were started in Los Angeles and Boston, and booksellers in a number of other cities were subjected to harassment by police and vigilante groups because of the book. Although all the suits were, of course, eventually decided in favor of *Naked Lunch,* the Boston case was of particular interest because the defense attorney involved in that one, Edward de Grazia, put on a very literary trial and brought Norman Mailer, Allen Ginsberg, and John Ciardi before the court as witnesses. Excerpts from the testimony of Mailer and Ginsberg are included in most editions of *Naked Lunch;* these are worth reading and reading carefully, for the remarks of both are very sharp and to the point. They provide a good and generally helpful introduction to the book.

Norman Mailer delivered an almost unqualified eulogy of the book. It is worth considering his testimony at some length here, for while what he said on one point in particular was unexceptionable, it may create some slight misapprehension on the reader's part regarding the particular quality of Burroughs' work. Mailer remarked at one point in answer to a
168     question by the court on the meaning of the work, "To me this

is a simple portrayal of Hell. It is Hell precisely." And then he went on to read from notes he had written for the occasion:

> William Burroughs is in my opinion—whatever his conscious intention may be—a religious writer. There is a sense in *Naked Lunch* of the destruction of soul, which is more intense than any I have encountered in any other modern novel. It is a vision of how mankind would act if man was totally divorced from eternity. What gives this vision a machine-gun-edged clarity is an utter lack of sentimentality. The expression of sentimentality in religious matters comes forth usually as a sort of saccharine piety which revolts any idea of religious sentiment in those who are sensitive, discriminating, or deep of feeling. Burroughs avoids even the possibility of such sentimentality (which would, of course, destroy the value of his work), by attaching a stringent, mordant vocabulary to a series of precise and horrific events, a species of gallows humor which is a defeated man's last pride, the pride that he has, at least, not lost his bitterness. . . .

Mailer goes on to talk a bit more about Burroughs' style of black humor, but the effect of discussing Burroughs as a "religious writer," refreshingly novel as this idea may seem, may well be to divert readers from the essential Burroughs and into what is sure to be an unrewarding search for his *meaning.* It may even alert some of the more ambitious to be on the lookout for religious symbols in his work.

No matter what has been or will be written about William S. Burroughs, the best possible introduction to his work is a phonograph record, *Call Me Burroughs,* that he has made on which he reads selections from *Naked Lunch* and *Nova Express.* Just text. You will find on it no explanations, no statement of purpose, and no artistic credo. Only the voice of William S. Burroughs reading from two of his books.

But what a voice it is! Dry, dusty, sardonic, a kind of nasal drawl that wavers somewhere between W. C. Fields and Ned Sparks. It is the voice of the con artist, the tout, the grifter, the man without illusions who must perforce create them. It is above all an American voice. The accent is middle-western (Burroughs was born and raised in St. Louis), and the intonation and phrasing is the kind you could hear until just after the war echoing through pool halls, railroad stations, and the lobbies of cheap hotels in every tank town from Minnesota to Oklahoma.

The voice is the man. It is a direct expression of the style of the personality and intelligence behind the books. William S. Burroughs—battered by his long history as a narcotics addict, scarred by his homosexuality, and bearing who knows what secret social bruises on his battered soul—is a man who has been around and knows all the answers to questions polite people don't ask. In his writing he draws on a wealth of personal experience that would have impoverished and utterly destroyed a lesser man.

The dry tales of old junk cons run through his novels, providing that firm springboard in reality that his surrealistic brand of humor must have to work. An example from *Nova Express:*

> ... stopped that night in Pleasantville Iowa and our tires gave out we had no tire rations during the war for such a purpose —And Bob got drunk and showed his badge to the locals in a road house by the river—And I ran into The Sailor under a potted palm in the lobby—We hit the local croakers with the "fish poison con"—"I got these poison fish, Doc, in the tank transported back from South America I'm a Ichthyologist and after being stung by the dreaded Candiru—Like fire through the blood is it not? Doctor, and coming on now"— And the sailor goes into his White Hot Agony Act chasing the doctor around his office like a blowtorch He never missed. . . .

This routine goes on at length, the action getting wilder, more bizarre and fantastic with each line—the troublesome doctor is finally ingested—but then suddenly we are back in "a naborhood of chili houses and cheap saloons with free lunch everywhere and heavy calm bartenders humming 'Sweet Sixteen.' "

This suggests a pattern to his humor, one that I think appears again and again throughout his novels. A typical Burroughs routine starts from a firm base in reality, takes a surrealistic leap, then having performed a devious turn or two

170

in mid-air, returns with a reassuring thump to reality. You can trace the entire progression through this single paragraph from *The Soft Machine:*

> "No calcium in the area you understand. One blighter lost his entire skeleton and we had to carry him about in a canvas bathtub. A jaguar lapped him up in the end, largely for the salt I think."

That is pure W. C. Fields. You can practically hear the old comedian's whining drawl delivering those lines, dropping that phrase at the end with a flick of cigar ash just to bring us back down to earth again. Much of Fields' humor followed this same pattern—and I'm not suggesting here that the comedian provided the source or inspiration for Burroughs. No, nothing of the kind. What I am suggesting is that both were fundamentally similar in style and share a common ethos. Their basic attitude, the force that activated the one and still drives the other mercilessly, is misanthropy. That may seem too strong for Fields—after all, he was a comedian, right?—until we remember not only the corrosive quality of his famous wit, but his horrible childhood and the systematic way that he went about drowning himself in alcohol through his adult life. As for Burroughs, the idea that he is a hater of mankind, once articulated, seems to fit quite nicely. His experience as an addict of what Norman Mailer calls "Hell precisely" was real and true enough, and precisely is just how he describes it. There is no saving grace of love—not so much as a hint of it—to be found in his work. And his visions and routines, funny as they are so often, are just as often ruthless, nightmare visions of brutality, torture, and death. The Burroughs who writes the books is like the God who is always absent from the Hieronymous Bosch paintings, stern-faced yet secretly snickering (having made his judgment) at the sufferings of mankind.

Yet what is a misanthrope but a realist who has drawn negative conclusions from his data? And William S. Burroughs is pre-eminently a realist. Allen Ginsberg commented on this eloquently in an important poem, "On Burroughs' Work," which he read to the court in the course of his testimony at the

Boston obscenity trial. It is short and worth quoting in whole because in just a few lines Ginsberg makes some very valid points in criticism that others have overlooked, ignored, or distorted in commenting subsequently on Burroughs' work:

> The method must be purest meat
> and no symbolic dressing,
> actual visions & actual prisons
> as seen then and now.
>
> Prisons and visions presented
> with rare descriptions
> corresponding exactly to those
> of Alcatraz and Rose.
>
> A naked lunch is natural to us,
> we eat reality sandwiches.
> But allegories are so much lettuce.
> Don't hide the madness.

Allen Ginsberg, incidentally, thought enough of this poem and its general statement to have taken a phrase from it and made it the title for the collection of poems, *Reality Sandwiches*, from which this one is taken.

And while we are on the subject of titles, what about *Naked Lunch?* Burroughs himself has something to say on that odd, provocative formulation. He tells us (in his essay "Deposition: Testimony Concerning a Sickness"): "The title was suggested by Jack Kerouac. I did not understand what the title meant until my recent recovery. The title means exactly what the words say: NAKED Lunch—a frozen moment when everyone sees what is on the end of every fork."

*The title means exactly what the words say*—there is an ultimatum implied there, something like a threat to the reader lurking just beneath the surface: either you take me at my word or you don't take me at all. He means it. Burroughs has made it clear that he thinks of himself as a realist and wants to be read just this way. The closest thing he has written to a description of his method of composition can be found in the next-to-last section of *Naked Lunch,* the part he calls an "Atro-
phied Preface":

> There is only one thing a writer can write about: *What is in front of his senses at the moment of writing.* . . . I am a recording instrument. . . . I do not presume to impose "story" "plot" "continuity.". . . In sofaras I succeed in *Direct* recording of certain areas of psychic process I may have limited function. . . . I am not an entertainer.

Thus he attests to the reality of his nightmares—"actual visions & actual prisons," as Allen Ginsberg calls them in the poem.

What is in front of his senses at the moment of writing can, of course, be either an observable, measurable, or precisely rememberable phenomenon—or it can be a vision, a fantasy. The distinction to be made here, of course, is between objective and subjective reality. But whether one or the other (Burroughs would insist), it is nevertheless reality to the writer at the moment of description.

The peculiar, terrifying, and often repulsive quality of Burroughs' subjective reality leads one to wonder where it all comes from. From dreams and simple fantasies, first of all. There is a brief mention in one of his notes to Allen Ginsberg in *The Yage Letters* to the effect that a routine he had written out and was sending on had come to him in a dream "from which I woke up laughing." This was on Burroughs' famous first expedition into South America in search of psychedelic herbs. Had these something to do with forming the shape and substance of that particular routine?* Probably. If not directly, then surely and ultimately, indirectly, for if psychedelics expand consciousness, they are certainly likely to alter the unconscious. And by the same reasoning, Burroughs' heavy, protracted, and varied experience with drugs of all kinds is sure to have left quite some impression on him. Or to be more specific, his drug experience must have left many different impressions, compelling visual images that occur and recur in transformations and metamorphoses of the most bizarre and surrealistic sort, images that he dutifully records, works into routines and narratives, and weaves into his texts. The drug image is often terrifyingly vivid. And in the truest sense it may

*It was "Roosevelt after Inauguration," which LeRoi Jones published in his magazine, *Floating Bear*. The issue was seized, and Jones was arrested for sending it through the mail.

be unforgettable: you want to forget, but you can't. This accounts, I think, for the repetition of certain fundamental images and visions in his writing sometimes with only minor variations from section to section and even from book to book.

Often, however, a good deal of imagination and conscious artistry goes into the creation and recreation of these little nightmares. For instance, in Burroughs' first published work, *Junkie,* which was written in straightforward fashion and published in 1953 under the pseudonym William Lee, he tells of the miseries he experienced when his source dried up, and he was forced to kick a habit temporarily with no more than benzedrine and juke box music to help him:

> Almost worse than the sickness is the depression that goes with it. One afternoon, I closed my eyes and saw New York in ruins. Huge centipedes and scorpions crawled in and out of empty bars and cafeterias and drugstores on Forty-second Street. Weeds were growing up through cracks and holes in the pavement. There was no one in sight.

Here, in compressed summary, is a veritable nightmare-temptation of St. Anthony. Burroughs has borrowed from these and other such drug memories time and time again in his writing. The centipedes, for instance, barely mentioned here, must be the ancestors of those monsters of the Mayan dungeons who appear in *The Soft Machine,* huge centipedes who by some malign metamorphosis have been generated from gobbets of flesh seared from torture victims.

There are indications that Burroughs himself is somewhat baffled by the perverse quality of some of the visions and images that he, as recording instrument, has transcribed, and perhaps he is even a little shocked by them. What else, after all, are we to make of his repeated claim that a good deal of his writing is taken in direct dictation from Hassan-i-sabbah, the founder of the eleventh-century cult of Islamic murderers, the Assassins? Isn't he asking, in effect, not to be held responsible for the nature of his dreams? How would Burroughs have us divide his work? What part of it belongs to him and what part to Hassan?

174

If I were to credit the notorious strangler-master as the source for any particular passages in Burroughs' writing, it would be the many instances scattered throughout his books in which the hanging image is repeated in certain slight variations of detail and circumstance again and again, quite literally ad nauseum. Yet in all of them the essential detail—orgasm at the end of a rope—remains the same. It is what this little story, in all its repetitions and variations, is all about. Yet on the strength of such textual evidence and Burroughs' testimony, can we accept Hassan-i-sabbah as author of these or any other passages in Burroughs' work? I think not. True, Hassan may also have been a homosexual misanthrope with sadistic tendencies but since that so neatly characterizes the Burroughs we know from the books, it does not seem reasonable or necessary to credit some ghostly collaborator beyond him as coauthor.

No. Perverse, grotesque, fantastic, ugly though they may be, Burroughs' visions are his own. They are of a piece with that part of his work that would be considered objectively realistic. Together, they comprise as total and frank a self-portrait as has ever been achieved in literature. *Naked Lunch, Nova Express, The Soft Machine, The Ticket That Exploded*— yes, and even *Junkie*—present William S. Burroughs the man, they show him inside and out. But—and I think this deserves emphasis—his novels have no meaning beyond the immediate one that is to be found right there on the printed page. There is no unifying idea, no grand plan, no myth underlying them. They are simply what they are, Burroughs' "reality sandwiches." Take a bite if you don't mind the taste of raw and sometimes putrid meat, for that's what you'll find there between the bread. "Allegories," as Allen Ginsberg suggests, "are so much lettuce."

The full name, William Seward Burroughs. Born February 5, 1914 in St. Louis, Missouri, the grandson of William Seward Burroughs, inventor of the adding machine and founder of the business machine empire that still bears the family name. Burroughs attended Harvard, graduated in 1936, and showing no inclination to enter the business world, dabbled in graduate studies in ethnology and archaeology without ever really settling down to academic life. His curriculum vitae even includes a brief stint at the University of Vienna in medical studies.

During this postgraduate period he read intensely and widely in a number of different areas. Without choosing a specific direction for himself, he began building up the store of erudition that he has displayed in bits and pieces in the writing of his novels. This was made possible by a steady income from a trust fund set up for him by his family. But the war came, interrupting this phase of his life. The army tried him out and didn't like him much, and returned him to civilian life—he is rather tight-lipped about this—in New York City toward the end of 1942.

Within a year he was on drugs. By my own estimate, this means that except for periods of involuntary withdrawal (centipedes and scorpions) he was an addict for better than fifteen years. He began on morphine and ended on heroin. Because of arrests and difficulties with sources, it was necessary for him to move around a good deal. He and his wife and son left New York for New Orleans and lived there over a year. Readers of *On the Road* will remember the visit to Bill Lee's household outside town near the levee—Burroughs, of course. The quest for good Mexican H and his continuing interest in the Mayan and Aztec cultures brought him to Mexico City. Kerouac visited him there. It was then that Jack met the Mexican girl he later write about in *Tristessa,* and it was on that visit, too, he wrote *Doctor Sax* and the endless choruses of his *Mexico City Blues.*

But Burroughs' stay in Mexico City ended rather abruptly when he shot and killed his wife, Joan. It came as the climax of a two-day party. Burroughs was known as a fair shot with a pistol, and in the right mood he used to give demonstrations. His wife urged him to show the party what he could do. After being teased, cajoled, and dared into it, he took his pistol, aimed at the glass his wife placed on top of her head, and missed—shooting her through the head. Although nobody suggested that Burroughs was guilty of murder, a Mexican police

official hinted rather broadly that a bribe—a large one—would be in order. Burroughs paid up, and the official confounded him by writing out a receipt for the amount and instructing him very seriously that if anyone else should try to shake him down, all Burroughs had to do was show this receipt and the matter would be dropped. Burroughs was subsequently brought to trial in Mexico City on a manslaughter charge from which he was acquitted.

Leaving Mexico City, he headed back for New York City where he lived with Allen Ginsberg briefly, working on *Junkie*, which he had begun as a series of letters to Ginsberg. Burroughs needed money. He worked quickly, and when he was finished, Ginsberg talked his old friend Carl Solomon into accepting the book for the paperback publisher that Solomon was working for as editor. Burroughs took the money and ran —to Tangier, where all is forgiven and most things allowed. It was there, off hard drugs and under the influence of nothing stronger than cannabis, that he wrote *The Naked Lunch,* which Olympia Press published in 1959.

Since 1962 he has been living in London. He had originally come to England some years earlier to receive apomorphine treatment for opium-derivative addiction in a program administered by a Dr. Dent. It was quite successful. He has been cured of his addiction and has become an ardent propagandist for the Dent method. He told Daniel Odier in *The Job* that apomorphine represented for him "the turning point between life and death," and said he would never have been cured without it. *"Naked Lunch* would never have been written."

Today, he lives on the top floor of an apartment building located in the center of London, about midway between Piccadilly and St. James Park. He travels a good deal, and is growing restless to move following a recent rent raise. But he stays on because he is used to it and, although the apartment has a bare and hardly lived-in quality, he now considers it home.

William S. Burroughs travels light. That, anyhow, is the impression he gave on first meeting. And true enough, he is a man with few encumbrances and no ties to speak of. He has a son, William S. Burroughs, Jr., but the younger Burroughs is now writing in America and has just published his first book, a documentary novel entitled *Speed,* which seems to do about the same thing for the methedrine user that his father's book *Junkie* did for the narcotics addict (so, perhaps, the cycle begins anew).

The face that appeared at the door, angular and slightly drawn, was rather strikingly reminiscent of the doleful face of Buster Keaton. Burroughs invited me inside without much enthusiasm, but warmed slightly to the idea as I explained why and about what I wanted to talk. He nodded, indicated a place at the table, and offered a drink. "Vodka all right? What about a vodka and lime?"

I said that would be fine. He ducked into the kitchen and re-emerged with two water tumblers, each about three-quarters full of nearly clear liquid.

"Cheers," he said without changing his expression.

Briefly I summarized my conversation with Alexander Trocchi and told him that Trocchi had said Burroughs would probably be less sanguine about the future than he had been.

"Probably so," Burroughs said drily.

"What do you think will happen?" I asked him. "Do you really think the future belongs to the control people like your Dr. Benway? That seems to be what you're saying in *The Job.*"

"I don't know, but it doesn't look very good. When I was answering Odier's questions—and in conversations with Alex Trocchi, too—I was speaking about the general world situation —inflation, soil exhaustion, fallout, overpopulation, the works. Altogether, it's a pretty dim picture, don't you think? But there are some good signs. Certainly, there's never been more worldwide resistance to control, nor for that matter has there been better reason for resistance."

Are there any other good signs?

"Yes," he allowed. "Yes, I suppose there are. There's the mass media. The underground press seems to have turned it on somehow, won it over. I'm hopeful as I see that gap between the administration and the mass media widening rapidly. What it really is, I think, is that the media people see there is a very real danger that they may be silenced. And I'll say this. The administration does seem to be plugging for all-out censorship."

178    Burroughs continued in this line, outlining the dangers he

saw from the right, the constant threat—as he read it—of superauthority and totalitarian control tightening over all America. He tended to go on a bit about this, dissipating what might be a good case by seeing devils beneath every bed and conspiracies behind every official pronouncement. He is intensely, avidly political—and that, somehow, surprised me.

"That's another one of the good signs," he was saying. "It's certainly a much more political movement in the U.S. today than it was. There is less and less of the old thing of the Beats and the hippies. None of that was overtly political in the beginning, you see. But Chicago changed all that, the Democratic convention. I was there for *Esquire,* you know. And I was rather agreeably surprised to see the Resistance so well organized on the one hand, without, on the other, letting the old-line Communists dictate their direction at all. The fact is that they've shown that the hierarchical control in the style of the Communists is absolutely not necessary. After all, Communism is about as outmoded as eighteenth-century laissez-faire capitalism, don't you think? Any movement that has such preconceived dogmatic postulates is handicapped because it always has to try to make the situation fit the postulate."

Burroughs was warming to his subject. He quaffed off his own glass of vodka and asked if I'd like another. While he was back in the kitchen, I called in to him, asking how all this contrasted with the Beat movement, as he has seen it develop.

"Oh that. Yes. Well, there certainly was a definite continuity from the 1950s to the present as I saw the thing take shape, although my personal acquaintances with Ginsberg and Kerouac goes back much further, to 1944, I'd say, somewhere around there. Actually, I'm not sure you could say that the Beat episode was terrifically successful, strictly as a literary movement. I mean when you contrast it with others like the symbolist movement or the surrealists. The situation with the Beats was never so clear-cut. Individuals—Kerouac, certainly —had tremendous influence. The kind of migrating that he described in *On the Road* has become practically a worldwide movement. People began migrating from Paris to Katmandu to Marrakech, and it all started with Kerouac. But no, not a literary movement. A social movement perhaps. You can see

I disagree because of individualism

that in the definite continuity there has been from then to now, in spite of the disparate aims of the people involved."

He had mentioned Kerouac a number of times and seemed to want to talk about him. I asked him when he had last seen him.

"Let me see," he said, "that would be in 1968, after the convention, when I was back in New York writing the *Esquire* story. He dropped in with his Greek in-laws. That was the night of his disastrous interview with William F. Buckley on television."

"What about that?" I asked. "Was Kerouac really sincere in his enthusiasm for Buckley and his conservatism? Did he really mean it?"

"Well, frankly," said Burroughs, "I would hesitate to comment on Kerouac's political change. After all, there's no doubt that the Beats ultimately had terrific radical political influence. And in the case of Kerouac, it was almost that he was frightened by what he himself had started. But as for Buckley, he's a conservative buffoon, not to be taken seriously—even by himself. I did advise Jack not to make the appearance. I knew it couldn't be anything but bad. Did you happen to see it? Yes? Then you know how awful it was."

Burroughs was right. Kerouac was treated brutally by Buckley. He showed up drunk, and perhaps because of that, he was used as the butt of every sally and jibe. William F. Buckley seemed to care not a jot for Kerouac's obvious sympathy: he ridiculed him mercilessly.

"But my God, yes," continued Burroughs, almost as if the image had suddenly clarified. "I remember that night very well. *Esquire* had been so cheap about the whole deal. I had agreed to do 1,500 words for them, and I got wound up and gave them 3,000, and they refused to give me a penny more. So I decided to take it out on them in room service when Kerouac came up with all those Greeks. By the way, Jean Genet was in on the same deal and did the same thing, but he had a real flair for it, and after he had taken *Esquire* for a few bills, Harold Hayes, the editor, called him a thief. Imagine calling *Genet* a thief!

180 "Anyway, Kerouac brought all his relatives and friends

down with him for his appearance on the William F. Buckley show. I could see the way it was going to go, and I implored him not to go on. But he wouldn't be talked out of it. Buckley was his idol. Pathetic."

I asked Burroughs how he would account for Kerouac's sympathy for the right. I asked if he really felt Kerouac were backing off from what he himself had helped create, or . . .

"Oh, partly," he said. "Partly. But in a way, you know, he didn't really *change* exactly, because to some extent he always had this in him. His father was a real old French peasant anti-Semite, Catholic Rightist, and Jack got a lot of his basic attitudes from him. And his mother! Talk about your old peasant types! She didn't want Allen or I to even come near him. She said we were being followed by the F.B.I." He paused, remembering. "But she was a great cook. I'll give her that. I guess that's why Jack stayed with her so long."

"It's remarkable, isn't it, a writer coming from a background like that?"

"Yes," Burroughs agreed rather somberly. "It is remarkable. I can't account for it." He paused a moment in reflection. "How about another drink?"

It turned out that he had arranged to have dinner that night with Panna Grady, whom he described as "a great literary hostess from the old Beat days." He asked if I would like to come along. It seemed like a good idea, and in just a little while we were at a nearby hotel, sitting down with Miss Grady in the bar. More drinks and Burroughs had opened up to the point that he seemed positively convivial. I don't mean to imply by this that the alcohol affected him. It didn't. He drank a good deal that night and showed no sign of it whatever. Yet sitting down with Miss Grady seemed to help a great deal. It put him at ease. She is charming and pretty, with a quick, nervous intelligence that complements Burroughs' own laconic manner—a fine companion, certainly, but what helped most, it seemed, was that she was an old friend. And Burroughs seems to put great store by his friends.

He began telling stories, expanding almost visibly. And as he did, the midwestern accent that is always there in his voice, lurking just below the surface, became more and more pronounced. By the time we had moved on to the restaurant, his a's had flattened and he had begun to drawl just slightly. He was telling us about that time in Chicago when, during his drug days, he had managed to earn as much as sixty dollars a week as an exterminator. He worked the South Side, he said, the Negro sections, because they were the most lucrative. "I've been in the old Mecca and most of the Negro whorehouses in that part of town. Places—this was during the war, remember —that you wouldn't believe even if you saw. We went after everything—rats, mice, roaches, waterbugs. And we managed to do it all in about two hours a day. How did we go about it? Well, I'll tell you, Panna, what you had to do was determine what the rats ate. Once you knew that you could start to work on them. Except that you could never tell who or what would eat the arsenic-sprinkled food we intended for the rats."

Talk about Chicago soon led him into a discussion of racketeers and bank robbers of the 1920s and 1930s. He knew his way around the subject, all right, who died of natural causes and who didn't, who bumped off whom. That sort of thing. He even came up with one name that I had never heard before —the Egans of East St. Louis, his territory, of course.

This led, quite naturally, it seemed to me, to a question about the film he has written, *The Last Words of Dutch Schultz.* I had seen a published copy of the script written by Burroughs, and I wondered if and when it would be produced. "Oh, eventually," he said. "Eventually." How did he come to write it? "That's an interesting point," Burroughs allowed. "The producer of the film was absolutely determined that I was going to do his script for him, and I was just as determined I wasn't. But he was smart. Instead of talking money, he began feeding me material on Schultz and Coll and that whole New York gangster scene back then. I'd tell him I had no intention of writing a movie, and he would send me some more. I kept saying no until he sent me the bit on Schultz shooting the guy in the mouth—the guy was a big-mouth and he was talking back to him—right in front of his lawyer. Well, when I saw that and the kind of scene it would make, I was sold."

Reading *The Last Words of Dutch Schultz* can provide an insight into all Burroughs' work. One thing that has bothered

182

even the most sympathetic readers of his books is their structure—or lack of it. Norman Mailer, for example, remarked in his testimony at the Boston trial of *Naked Lunch:* "But what is fascinating to me is that there is a structure to the book, you see, which is doubtless imperfect. I think one reason we can't call it a great book like *Remembrance of Things Past* or *Ulysses* is the imperfection of this structure." Considered from a conventional literary point of view, this is really most generous. For to look at *Naked Lunch* in the same way we would either of those great works Mailer mentioned, we would have to concede that it has no structure at all. The sections of the book jump back and forth and repeat in no apparent order. And what is true of *Naked Lunch* is even more true of the books that follow. In them—take *Nova Express* as an example—we see image merging with image within separate sections, and we sometimes perceive the voice of the author changing even in mid sentence. What are we to make of it? The answer, I think, comes with a reading of *The Last Words of Dutch Schultz,* Burroughs' movie script. For as nearly plotless as it is, it still makes sense, for mixing his images with the same speed and variety that he does in his later novels, Burroughs manages to achieve a flow, a structure that gives continuity and form to the whole. The point is that fundamentally the technique is the same. The structure of Burroughs' novels is essentially cinematic. As film, *Naked Lunch* makes very good sense indeed—and it is perhaps *only* as film that the more extreme *Nova Express* and *The Soft Machine* might be made to work. William S. Burroughs is essentially a writer of head movies.

That allowed—or at least put to one side for the moment—Burroughs' opinions on recent films might be of some interest here. They were to me, for even at the time I talked with him there in London I had begun to perceive some special movie sense in his work. I didn't question him about particular films. They simply came up, as they might in any conversation. I remember he remarked after we had talked a little about *Dutch Schultz* that last year (1969) had been "a great year for movies."

"Take *Easy Rider.* Now that was pretty good. Those great wide vistas that are really America. Kerouac would have loved that movie. I wonder if he got to see it. Or maybe he wouldn't have liked what it said the way he was talking those last years you could never be sure. Odd about that.

"*Medium Cool?* Not bad, a step in the right direction, certainly, with the *cinema verite* stuff, but not an exceptional movie, though, like *The Wild Bunch.*"

He asked if I had seen *The Damned.* "Now that was something. There was a movie by a real master. If any American director had tried to do that movie with the biggest budget and the greatest actors, he would have gotten it wrong. You know why? Because Visconti is a European, a real European with roots that go way back. He knows how the European family works—and that is really what that movie is all about."

Thus the conversation dithered off—as it will on even a good evening—into small talk. Was it worth quoting some of it here? I think so. Not because Burroughs is so great a writer that even his small talk is of great interest, nor yet because it adds much to see him here, as it were, in his shirtsleeves. But rather to prove—as it evidently must be proven to some—that he actually does indulge in the sort of half-serious conversational grabass with which all the rest of us fill our days.

There is a tendency among Burroughs' readers to regard him as a kind of holy monster. His books so obviously go beyond art into an area of purest, rawest experience that it is easy to forget the writer, the maker, the man behind them. There is a writer at work there, all right, and not some mad, glassy-eyed Rasputin who spends his time belching, and cursing, and torturing children for pleasure.

And as for Burroughs, the man—that Buster Keaton with the Ned Sparks voice—he may not be quite as rare a type as the writer, but he is infinitely more likable. I had begun by wondering how Jack Kerouac and Allen Ginsberg could have coexisted with the author of a book as brutal as *The Soft Machine.* Not having found the answer to that, I also began to wonder how William S. Burroughs had managed to live with him so long.

# PART III

# "They Sure Weren't Laughing on the Way Back to the Fairmont Hotel"

On a Saturday afternoon in August 1960, a thirty-nine-year-old member of the Harvard University psychology faculty sat with a group of friends and fellow researchers on the lawn of a rented villa in Cuernavaca, Mexico. In all, there were six men and women there, ranged in a circle around two large bowls of ugly black mushrooms. These were the so-called magic mushrooms that grow on the mountains around Mexico City. When eaten, they produce altered states of consciousness in the individual, a heightening and release of the senses, and ultimately visions as well. The Indians of the area have eaten them since long before the coming of the Spaniards; in defiance of the prohibitions of the Catholic Church they maintain a cult for the consumption of the sacred mushrooms.

None of those present that afternoon in Cuernavaca had ever before sampled the mushroom. The Harvard psychologist had taken no mind-changing drug stronger than alcohol, and so he quite naturally felt some trepidation when his turn came: "I picked one up. It stank of forest damp and crumbling logs and New England basement. Are you sure they are not poisonous?" Receiving some assurance, he put one into his mouth, then another and another, fighting back the nausea that swept over him in response to the foul, bitter taste of the mushrooms. But he washed them down with beer, and managed to swallow seven of them in all, without vomiting.

What happened then was four hours and seven minutes of an experience so unique and powerful that it not only changed the life of that psychologist, whose name of course was Timothy Leary, but it may ultimately also alter the shape and substance of life here in America. For from that "classic visionary voyage," Dr. Leary's first, followed the psychedelic revolution that swept America in the 1960s. Nothing has done quite so much to spread the fissure between generations as the passion of the younger one for drugs that alter or intensify consciousness. And no one has done quite so much to accelerate and propagate this passion as Timothy Leary. Whether or not the psychedelic revolution would have happened just as it did without him is open to doubt. The drugs were there certainly, and others—such as Aldous Huxley, Gerald Heard, and Alan Watts—were working to get them better known. But Dr. Leary had so many qualities that made him just the right man for the moment. He was, among other things, a respected research psychologist and a man unafraid to break the rules and buck the establishment; he was an apostate Catholic who through most of his life nursed an unsatisfied desire to play the role of messiah; he was, in his own way, quite modest, yet willing to do almost anything to publicize his cause and win converts to it; he was utterly sincere and at the same time a bit of a charlatan.

In the beginning, not even Dr. Timothy Leary knew all this about himself. At the time he sat down in Cuernavaca to eat those mushrooms in fact, there were a good many things he did not know. He knew nothing of Aldous Huxley's experiment with the drug mescaline (synthetic peyote) described so vividly in *The Doors of Perception*. He had not heard about the synthesis of the spectacular mind-expander, lysergic acid dithylemide, by the Swiss research chemist Dr. Albert Hoffman. And when he went so far as to describe his visionary experience to another psychologist, he was told that it all sounded very much like marijuana. But Dr. Leary didn't know, for though he had often heard of the stuff being smoked by Beats in San Francisco and Greenwich Village, he had never actually tried it himself. He then reflected: "This was some development! Was that all I had experienced? Were the mystic visions and the oriental dreams just a stronger version of a Greenwich Village pot high? I had been sure we were on the verge of something new and great. A pushing back of the frontiers of consciousness. But now it looked as though I was just a naive, sheltered intellectual discovering what hip teen-agers on the North Beach had been experiencing for years."

But no North Beach teen-ager could have proselytized for marijuana as he did for the mushroom. As soon as he got back to Harvard, he and his coworker there, Richard Alpert (who was also present that afternoon in Cuernavaca), got to work on projects to legitimate the taking of the drug. They wanted to find out what it could do. They wanted to discover what its uses might be as a tool in clinical psychology. Thus the Center for Research in Personality was founded, and from it came a number of interesting projects, the most successful of which was a group counseling program at the Massachusetts State Prison in Concord in which inmates were given psilocybin on a regular basis to break down psychological patterns that confirmed them in recidivism.

The Center gave Dr. Leary a base of operations from which he planned the strategy for his campaign to turn America on to visionary drugs. He thought of it, truly enough, as a religious crusade, and no zealot ever went after converts with a more intense missionary zeal. Faculty members, graduate students, anyone in fact who seemed mature enough to handle such a powerful drug was given the chance to do so by Timothy Leary.

He was especially avid to attract writers and intellectuals who had—or might be persuaded to have—some interest in this area. Arthur Koestler, for instance, was known even then for his investigations into the physiology of thought and consciousness, and he had just published a book called *The Lotus and the Robot,* in which he had dismissed the mysticism of the East as having virtually no worth to modern man. Leary wanted to see him on both counts—to discuss his investigations and to send him on a psilocybin trip that might change his mind regarding the Orient. And so he wrote Koestler a letter so full of boyish enthusiasm that it must have made even the dour Hungarian smile. Leary concluded, urging him to give the mushrooms a try: "We are offering the experience to distinguished creative people. Artists, poets, writers, scholars.

We've learned a tremendous amount by listening to them. . . ." Eventually Koestler did show up, had a disastrous paranoiac experience, and left even more hostile to drugs and visions than he had come. "This pressure-cooker mysticism seemed the ultimate profanation," he later commented.

But Koestler was only one of many who came by. Among those "distinguished creative people" mentioned by Leary were Charles Olson, William S. Burroughs, and of course, Allen Ginsberg. Ginsberg rates an "of course" here because Timothy Leary himself has given an enormous amount of credit to the poet for the part he played in furthering the work. He is so generous in his praise ("Allen taught us courage—taught us not to be afraid in facing those unknown realms of consciousness which are opened by psychedelic drugs") that Allen Ginsberg is thought by some to have played a much more active role in the psychedelic revolution than, in fact, he did. But from the beginning, apparently, Ginsberg and Leary have felt quite close. And the reasons for this seem to stem directly from that first psychedelic summit which took place at Leary's home in Cambridge.

Allen Ginsberg, of course, was no newcomer to the drug scene. As early as his Columbia years in New York, he had become well acquainted with the narcotics milieu through Burroughs and Herbert Huncke. In San Francisco he had smoked marijuana and taken drugs of the amphetamine variety. And he had heard—again, from Burroughs—of the effects of various mind-opening drugs encountered on expedition through parts of South America.*

At the time Dr. Leary invited him up to Harvard for his session in December 1960, Allen Ginsberg had recently followed Burroughs's trail to the Peruvian jungles and had had some experience with the psychedelic drugs, mescalin and LSD-25—all documented and dutifully recorded in poems from the period. As with all the early Leary sessions, however, this one was to involve the taking of the synthetic mushroom drug, psilocybin. In fact, Timothy Leary did not himself take LSD, the drug with which he became so closely identified,

*Correspondence from Burroughs to Ginsberg on this trip was published as *The Yage Letters.*

until just about a year later. He welcomed Ginsberg as a visiting guru and interrogated him closely on matters of primitive belief and ritual practice among Indians that involved the taking of drugs. The poet regaled him with bits of narcotic lore learned from Burroughs, and he told him what he himself had seen, heard, and experienced in New York, Berkeley, and Morocco.

As for the session itself, there is a long and complete account of it in Leary's book, *High Priest*. It reads like a chapter in the great comic psychedelic novel that he may, after all, someday come to write—we see Ginsberg capering naked through the halls of Leary's home, then running to the telephone to call Jack Kerouac and tell him all about this great experience he is having. The action ends in the kitchen. Ginsberg, now back to earth, puts his mind to what he can do to promote the psychedelic experience to the media. He goes through the address book he always carries with him and considers his list of friends and contacts, promising to turn them all on. Leary was delighted. He concluded that shouting it from the housetops the way this "Zen master politician" urged him to might, after all, be the best course: "Allen Ginsberg came to Harvard and shook us loose from our academic fears and strengthened our courage and faith in the process."

Regarding the visit of William S. Burroughs, Timothy Leary was somewhat more equivocal. Burroughs seems to have scared him just a little—or, in any case, left him feeling a little less certain of his mission. Ginsberg had urged him to invite Burroughs for a session: "He knows more about drugs than anyone alive. What a report he'll write for you!" Leary sent him some psilocybin pills; he heard in a short time that Burroughs had had a bad trip on DMT, a related drug, and wasn't much interested in the pills from Harvard. He and Leary met on a couple of occasions in Morocco and London, sparred tentatively without decision, and finally got together at Harvard in the summer of 1961. Burroughs had then only recently kicked heroin with the help of apomorphine, and with one bad psychedelic trip on DMT behind him, he was understandably less than sanguine about this grand new experience that Leary was urging upon him. Although he got him to *smoke* a little of the magic mushroom that had been dried and sent up from Oaxaca, and Burroughs conceded along the way that he was feeling a little high, Leary never really broke down his resistance. He left the Harvard researchers high and dry. And the impression was clear that they had failed to measure up to some high standard that, though never articulated, was carefully maintained. They had to accept that. William S. Burroughs is a man to whom it is very difficult indeed to feel superior.

It may seem to some that in emphasizing the link between Leary and the Beats I am doing a disservice to them. For he did, it is true, go to rather giddy extremes in promoting drug-taking as a cult, coming on, as he did, as a kind of pill priest whose half-baked religious ideas and vocabulary were borrowed from the Roman Catholicism into which he had been born. He became so enthusiastic about psychedelics—LSD, in particular—that he began recommending them almost indiscriminately, refusing to concede even the possibility of ill effects. And if he was railroaded on that marijuana charge (thirty years for a stash discovered on his daughter's person), nevertheless, he seemed by then almost to have sought imprisonment as martyrdom.

There are a couple of things, however, that should be said in Timothy Leary's behalf. First, and most obvious, he is sincere. He believes quite honestly in the general efficacy of the psychedelic drugs; he is certain that their real importance to man is as a means to direct religious experience; and he is also probably convinced personally that reports of recurring psychosis and genetic damage from LSD have been greatly exaggerated.

There is also this: While Leary has always laid doubtful claim to the future as being on his side (after all, only time will tell), he and all the little Robespierres of the drug revolution can make more certain claim to the past. Drug-taking of one kind or another has been with us so long in so many different cultures and forms as to make it seem universal. The practice springs, in the view of Aldous Huxley, from something deep in

man's very nature:

The urge to transcend self-conscious selfhood is, as I have said, a principal appetite of the soul. When, for whatever reason, men and women fail to transcend themselves by means of worship, good works and spiritual exercises, they are apt to resort to religion's chemical surrogates—alcohol and "goof pills" in the modern West, alcohol and opium in the East, hashish in the Mohammedan world, alcohol and marijuana in Central America, alcohol and coca in the Andes, alcohol and the barbiturates in the more up-to-date regions of South America.

It is also possible for us to trace through history a record of man's efforts to transcend himself by artificial means of one kind or another. He has been at it since time immemorial. Alcohol, of course: the earliest written texts of all languages and every culture carry some record of the drinking of fermented spirits and at least give some suggestion of the transcendental joys of intoxication. But far stronger modifiers of consciousness have been known to man and used quite commonly for just about as long. Opium, the most powerful and most addictive of them all (heroin, of course, is an opium derivative), is also the one with the longest history. It is first mentioned in an Egyptian medical text that has survived from the sixteenth century B.C.

In eighteenth- and nineteenth-century England it was available as laudanum, which was opium in a raw state dissolved in alcohol. Many had it prescribed by physicians to provide relief from some illness or disorder, stayed on it as long as pain persisted, then found they could not do without it. Robert Clive, the eighteenth-century empire builder who won India for the king, became addicted in this way and eventually died of an overdose at the age of forty-nine. William Wilberforce, the English clergyman who was greatly responsible for the repeal of slavery in the British Empire, took laudanum to help him through a digestive illness, and then continued using it daily to the end of his long life. But illustrious addicts aside, it is not generally appreciated today just how widely available the stuff was in the eighteenth and nineteenth centuries. In 1830, 22,000 pounds of solid opium were imported into England, and by 1860, the count was close to 100,000 pounds.* Cut with alcohol and sold as laudanum, it was actually more cheaply-priced than gin. Not only that, but an opium tincture called Godfrey's Cordial was also used by mothers all through the nineteenth century for keeping noisy babies quiet. Very quiet.

And should Americans begin to feel in the least complacent regarding the nasty habits of those in the Old World, then they should know that opium addiction was at least as common in the United States during the nineteenth century as it was in the British Isles or on the continent. Even before the American Revolution, Hector St. John de Crèvecoeur, in his *Letters from an American Farmer*, described the singular practice of the ladies of Nantucket: "They have adopted these many years the Asiatic custom of taking a dose of opium every morning; and so deeply rooted is it, that they would be at a loss to live without this indulgence; they would rather be deprived of any necessary than forego their favorite luxury." American physicians, however, considered it not a luxury but a necessity, and they prescribed it in a wide variety of cases, including ordinary toothache.

It was an American, too, who was probably indirectly responsible for the appearance of a new figure upon the literary scene: the poet drug-taker. Edgar Allen Poe may or may not have been an addict, for he claimed to take laudanum and wrote about opium often in his stories. But there is no other evidence to support this—and Poe, an awful mythomaniac, may well have lied about this as he did so many other things. He did, however, manage to convince Charles Baudelaire, who began experimenting with drugs in what he supposed was imitation of Poe and wrote excitingly of opium and hashish in *Paradis Artificels.* Thus the archetype of the poet drug-taker, which has survived to the present day in the persons of Allen Ginsberg, Alexander Trocchi, and William S. Burroughs, has come down from Poe through Baudelaire, Verlaine, Rimbaud, and other French poets. The rationale here follows the line that it is the proper role of the poet to test himself with every sort of new sensation; drugs provide experience far beyond the

*These interesting facts and figures have been plundered from an excellent text on the subject, *Opium and the Romantic Imagination,* by Alethea Hayter.

194

range of the ordinary; ergo, drugs must be taken.

Far less colorful and far less ready to justify themselves were the number of English writers who became laudanum addicts. The roll is an interesting one. Although because of its ready availability and its medical respectability laudanum was used at some time or other by just about every literary man (and woman) in the nineteenth century, true addiction has been documented for only a comparative few: George Crabbe, Samuel Taylor Coleridge, Thomas DeQuincey, Wilkie Collins, and Francis Thompson are the most prominent among them.

The striking thing about this list is that it is rather undistinguished. Nobody—surely not even Timothy Leary—would seriously maintain that George Crabbe and Francis Thompson were great poets, or Wilkie Collins a great novelist. With the exception of Coleridge, these are all writers of moderate talent who may have derived some initial benefit from opium as a modifier of consciousness (as a source of imagery for poetry, in particular), but were ultimately defeated by it. All achieved less than they would have without it. Dependence on the drug occasioned DeQuincey's finest piece of prose, *Confessions of an English Opium Eater,* but it also prevented him from developing as he might have as an essayist and critic, and in his later years it reduced him to a routine of plagiarizing contemporary German authors. Coleridge is allowable as an exception here only in that his was a first-rate talent; the course of his career was the same, however. There was the early flowering of his poetic gift, which was cut off in bloom and soon bled out from him like the poppy resin that enslaved him.

The point is that in spite of Dr. Leary's enthusiastic endorsement, and notwithstanding the now old and nearly honorable tradition of the poet drug-taker, it is nevertheless verifiably true that nothing anybody ever drank, smoked, or punched into his arm with a needle ever made him write better. Those who have had much experience with drugs—including alcohol—have eventually come around to this opinion. Nevertheless, people have taken drugs in the past and will no doubt continue to do so in the future in the firm expectation that the experience will make them write well, play music better, or perhaps more fully comprehend the secrets of the

195

universe. Aldous Huxley sees those who resort to "religion's chemical surrogates" as having failed to transcend themselves by worship. Timothy Leary has turned Huxley inside out and tried to dignify drug-taking as its own religion, one that is three-quarters mystical experience and one-quarter do-it-yourself ethic. Nevertheless, in spite of Dr. Leary's missionary zeal, his is not the sort of religion to attract great numbers of true adepts. Whether by meditation or by chemical means, most people are incapable of mystical experience and are not much interested in it either. As DeQuincey very wisely and matter-of-factly put it in his *Confessions,* "If a man 'whose talk is of oxen' should become an opium-eater, the probability is that (if he is not too dull to dream at all) he will dream about oxen. . . ." Drugs, in other words, can work no fundamental change in the drug-taker; he takes with him on his trip all his incapacities as well as his capacities, his faults along with his virtues, and all of his predispositions, too.

And with respect to DeQuincey, most men *are* too dull to dream at all. So why then do they take drugs? For all the very old and very usual reasons—to get release from the tensions of life (*any* sort of life has tensions); to find a place in an open and not very critical society; or perhaps in desperation, to seek the very extinction of personality; or finally, simply because they have started and can't stop. The great majority of drug-takers —those who filled Gin Lane in London, the opium dens of Shanghai, and the acid pads in the East Village—have had such motives as these. A very few seem to have gained something more than dreams of oxen from the drug experience. Perhaps for them it does serve as a sort of substitute religion. Yet no religion ever demanded so much of its believers and gave so little in return.

If hippies are, as Alan Harrington suggested to me, "no more than Beats plus drugs," it may be worth studying the quantities of that equation to see just how they happened to fall into place. It all began, legend has it, with Ken Kesey. He had a far more substantial and direct influence on events than did Timothy Leary. It was Kesey, they say, who made it all happen.

While attending Stanford in 1960, Kesey had a job as an aid in the psychiatric ward of the Veterans Administration Hospital in nearby Menlo Park, California. Partly to pick up a little extra money and partly, too, because he was curious, he volunteered as a subject for tests that doctors there were running on psychedelic drugs to test their value for use in psychotherapy. In one test after another they fed Kesey the whole menu—LSD, peyote, mescaline, psilocybin—and whatever they learned from him during these experiments was nothing to what he himself learned.

"Before I took drugs," he later told writer Burton H. Wolfe, "I didn't know why the guys I saw in the psycho ward at the VA Hospital were there. I didn't understand them. After I took LSD, suddenly I saw it. I saw it all. I listened to them and watched them, and I saw that what they were saying and doing was not so crazy after all. And so I was able to write about that in my first novel." Which was, for the record, *One Flew Over the Cuckoo's Nest.*

Ken Kesey was then enrolled in the Stanford University creative writing program as a graduate student. He had come down from Oregon, where the year before he had come out as a champion wrestler in the AAU's Northwest Division and had barely missed qualifying for the Olympics. That was Kesey then, sort of an All-American boy in the old Kerouac mold. He had, in fact, out-Kerouacked Jack both as an athlete and a scholar, for he had managed not only to graduate from the University of Oregon, but had done so with distinction and had gone on to Stanford as a Woodrow Wilson scholar. And there he intended to prepare himself to write great American novels.

And he did produce a couple that, if lacking greatness, were at least grand, before turning his back on writing and becoming guru to a group of wacked-out psychedelic gypsies who called themselves the Merry Pranksters. They gathered around him in a kind of free-form community on his six-acre place near La Honda in San Mateo County. He had bought it from the proceeds of his first novel, and at that time was still writing, hard at work on his second novel, *Sometimes a Great Notion.* Kesey's adventures with the Merry Pranksters were the subject of Tom Wolfe's wildest essay in the New Journalism to date, *The Electric Kool-Aid Acid Test.* They partied a lot, dropped a lot of acid (which, of course, was still legal then), but got going when Ken Kesey bought the bus.

The Merry Prankster bus, gaudily painted in wild psychedelic colors, took them back and forth to San Francisco and up and down the coast, as they spread their doctrine of fun, love, and acid. Kesey even took them in a long, epic haul in the magic bus to New York City in 1965, where they visited the World's Fair and renewed old acquaintances along the way.

The bus driver on that trip was one who knew the route well. Neal Cassady was his name, and he will be remembered as Jack Kerouac's friend and fellow traveler, the original for Dean Moriarty in *On the Road.* Yes, when the Beat thing exploded, and reporters were rushing around interviewing everyone who had been even peripherally associated with Kerouac, Ginsberg, & Co., Cassady was unavailable for comment, for he was serving time on a California prison farm for possession of marijuana. Not long after he got out, he met Kesey, hit it off well with him, and settled in with the bunch at La Honda. He was number two Prankster, not so much the man they counted on to get things done (Cassady, after all, was never as dependable as all that), but the one who inspired them all with that demonic energy that so awed Kerouac. And he came up with the kind of ideas and insights that kept them loose during some of the tougher days that lay ahead.

The presence of Neal Cassady in the Merry Pranksters offered to those who might otherwise have looked with skepticism on the group some evidence of continuity. He was a link with the genuine Beat past. Cassady had a terrific underground reputation by this time. He was thought of as the only true Beat, for after all, he was the only one who made no money from it all. The others wrote about it—so the argument went—but Neal Cassady had lived it. To some, the fact that Cassady was one of the Pranksters certified Kesey's bunch as authentic.

Kesey, Cassady, and their friends made frequent forays into San Francisco and became well known around the city.
198  How could they keep from being noticed when they came and

went in that wildly painted bus? By that time, of course, the locus of the action had begun to shift from the North Beach area that had offered the Beats their first home in the city. They had begun drifting away as soon as the tourists started coming to gawk at the Beatniks (as *San Francisco Chronicle* columnist Herb Caen had dubbed the North Beach residents). The process of commercialization and exploitation of the Beat phenomenon followed the same course there that it did all around the country—though at an accelerated rate and on a much grander scale. Coffee shops and bars opened up on every block suitably decorated and with house Beatniks hired to chant crude verse and insult the squares. The squares loved it for a while, and when their interest began to wane, Carol Doda and the topless craze took over and brought them back in droves.

But by this time, most of the real Beats were long gone, some of them to surrounding communities—Berkeley, Sausalito, and Mill Valley—but many to an area across town called Haight-Ashbury after the intersection at its center. In the early 1960s, it was a working-class district, not particularly hip, and that appealed to the Beats' proletarian instincts. In the beginning, they hit it off fairly well with the old-timers there, blended into the background, and took on a kind of protective coloration. They felt enough at home to be indignant when the city announced plans to build a new freeway that would cut the neighborhood off from nearby Golden Gate Park. In response, some of the new residents joined with the old to form the Haight-Ashbury Neighborhood Council and began the long fight to keep the freeway out. It was one that was not finally won until 1966, and by that time, Haight-Ashbury had altered drastically. The newcomers then outnumbered the old-timers and were, on the whole, much younger than those who had first moved in. They were colorfully and outlandishly dressed in hand-me-downs, they frequented crazy stores (like the Thelin brothers' Psychedelic Shop) that had opened just to serve them, they lounged around in bunches, and seemed to bestir themselves only when the police came by to hassle them. And now the tourist buses that once brought in Mr. and

199 Mrs. Middle America for a closer look at the Beatniks were

stopping by Haight-Ashbury to give them a peek at the Hippies. The term was evidently coined by a *San Francisco Examiner* writer Michael Fallon and first used by him in a piece published on September 5, 1965. For a while it was used interchangeably with Beatnik, until gradually it supplanted the older word completely.

This was the neighborhood that Ken Kesey and the Pranksters blew sky-high earlier that same year when they rented a broken-down old ballroom called the Fillmore and threw it open to the Haight-Ashbury community for what Kesey called an acid test. There were a thousand people on hand. Their ears were blasted with the thunderous rock music sounds of the Grateful Dead; their eyes were blinded by the spectacular strobe colors of the Fillmore's first light show; and their minds were exploded by the LSD-spiked punch that Kesey made available to one and all. What Kesey did was to turn the whole district on to LSD.

Although none of the psychedelic drugs were then illegal, they were not generally available. Through the efforts of Kesey (bigger and better acid tests culminating in the great Trips Festival in early 1967) and a few others such as Augustus Owsley Stanley III, the acid producer, LSD was made so easily and generally available in the Haight that what they soon had going there was a complete acid culture. Groups that played the Fillmore, the Avalon Ballroom, and the Matrix played a brand of music they called acid rock—not just loud, but with lots of crash, jangle, and quiver, too. The few small galleries in the area featured paintings of a peculiar sameness: all seemed to feature swirls of livid colors in direct imitation of common LSD hallucination patterns. The talk up and down the street was in the argot of "trips," "downers," "highs," and "freakouts." And although it was all graphic enough to be easily understood, this special vocabulary gave the young men and women who used it a sense of belonging, a sense of being a part of something secret, a conspiracy, a whole new culture that was being created by them on the sly.

And it was a culture that was creating its own rituals for celebration. In the Haight and outside it there was a keen sense of ritual and role that seemed to distinguish the hippies from the Beats of a decade before. Yet even here they seemed to look to their elders for the formulation of the very ceremonies in which they took part. As a prime example, the preparations for the great Human Be-In held in Golden Gate Park in January 1967, were handled, for the most part, by Allen Ginsberg and Gary Snyder (who had then only recently returned from Japan), with an assist from Dr. Timothy Leary. "We went to considerable lengths to follow the way a Hindu *Mela,* or gathering of holy men and seekers, is conducted," Ginsberg later explained. "We began by chanting a special mantra, or incantation for removing disasters. There was a purificatory circumambulation of the polo field, to drive away demons and bad influences."

All in all, that was quite a day. If the "bad influences" Allen Ginsberg spoke of meant the police—and to most of the hippies present in the park it did—then that purificatory circumambulation must have worked, for most of the cops did stay away, and the few who were present carefully looked the other way while literally thousands of young people smoked pot. At the end of it all, those who were present turned and faced the setting sun, listening to a closing mantra, as Allen Ginsberg blew a blast on a conch horn, ending the day's festivities.

Of course it was exciting—and not only to those who were there on the scene. For by now, the media were covering the hippie scene in the Haight-Ashbury district with the same breathless, eager thoroughness that they had the Beats a few years before. But this time, oddly, the tone of their comments was far more approving than before. *Newsweek* described the hippies as "mystical" and "ethereal," and "mostly young and generally thoughtful Americans who are unable to reconcile themselves to the stated values and implicit contradictions of contemporary Western society, and have become internal emigres."

America's young people read the magazines and they watched the television reports that were coming out of San Francisco. The teen-age grapevine was suddenly humming with what was happening "out there." And even the music they listened to on the transistor portables they carried with them everywhere began to change perceptibly in form and content under the influence of the San Francisco drug culture. The bubble-gum sounds that were for years the staple of the Top 40 stations began, little by little, to give way to the harsh, jagged tones of acid rock. The new music propagandized quite blatantly for the drug scene. When, for instance, Grace Slick of the Jefferson Airplane sang

> One pill makes you larger
> And one pill makes you small.
> And the ones that mother gives you
> Don't do anything at all.

then the kids rolled their eyes knowingly at one another because they knew what *that* meant!

They knew where it was happening, too. The word went out to them on those same Top 40 stations in the spring of 1967, summoning the multitudes to San Francisco for that "summer of love." And the city—the other, workaday San Francisco—quivered in dread of the 100,000 who were expected to descend on them. The City Council passed a resolution urging them to keep away. But they came anyway, most of them very young—runaways, drop-outs, or kids who had just taken to the road for the fun of going, as Jack Kerouac and Neal Cassady had a decade and a half before. But in spite of the dream of love and understanding that their songs promised, what most of them found there in Haight-Ashbury was pure nightmare. The district was filled to bursting by midsummer. A few doors were thrown open to the young visitors. The Reverend Larry Beggs' Huckleberry's for Runaways, a shelter for minors, began "temporary" operations in June 1967, but kept right on going as the kids kept pouring in. A few families took in some of the kids but were discouraged from this by the San Francisco police. For the most part the kids melted into the district's population, sleeping in crash pads or out in Golden Gate Park, copping a free meal now and then from the Diggers (the hippies' own do-it-yourself social workers), panhandling from the tourists when their money gave out.

By summer's end, 1967, things were going a bit grim. It

wasn't just the crowding and the logistical difficulties involved in feeding and housing all those young "seekers"—though these were certainly serious enough—but in addition, the indirect results were even more damaging to the district and its way of life. Since the end of 1966, LSD had been illegal in the State of California, but enforcement of the ban in the Haight had been fairly lax until the great migration of 1967. With so much national attention focused on them, the San Francisco police then cracked down with a vengeance. They shut off the old, reliable sources for acid and marijuana, staple drugs in the district, and the kids began to turn on with whatever was available—banana peels, bad acid, chloral hydrate, methedrine, even belladonna, and eventually heroin. This—at least according to the going local accounts—was what finally brought in the Mafia. Prices were upped. A heavy sociopathic element moved in. Prostitution, which the hippies had righteously mocked as an adult, middle-class enterprise, began to flourish up and down Haight Street. The crime rate—strong-arming, mugging, burglaries, and holdups especially—began to rise alarmingly. The district was no longer safe for the tourists who came to snicker or be shocked. Even less was it safe for those original Haight residents, square and hip, who hung on there bravely waiting for things to get better. They haven't yet.

But what happened to Ken Kesey, the novelist-cum-guru who had helped turn on those ur-hippies to LSD? He was arrested in 1966 for possession of marijuana. After delaying the case on a continuation or two, Kesey, who was out on bail, fled as a fugitive to Mexico. Neal Cassady was with him then, and eventually all the Merry Pranksters came down across the border to visit him. He returned with them to San Francisco, and still a fugitive, made fools of the police by popping up in very public places, then disappearing before he could be captured. In one instance he even sat down for an interview on a local radio station and managed to step out just five minutes before the police showed up to cover all the exits and make the arrest.

Eventually, however, Kesey tired of the game and turned himself in. As it turned out, the state didn't have much of a case, and so settled for a nolo contendere on a lesser charge. And so Kesey was sentenced to six months for "knowingly being in a place where marijuana was kept." He served his time in a minimum security prison camp only minutes from his old place at La Honda.

He was there, working in the tailor shop and nearing the end of his sentence, when Burton H. Wolfe came and talked with him about the direction the hippie movement had taken since Kesey had more or less dropped out of it. The interview, in its own way a rather moving document, serves as a sort of epilogue to Wolfe's good journalistic account of the happenings in the Haight, *The Hippies*.

The point pressed by Wolfe was a remark or two that Kesey had dropped before he left to serve his sentence. It was being passed around the community by word of mouth and was, by this time, available in a number of versions. It seemed Kesey had put the hippies down. But what had he really said, Wolfe wanted to know.

"What I told the hippies was that LSD can be a door that one uses to open his mind to new realms of experience, but many hippies are using it just to keep going through the door over and over again without trying to learn anything from it. They don't understand, and I got hate letters. But those in the hip community who really understand, people like the Thelin brothers, know what I meant; and they will continue on. So long as people like the Thelins are there, I have confidence in the whole movement."

But though he wished them well, Kesey was prepared only to watch from afar. He went up to Oregon, bought a farm, and settled down there with his wife and kids. Some of the Pranksters came up and settled on his place commune-style, but that didn't work so well, and one by one they took off in separate directions.

That might be all there was to tell except that a little earlier —February 4, 1968, to be more precise—Neal Cassady was found dead down in Mexico. Cassady, the original hipster, had run out of go at last. He had been feeling bad because he thought he was getting old, they said, and one night by the side 204 of a railroad track, his heart just gave out.

If the hippies are just second-generation Beats—and a continuity can certainly be seen in attitudes and the personalities involved—it is nowhere more clearly so than in the city of San Francisco. The reason for this is that so many who have been involved under one banner or another in the cultural life of the city have remained right there—or left for a time eventually to return: Kenneth Rexroth, father of the Beats and grandfather of the hippies, is there still today; Robert Duncan is settled there; and Lawrence Ferlinghetti, poet, publisher, and bookshop proprietor, has apparently not been tempted to leave after arriving in 1951. And so on.

It was precisely that "and so on" that I wished to explore at first-hand when I came to San Francisco and talked with writers there, some of whom I have already quoted at length. In addition to those whose names were inevitably and necessarily associated with the Beat movement, I wanted to see some others, too, perhaps not so well known, who had come to live and work there during the latter stages of the so-called San Francisco Renaissance and had come to be known as writers of the 1960s. Because of this they were thought of by some as "hippie writers." But distinctions break down as the movements merge —and what constitutes a generation, anyway? Fathers and sons? Twenty-five years? Or merely a distinct group of a certain age who share certain basic attitudes and characteristics? (By that last standard the hippies and the Beats are the same.)

At the top of this list of younger writers was Richard Brautigan. Born in 1935, he came down to San Francisco from his native Oregon in 1958, the big year of the Beat movement, and he has stayed there since except for brief interruptions for fishing trips, readings, and a stand or two as poet-in-residence. His poems are charming, often witty, sometimes successful— but rather slight. He gets his best effects from those brief, spontaneous bits of word play in which a single idea is twisted into the shape of a poem, almost in the manner of a haiku. For example, the title piece of his first collection, "The Pill versus the Springhill Mine Disaster":

When you take your pill
It's like a mine disaster.
I think of all the people
lost inside of you.

And even more simply put, this little opus titled "Critical Can Opener":

There is something wrong
with this poem. Can you
find it?

Anyone who can put the New Critics in their collective place in just three lines surely deserves to be called a poet.

Nevertheless, I'll call him a novelist because it is for his novels, *A Confederate General from Big Sur* and *Trout Fishing in America,* that he is best known. There are no books quite like them and no writer around quite like him—no contemporary, at any rate. The one who is closest is Mark Twain. The two have in common an approach to humor that is founded on the old frontier tradition of the tall story. In Brautigan's work, however, events are given an extra twist so that they come out in respectable literary shape, looking like surrealism. *A Confederate General from Big Sur* is a kind of Huck Finn–Tom Sawyer adventure played out in those beautiful boondocks of coastal California where Jack Kerouac flipped out in the summer of 1960. But it is with *Trout Fishing in America* that Brautigan manages to remind us of Mark Twain and at the same time seem most himself. As you may have heard, this one is not really about trout fishing, but it is really about America. In the book—call it a novel if you will—whopper is piled on dream vision with such relentless repetition that the ultimate effect is a little like science fiction. The narrator's visit to the Cleveland Wrecking Yard, for instance, is at once quite funny and a sadly serious comment on the awful junkyard America is fast becoming. This one, like every other episode in the book, is delivered in Brautigan's distinctively oblique, understated, and offhand manner.

And make no mistake: the style is the man. For Richard Brautigan—quiet and somewhat withdrawn—is a little like the

man on the old television commercial who taps thin air and

says, "Just as I was protected by this invisible shield . . ."

I tracked him down in his apartment in an old stucco building above North Beach. Could he talk to me? I asked. He obviously wasn't much excited by the prospect but said to check back later on. In the meantime, a third party put in a good word for me, and Brautigan agreed to meet me the next morning at a coffee shop nearby.

At the appointed hour he showed up with a pretty girl whom he introduced by her first name only, sat down and drank coffee, and submitted to a few questions. But only a few.

After discovering where he was from and when he had come to San Francisco, I remember asking why. What had he heard about the city that attracted him? And Brautigan explained patiently that he had come to San Francisco just to come to San Francisco. He had no ambitions to be a Beat writer or anything. No ambitions at all, he said. Just got to know some of the people around town after a while, that was all. "But my involvement with that was only on the very edge and only after the Beat thing had died down."

And whom had he known? "Oh," he shrugged, "most of them. Ferlinghetti, Duncan, Phil Whalen—used to live with him in a place south of Market Street—and Michael McClure. McClure's a good friend. You ought to talk to him about this stuff. Not me."

We talked around the edges of his books then—when he had written what and how little he had made from that. It seems that between 1965 and 1968 he made less than $7,000 from his writing. Nothing much happened, in fact, until the little Four Seasons Foundations in San Francisco published *Trout Fishing in America*. That not only sold pretty well around the country, it got a New York publisher interested in his work. Eventually, all of Brautigan's Four Seasons books— and by then there were three—were issued by that publisher who now keeps him pretty well sustained on advances and royalties.

Then there were the readings. They helped, too. Even though Brautigan himself never attended college, he is much in demand on campuses all over the country. He even put in
a stretch of a few weeks during the year before as poet-in-

residence. Where? "Cal Tech," he says with a rather pained look. "I can't explain it. Maybe they brought me there thinking of me as some kind of exotic influence or something."

He also gave an account of just how he works that was strangely reminiscent of Jack Kerouac's old Spontaneous Prose technique: "I get it down as fast as possible," he said, "and on an electric typewriter, 100 words per minute. I can't spend time on character delineation and situation. I just let it come out. And when it doesn't want to come, I don't sit around and stare at the typewriter or anything. I just go down and see about two or three movies—the worse they are the better. And for some reason that loosens me up and gets things going again. That's what I do when I'm stuck."

He went over that a time or two more to explain it, just so I would be sure to understand that this wasn't some big literary point he was making. "It's what I do when I'm stuck," he repeated, suddenly spooked, uneasy, perhaps afraid that he had said too much already. And then he left in such a hurry that he almost forgot the girl.

He did, however, remember to repeat, "See McClure. He's really the guy you should talk to."

But not that night. It had been arranged earlier that I would visit Lenore Kandel at her place on Ashbury, just off Haight. Although a comparative latecomer to the San Francisco scene, she has a big and well-deserved reputation around town as a tough lady and a fine poet. She is both. Born in New York, raised in Los Angeles, she had seen a bit of the world before she came to San Francisco for a weekend sometime in the middle 1960s, liked what she saw, and moved into the Haight-Ashbury district to stay. She is an ex-model, -folksinger, -bellydancer, -cocktail waitress, -schoolbus driver. But, she insists, always a writer, too: "I've written since I could scribble, and before that I made up songs. And so for all that other stuff —where I've worked and what I've done—I've really just been following my impulse, wherever it has taken me."

Lenore Kandel became a kind of local celebrity in 1966, when her first collection of poems, *The Love Book*, was seized by San Francisco police, and the city was treated to its first big
obscenity trial since the case against Allen Ginsberg's *Howl*

*and Other Poems* just ten years earlier. ("Sure," she says, "I've gotten a lot from him. We all have. I think Allen Ginsberg has remarkable guts. That's what it took for him to stand up and let his asshole hang out in public. He gave a lot of people the courage to admit they had one, too.") She survived the trial and published a second book of poems, *Word Alchemy*, one that is about as erotic in theme and diction as the first, yet is in just about every other way possible a better collection of poetry. While in *The Love Book* she was inclined to be a little solemn and fierce about it all, there is a feeling of wit and play that sustains most of *Word Alchemy* and is most clearly in evidence in the long poem, "Circus," that begins the book. There is a wry sense of all that is false in her own new-found reputation as a "hippie love goddess" in the brash pitchman's promise of

> love lyrics of the homesick tiger
> the secret mating dance of
> everybody

which she tosses off as a preface to the poems that follow.

Kenneth Rexroth had urged me to see her. "Maybe if you're lucky," he had said, "you'll see her lodger, Frank, there, too." Arrangements had been made for me to come by to see her fairly late in the evening. Friends I was staying with prevailed on me to take a taxi into the Haight. At first I argued: after all, I said, I've been down there before. "Yes," I was told, "but that was last year. Things are a lot different in the district now. You'll see."

They were right. I did see. And on the way there, I heard about it, too—from an especially garrulous cabdriver who had, he said, seen Haight-Ashbury change from not-so-bad to unbelievable. Fundamentally, he was sympathetic: "I'll tell you," he said, "it breaks your heart to see them. It really does. They wander around and can't even take care of themselves. The cops pulled a little girl out from under the bushes in Golden Gate Park just this morning. Dead from an overdose—and she's just seventeen years old. Now, I ask you!" He paused to make his point and then continued. "The murders and the strongarm stuff, that's every day now down here, and it's all because of the drugs. There's a lot of the hard stuff now down on the scene."

He went on to tell of how he had picked up Senator and Mrs. Edward Kennedy and another couple one night not too long ago at the Fairmont Hotel. "They told me to take them down to where the hippies are. Oh, they was laughing and giggling like anything about how they were going to catch the hippies doing their thing. Well, we got down there, and I drove them around, and they got a good look, all right. No, they didn't want to get out. They saw plenty, and let me tell you they wasn't laughing when I drove them back. It sobers you up to see all those kids messing up their lives, wandering around half-dead. They sure weren't laughing on the way back to the Fairmont Hotel."

Haight, where he let me off, was a dark street that was apparently quite heavily patrolled by police (a pair on each side of the street at either end of the block), and there seemed to be nobody else around just then. Lenore Kandel answered my knock on her door and turned out to be just as beautiful as she had been billed—though reserved and obviously skeptical. She led the way back to her kitchen, asked whether my preference was coffee or tea, and set about brewing a pot before she sat down to talk. When at last she did, she gave my questions and her own answers almost too much consideration.

I began, I remember, by asking her if she had decided to stay in San Francisco because there were a lot of other poets around then, too.

"You mean the 'community of artists' and all that?" she cut me off.

I nodded.

"Frankly, no. I think the idea of a community of artists is appalling. You don't have communities of plumbers or housepainters, so why should you have communities of poets? I don't believe in these in-grown groups who just talk to each other and think the same. Different kinds of people should get together, so they'll realize that there are other kinds of people on other kinds of trips. It's not that I don't know poets. It's just that a lot of my friends *aren't* poets, too."

"But why San Francisco then? Could it just as well have been some other place for you?"

"Well, I like it here," she admitted almost reluctantly. "It's part of the physical structure of the place. The wind blows clean here, and it's a kind of birthing place. It always seems to be a few steps ahead of the rest of the country."

I asked her if she associated all this with the Beat movement and the San Francisco Renaissance.

"No," she said, "I've never been concerned with who were Beats and who weren't. I've never had a big thing with labels —a rose by any other name and so forth."

She got up then, poured a cup of tea for me, and looked at me sharply. "I resent this," she said suddenly. "Everything you've asked me so far says you think I came here guru-hunting. And I didn't. I'll admit I liked the work of some of the poets they were calling Beat back then, but even when I liked the work it didn't mean I especially wanted to meet the person. I wouldn't try to tie things too closely together if I were you—influences and all that. We all work out of the same culture. We all work out of the same world. That's where the influences are."

We talked on desultorily along these lines. She was quite emphatic that she was her own woman and that she was a poet without a master—and from what I had heard and read this certainly seemed to be true enough. At last she declared—and she does have a way of making declarations—that I was making a mistake if I were limiting all this in my own mind strictly to San Francisco. "There's a lot happening all over the whole country right now. All the lies and hypocrisies that have been a part of it for so long are now being shattered. This goes back a long way, and what you've got here and now is like what they talk about in the Bible—when they compare the house founded on sand with the one founded on rock. So right now I'd say we've got a lot of sand underneath us in this country, and the sand is starting to shift."

Just then I heard a key in the front door. The lock turned and a moment later, I heard the sound of the door slamming. Down the hall and into the kitchen came Lenore Kandel's boarder, Frank—who turned out to be none other than Freewheelin' Frank, secretary of the San Francisco chapter of the Hell's Angels Motorcycle Club. The introductions were awkward. He fixed me with a skeptical look as he heard who I was and what this conversation in the kitchen was all about. When I had it all out then and arranged neatly before him, he looked it over rather severely and said to Lenore Kandel, "A book, huh? He better talk to McClure." And that was the end of the interview.

That was two votes cast in a single day for Michael McClure. Of course, it hadn't been my intention to neglect him; it was just that I had no telephone number for him, and I had received no answer to the note I had sent him before coming to San Francisco. At first I wasn't even sure he was in town, but what Richard Brautigan and Freewheelin' Frank had said made it fairly certain he was. Perhaps the best thing to do was simply to present myself at his door and hope for the best.

Perhaps more than any other writer, Michael McClure's career neatly spans the first and second generation of the Beat movement in San Francisco. Born in 1932, he was the youngest writer to be represented in the 1957 San Francisco Renaissance number of the *Evergreen Review*—and at twenty-five, the youngest of the Beat poets when the roll was called by Kenneth Rexroth in the introductory essay he contributed to that issue. McClure remained in San Francisco, writing the strange and original poetry for which he has become so well known. But perhaps even more influential than his poems has been his continued presence in the city. He's looked on as nothing like a guru—he's far too plain and direct for that. Nevertheless, just having him around to talk to has been important to many who were developing as writers—or just beginning to make it as human beings—in North Beach and Haight-Ashbury during the 1960s.

Take his relationship with Frank Reynolds—Freewheelin' Frank of the Hell's Angels. Not only did Michael McClure serve as amanuensis when Frank decided it was time to write his autobiography, but as the two got to know each other better during the long sessions that brought forth the book,

McClure began to interest Frank in his own style and values. As a result, Frank Reynolds began not long ago to write poetry himself. His first efforts are there for the world to see in a little sheaf of verse printed and illustrated by himself and distributed locally. Some of it is not so bad, most of it positively awful, and all of it is . . . well, interesting.

But the smugness of that "interesting" simply would be unknown to Michael McClure. For if he is no guru, then even less is he the sort of alert literary sociologist who makes careful, controlled contacts with the *Lumpen* for the quick little thrills they may give and whatever creative stimulus they may provide. No, that's not McClure. He is, after all, half a Hell's Angel himself—dragging up and down 101 on a big Triumph motorcycle—and as for the half that *isn't* a Hell's Angel, it cheerfully declines to make judgments except on personal terms. And should you wonder, it is neither one half nor the other who does the writing but the *whole* man of meat and spirit—the *mammal,* as he would have it.

Michael McClure's life as an artist has been one long, arduous struggle to unleash the animal inside him and get him to write. It hasn't been easy. That wild, slapdash, and terribly personal novel of his, *The Mad Cub,* reveals the cost to him in pain and loss of self. But release the animal is what he most certainly has done, and if the results have sometimes been rather intimidating, they have always been spectacular. *The Ghost Tantras,* strange amalgamations of beast language and pure revelation, are about the most pungent examples of McClure *in extremis,* the animal meat and the spirit meat trapped into collaboration. In this one, for example, we see it served up almost sandwich-style—the vision caught between great raw, juicy slices of roars and growls:

PLEASURE FEARS ME, FOOT ROSE, FOOT BREATH,
BY BLAHHR MOKGROOOOOOO TARR
nowp tytah broooooooooooooooooooo

In the middle of the night I dreamed I was a creature
   like the great Tibetan Yodi Milarepa
     I sang a song beginning:
     "Home lies in front of you not in the past.

    Follow your nose
        to it."
It had great mystic import, both apparent and hidden.
    I was pleased with it.
        GOOOOOOOOOOOOOOOOOR!
        GROOOOOOOOOOOOOOOOOOOOOH!
        GOOOOOOOOOO.
        ROOOOOOOOOOOOOOOOOH!
    POWFF! RAHH! BLAHHR!

Those who blunder unbriefed into this may well fear that some awful error has been made by the printer. But no, McClure means it. The howls of the *Ghost Tantras,* all passion and rage, are delivered *de profundis.*

It is probably unfortunate for Michael McClure's reputation as a poet that he has gained such notoriety for this sort of thing. His best-known work, *The Beard,* although written for the stage, expressed the same spirit of rage and agony as his beast language poems in terms that are nearly as crudely and willfully inarticulate. It is in the nature of a fantastic encounter between Jean Harlow and Billy the Kid in some private room in hell. The essence of the play is nothing more or less than the desperate rage of its protagonists.

All of which makes Michael McClure's work seem more limited in theme and tone than it really is. There are many more moods than one expressed in his writing. McClure himself is partly to blame for the impression of his work that is now so widely held, for he is, as Isaiah Berlin said of Tolstoy, a fox masquerading as a hedgehog. ("The fox knows many things, but the hedgehog knows one big thing.") His heady pronouncements in his *Meat Science Essays* notwithstanding, he is certainly not a philosopher, but a poet. For an indication of the variety and depth to be found in McClure's poetry, just look at "On Beginning Romeo and Juliet," as beautiful and gentle a poem as any to come from the Beats, or at any one of the others collected in his *Little Odes.* All are done with gentleness and a genuine sense of poetic propriety.

This gentle quality, so seldom noticed in his work, is clearly enough in evidence to anyone who meets him. McClure has had his season of rage, spent himself, and now seems to have come to terms with all in life that one must finally come to terms with.

I simply presented myself at Michael McClure's door—except that at the moment of my arrival he was outside the house tugging away with a friend, trying to struggle a new mattress up the stairs. I hung back a moment to make certain it was he, and then I introduced myself.

"Oh yeah. I got your letter," he said. "Grab an end."

I did, and after a few difficult moments found myself inside his third-floor apartment, helping haul that flopping mattress over to the corner to which Jo Anna McClure directed us. She rewarded me with an invitation to supper and set an extra plate. And as I explained the sort of things I wanted to talk to him about, she called in their daughter, Cathy, and dished up a meal for us all. We talked. And in the course of it all there was some reference—by Jo Anna?—to McClure as "the Irishman." I picked up on that immediately.

"Of course," said McClure with good humor. "I'm the last member of the Celtic Renaissance, a man like the rest of them with supreme feelings. And where else would such a man be born but Kansas?"

His joke. But he enlarged on that at my urging and said that, yes, the name of his home town was Marysville, and that was probably important. "Because no matter where it is you're born and grow up, you get something of the genius of the place in some way or other. Maybe it's orgone energy." Probably far more important, he allowed, than his being Irish and the last member of the Celtic Renaissance. Or whatever.

He pieced together a sort of informal autobiography for me as the evening wore on. He told how when he had met Jo Anna she was married but that he had refused to let that discourage him. "She ran away to Arizona to get away from me, but I followed her there—you can see I wasn't easily discouraged. And then she came to San Francisco, and that's how I happened to get here. I kept after her until she finally got a divorce and married me."

When he arrived in the city he enrolled at San Francisco State in Robert Duncan's poetry workshop. He had done some writing earlier but without much real success. "I bugged Duncan by writing villanelles and sonnets, but I was terrifically impressed with him because he was the first poet I had ever known, and he also turned out to be one of the finest men. So here I am doing Petrarchan sonnets almost to spite this man who is one of the masters of twentieth-century verse. Looking back, I find my attitude unfathomable. But out of it grew a sort of friendship made up of mutual bewilderment and admiration. I'll be honest, though, it wasn't until much later that I was able to dig Duncan's poems for what they really are."

Now, perhaps a bit ironically, McClure is engaged in a similar enterprise, teaching a poetry workshop at San Francisco College of Arts and Crafts. He's doing it for a living, he says, for the same reason everyone else turns to teaching. "It's either that or write movie scripts, which they want me to do after *The Beard,* or try to write a best-selling novel."

And yet Michael McClure is a little uneasy about the value of his teaching—to himself, first of all: "This professor bag just doesn't fit me so well. In spite of the fact that they're pleased at the college and keep asking me back I'll admit I'm kind of uneasy about it." And even uneasy, too, about how he's getting through to his students: "Most of them are capable of basic decent prose, and they're sensitized to words from listening to the lyrics of Dylan, and Donovan, and the Doors. They are really enormously sensitized to poetry, but most of them are carrying around a terrific anti-intellectual bias. Some have a prejudice against poetry as poetry—as music it's okay. That way it's in the milieu of their attitudes, postures, and viewpoints. A kid can be great with a guitar singing and so forth, but still be a squirt as far as poetry and real beliefs are concerned. They're not going to save themselves. I've got to do what I can with them and hope it works. I'd like to build their morale and give them something to do."

I asked about his own writing, the direction his work was taking. "Well"—with a shrug—"my poems always take care of themselves. They come. I put them down. All I have to do is not publish most of them. The poems that always seem to turn out best are the ones I wrestle with hardest."

McClure has probably experimented more boldly with poetic forms than any other poet called Beat. Why? What has he derived from it all? Where has it led him?

"Let me see. The first poem I ever published was in *Poetry* magazine in 1956. It was a perfect villanelle. And even when I began writing what was considered Beat poetry, I was working at least part of the time in Blakean quatrains. I was attracted to this sort of trial and exploration in the beginning. But then I decided I'd better do the kind of long-line free verse people were trying then. But after trying that for a while, I got tired of repressing rhyme, and so when the rhyme wanted to come, I'd let it. For a while everybody was bit with the idea of Projective Verse. Very exciting. But I found that for myself Olson's methods dissolve in practice. So what have I settled on? An energy line based on seven principles that . . ." He smiled and shrugged, breaking off suddenly. "But all this is a priori, intellective, after-the-fact. What it really amounts to is that I want my prosody to take the shape of the energy behind it. For me it does."

Has he learned from other poets? "I learn from everybody. But in the way you mean, no. I don't think I've made myself a pupil of anybody. I can look at what Allen, and Corso, and Gary Snyder are doing and appreciate and understand it, because I appreciate and understand them. But no poet needs another poet's techniques. When I do turn off, though, is when I try to read academic poets who write these tremulous little odes about lawnmowers running over frogs—but neither the lawnmower or the frog they write about are real. Furthermore, they think that what they write is good, more genuine, because it's written in iambic pentameter. *Imagine!* Why, you ought to be able to teach any reasonably attentive twelve-year-old child to *speak* in iambic pentameter in about an hour. So what's so great about writing it?"

What about language? McClure has pioneered in the use of violent invective and erotic language that some consider obscene and nearly all call daring. Will he continue? Is there anything left unsaid that still needs saying?

"There's probably no reason to be pornographic anymore. Most people, I think, have had their gut full of it. They are now ready to go beyond this. I am myself. I just read a novel of E. M. Forster's—and he didn't need it. Sure, of course, I dug it.

Who wouldn't? So obviously you don't *need* pornography for art. But the reason for using such language in the first place, and the only argument justifying maybe even more of it, is this: It's not until so much pornography has been used that Nebraska is absolutely saturated with it that people out there will be able to ignore it as unimportant, and then we can get on to other things. I mean, after all, some people still pick up a book and think, 'Great! It's a sex novel. Wow!' But oh man, we're already beyond that.

"Look, in fifty years people are going to read 'fuck' and 'shit,' and it's not going to seem unusual at all. It will be just like 'Ah' or 'Oh' or 'I fall upon the thorns of life! I bleed!' And once we get them to that point out in Nebraska, *then* they're going to worry about what the poem is about."

I remarked that he had sounded a little worried when he had talked about his students a little while before. Was he pessimistic about them? About young people in general?

"No more than I am about everybody. Sure, I'm worried. Our whole civilization seems to be stuck in little stagnant pools. I mean, they stink. They really are stagnant. It's this whole interlocking socialist-capitalist bullshit. What we've got to do is have new pools where geniuses will come together and make clear to us just where we're going. Is this the answer? No, but it's *an* answer. Too many little chest-beating messiahs are around today with answers that are everything from eating health foods to manning the barricades. So I say no to all that. And I'm putting this forward tentatively—a proposal. People who believe in the future but feel trapped in the present should get together and start planning their way out. How do they do this?" McClure suddenly threw up his hands in a desperate gesture. "Yes, how? I'm just beginning to think about it. No answers."

Is it a crisis?

"Sure it is. I think this whole technology we've developed is worth saving, but only if it can be controlled. We've got to think it through so that the whole thing will benefit us instead of just dominating us. Gary [Snyder] really turned me on with his *Earth House Hold,* and this whole ecology thing he's into. Now I'm into it, too—all the way. There's where your crisis is.

218

It's got nothing to do with time or history or politics. It's biological! And it's biologically that it's got me so worried. I'm a mammal, not particularly a man, but a piece of meat that's related to bacteria, cedar trees, lions, and ears of corn. I'm not really related to the political-social thing, except in what I've inherited. I want to see these old pools broken up, so you get a new sense of community. There's so much old-pool thinking still around. All these people who say they've got the answers —they're full of shit. There's no one answer, no one solution. But if we talk in this new, open way—new communities, new combinations, maybe we can come up with some answers that will work. We'd better. Because if we fail . . . well, there might suddenly not be any mammals anywhere. And that would be a shame because they're some really nice forms. All gone—just like that."

We talked a long while that evening and might have talked longer still but the doorbell interrupted us. McClure went to answer it, turning on lights as he went, for it had gotten dark as we sat in conversation. The callers turned out to be a couple neighborhood poets who had come up on impulse just to talk to McClure. And so I got up to go.

He came down the stairs with me to the street and instructed me on the quickest route to Ashbury. There was a bar there. I was to go in and call a taxi. Cab drivers don't like to make pickups at houses after dark here in the Haight, he explained. We shook hands, and I started away. "One more thing," he called after me. "It might be a good idea to walk down the middle of the street. It's better lighted along there."

"It's not that bad a scene here, is it?"

"It's a pretty bad scene," he said.

# CHAPTER 12

# The Silence at Woodstock

In their own time the Beats made a tentative, awkward, and rather fruitless attempt at union with jazz. It was *their* music, they felt, and their passion for it reassured them they were a different breed from those purse-lipped academic poets who lived for their precious little evenings of Bach and Mozart. No, jazz was what was real. It was the sound of the nervous life humming around them. They felt that in the tension in the music, in its drive, and they heard it in the lyric statements of the soloist who would stand up and blow chorus after chorus, one man against the world, a model for very poet, every artist. This was what the Beats found in jazz, yet not this alone, for if jazz were then as respectable as it has since become, it would not have seemed half so attractive to them. It was the illegitimate atmosphere of the jazz milieu, with its overtones of criminality, sex, drugs, and violence, that brought them back night after night to spots like Birdland, the Five Spot, and the Half Note in New York, the Bee Hive in Chicago, and the Black Hawk in San Francisco.

"Furtive"—that was Kerouac's word for the Beats, and that was the word for the jazz of the 1950s: quick, elusive music, given alternately to uneasy skulking and pell-mell escape dashes. And it was just such qualities that all the Beat novelists tried to capture in their fiction. Every early Beat novel had an obligatory jazz scene (Paul Hobbes realizing the true meaning of "cool" as he listens to the music at the Go Hole and studies its effect on the audience; Sal Paradise and Dean Moriarty calling encouragement to the alto sax man who ends his solo blowing to "the children of the American bop night"). And in a few they even took musicians as protagonists. In such novels as George Lea's *Somewhere There's Music* and John Clellon

Holmes' second work, *The Horn,* the jazzman was presented as a sort of ultimate Beat hero.

Jack Kerouac was probably the one most obsessed by the jazz ethos. It was not just in the occasional scene that Kerouac would try to inject something of the jazz feeling; he attempted, rather, to infuse all his work with the urgency and continuous flow of the music. He took the inspiration for his technique of Spontaneous Prose, discussed earlier, directly from jazz improvisation. Allen Ginsberg referred to it from time to time as "spontaneous bop prosody," embellishing it thus slightly so that its origins would be appreciated. And Kerouac's single effort at formal verse, a book of 242 poems (or "choruses"), *Mexico City Blues,* is prefaced by a note in which he says, "I want to be considered a jazz poet blowing along blues in an afternoon jam session on Sunday. I take 242 choruses; my ideas very and sometimes roll from chorus to chorus or halfway through a chorus to halfway into the next." Which is, alas, a fair description of the helter-skelter jumble that pours across the pages. Some of the poems work, though most of them don't, and those that seem least necessary are those whose purpose is to convey the kind of corny-cute nonsense bop sounds popularized by Dizzy Gillespie in the late 1940s: "Mexico City Bop/I got the huck bop/I got the floogle mock . . ." etc.

It was also Kerouac who provided most of the push behind the abortive poetry-with-jazz movement. That may be remembered still by some from readings once attended in the Village or North Beach. Most of the Beat poets at one time or another found themselves up on a stage, declaiming their verses valiantly above a walking bass, until the horns would come in raggedly in the open spaces with a run or a crescendo chord that may or may not have been appropriate. It was all rather haphazard and uninteresting, but it could hardly have been otherwise, because for one thing, it was based on a fundamental misconception of the nature of jazz as music. The Beats, none of whom (I think) had had even rudimentary musical training,* held quite naively to the popular notion that in

*The exception is Allen Ginsberg, who sings well and has even composed melodies on the recorder for William Blake's *Songs of Innocence* and *Songs of Experience,* but Ginsberg, significantly, took no part in the poetry-with-jazz exercises.

jazz it is possible to achieve something like total freedom, that each member of a jazz group can blow what he feels like and yet by some special magic have it all come out right together. Some—and this certainly seemed to be the case with Kerouac —had the idea that if the poet added himself to the combo, he could swing with the horns just by reading out his words. But it takes more than sharing a stage with musicians of the right persuasion to metamorphose a poem into a jazz song.

The reason it didn't work this way, of course, is that jazz is far more complex and far less free than they supposed it to be. For if, in the fifteen years or so before the Beats became nationally known, jazz musicians had begun to experiment a bit in harmonies and tempos, their experiments certainly had not opened things up enough to make possible true improvisational settings of the sort the poets may have hoped for. Actually, the music had been going, and has continued to go, in the opposite direction, becoming increasingly sophisticated and less flexible—less public in its appeal. Jazz, at least the jazz of the late 1950s and early 1960s, was simply not the proper mode for them to achieve the song-poetry effect they were striving for.

Rock was. For with almost mathematical precision, that rough amalgam of country music and Negro blues that in the beginning was called rock-and-roll began to increase in popularity as jazz became more complicated, less emotional, and more limited in its appeal. Rock, in its earliest forms and even more so today, is no more than a kind of ur-jazz, representing a conscious return to simpler forms that lay closer to the roots of American music. Jazz had ceased to be sung, was no longer danced to, and could only be really appreciated by those with some musical education. And that was where rock came in. It was the most accessible of music, offering a heavy beat to dance to and easy melodies to sing; it was a music so simple that it not only could be appreciated for all it was worth by anyone, but it could be performed and even written by high school boys who knew only a few simple guitar chords. In the beginning, of course, it was pretty awful stuff. With the exception of a few performers who came up through country and western or rhythm and blues, the early rock-and-rollers were so limited musically and emotionally by their extreme youth that they had little to offer any audience but their sincerity, and that wasn't enough.

Gradually, however, rock began to improve. Musically, this was inevitable: as young musicians grew older and gained facility on their instruments, they were sure to grow bored with the same old thump-thump-thump-thump reiterated on the same old chords. And so they tried new things, listened carefully to other kinds of music, accepted and accommodated new influences from inside and outside the fraternity.

Among the latter influences were the poetry and prose of the Beats. It was, after all, when the fad for the Beat Generation was at its height that popular music was going through these throes of transformation that eventually brought forth rock in its present sound and shape. The Beats had led them a couple of steps in the right direction. There was, as noted, the poetry-with-jazz experiment. Unsuccessful though it may have been in practice, the *idea* was a good one. It suggested a return to the old conception of poetry as song, and it indicated possibilities for rock that the square world could not then even conceive. But music aside, it was also important that so much of the poetry called Beat was written for the human voice. It made use of old bardic devices of chant and simple rhythmic repetition to stir audiences. And anyone who ever attended a Beat reading will remember how well such devices worked. The tension generated on such occasions was of the kind one had only felt until then at old-fashioned *swinging* jam sessions and would only feel again when rock had developed to its present high level of musical sophistication. And audiences responded as if to music, too. There was nothing of the solemn-occasion-sponsored-by-the-English-Department when the Beats appeared for a reading. All those present participated: applauding, answering back, shouting encouragement. I remember on one occasion hearing an audience clap rhythm as Allen Ginsberg half-read, half-chanted the "Moloch" portion of "Howl." It seemed entirely appropriate. The audience was happy, and Ginsberg was obviously pleased with this response.

It was public poetry. What the Beats did was to demonstrate convincingly that poetry might be restored to its old place among the performing arts. They made it accessible. They showed that the poetry of direct utterance could be easily understood and yet still be exciting. Theirs was the kind of poetry that not only inspired but encouraged others to write. (It didn't really sound so difficult, after all, did it? Maybe you could just put down what you felt, what you believed!) As a result, of course, there was probably more bad poetry written in emulation of the Beats during the five years or so they held center stage than at any other comparable period in history. But—and bear this in mind—not all of it was bad. As I suggested earlier, most of the younger poets of the so-called New York School were strongly influenced by the Beats. Others, who may not fit quite so neatly into categories and whose work may eventually have taken a much different turn, were nevertheless first turned on to writing after hearing (usually rather than reading) Allen Ginsberg, Gregory Corso, Lawrence Ferlinghetti, or one of the other of our poet-performers.

Did the Beats influence rock? Yes. A direct link of sorts can be established through the Fugs, that notorious trio of scato-porno-rockers who have a large following in and outside of New York, even though their records cannot be played on the air. A sample Fug lyric, "Supergirl," will tell you why:

> I want a girl that can fuck like an angel
> Cook like the devil
> Swing like a dancer
> Work like a pony
> Dream like a poet
> Flow like a mountain stream
>> Supergirl
>> Supergirl
>> Supergirl
>> My supergirl, *etc.*

That one, as well as about half the Fugs' songs, was written by one Tuli Kupferberg, a bald-headed Beat poet and little-press operator now well into his forties. The result of the group's material is the work of Ed Sanders, a younger poet who was

224

inspired to leave Kansas and head for New York when a copy of *On the Road* fell into his hands. There, Sanders soon became known when he began putting out a little magazine with a very distinctive title: *Fuck You/A Magazine of the Arts*. It was mimeographed monthly from 1962 to 1966, and among its rather distinguished contributors were Allen Ginsberg, Peter Orlovsky, Norman Mailer, and William S. Burroughs. Sanders himself began to establish a reputation as a belated Beat poet and was well known also as the proprietor of the Peace Eye Bookstore, a popular meeting place in the East Village. In 1966, however, the police raided Peace Eye and confiscated all the copies of *Fuck You*—and that was the end of that magazine of the arts. Sanders shed no tears, however, for about that time he had been discussing with Kupferberg and Ken Weaver, a young drummer from Texas, the possibility of starting a rock group—*their* kind of rock group. It all came about, Tuli Kupferberg told writer Martin Cohen,* as the result of an evening out with Allen Ginsberg: "I had always kind of looked down on rock-and-roll music. So had Ed. This night we were out with Ginsberg and stopped in a joint that had a rock band. Allen got up and danced and then we did. It felt great, you know. You just danced and moved the way you felt." The two began writing songs, rehearsing them, and developing the distinctive repertoire of gross, satirical material that is so uniquely their own. In a peculiar way, the Fugs are a most literary kind of group: the words do count with them. Their melodies, such as they are, serve only to support their crudely witty poem-lyrics. Ed Sanders owns that this is so and explains: "We came to music through literature, through being well read and literate. A lot of poetry was written with regard to music and meter. Most of the ancient poetry was sung. We've put a lot of good poetry to rock—Ginsberg's, Matthew Arnold's, Ezra Pound's, Sappho's, and so forth."

It would not be too much to claim, then, that if the Beats had not given poetry a firm push in the direction they did, and if the Fugs first had not shown others the way, then what many are now calling the rock poetry movement might never have

*As quoted in his article, "The Fugs: Nextness Is Godlier than Cleanliness," *Avant Garde*/Number One.

happened. Beat, in this way, was a necessary precondition to rock in its present form. Many may leave me here. For though it is a point often argued in the press, the notion that rock lyrics may qualify as poetry is not really a very popular one.

Nobody, I think, who has given the matter much attention would dispute that popular song lyrics have come a long way since the days when Steve Allen could break up an audience simply by reciting in solemn tones the words to the latest rock-and-roll hit right down to the last sh-boom-sh-bop. Nevertheless, most argue with good reason that even the good, intelligent, sensitive lyrics that have been written in the past few years are far more captivating when sung than when read on the page. A collection of rock lyrics put together by Richard Goldstein, *The Poetry of Rock,* was intended to demonstrate that Bob Dylan, Paul Simon, John Lennon, et al., are true poets, more than worthy of the name. Mr. Goldstein sought to prove this simply by displaying their lyrics in the ragged-line format usual for poetry. Yet in all but a few cases this had quite the opposite effect from the one intended. Seeing the pitiful little bare bones of the things on the page in that way diminished rather than enhanced their value.

And that, after all, is not so surprising, for as songs they were written to much different requirements. A few of the so-called rock poets—Janis Ian and, of course, Jim Morrison come to mind—have actually written and published poetry. It is of an uneven quality but shows evidence of the genuine poetic talent that is indicated in some of the song lyrics they have written. And it also shows signs that their ideas of what poetry should be have been formed by close and frequent reading of the Beats. The Canadian poet Leonard Cohen is a special case. He was well established as a writer, with two novels and a number of books of poetry behind him, before ever he undertook to write songs. His influences, in the beginning, were English and university-acceptable American, but these he digested and absorbed long ago. An interesting change can be detected in his recent work: since he began writing songs (some of them such as "Suzanne" and "You Know Who I Am" very good indeed), his poems have become smaller somehow and more songlike.

I'm of two minds about the rock poetry phenomenon myself. As a member of this vast, captive pop-music audience we call America, I'm as glad as the next man that the intellectual quality of the lyrics heard day-in and day-out has now improved so markedly. And while I occasionally detect flashes of real wit and intelligence in them, as in Paul Simon's "Mrs. Robinson," just as often, I'm afraid, my shit detector begins jumping wildly as it did when I started listening closely to the words of that same Mr. Simon's "Bridge Over Troubled Waters," which sound *serious* but mean absolutely nothing. There is an awful sameness, a deadly predictability to the ideas and attitudes of so many rock lyrics (though not in all). Just as composer-critic Ned Rorem does, I object to their "commercial up-to-date before the fact intent"; theirs is the sagacity of the easy generalization, the sort of pseudo wisdom offered by the mass media. And finally, I object to the increasingly heavy literary emphasis in rock because as a result of it the music itself is beginning to suffer. What is and should be fundamentally simple blues-based music is beginning to show perceptible signs of strain because it is made to bear messages of revolution, mystic experience, and sexual liberation. Melodies often have been made so complex in order to accommodate ponderously meaningful lyrics that they are scarcely recognizable any longer as melodies.*

But no matter, really, whether rock lyrics please Ned Rorem, satisfy me, or convince someone else that they deserve to be called poetry, for there are a great many they do please and satisfy, and they comprise the vast under-twenty-five rock audience. To most of them rock provides all they need or want in the way of poetry. To them the lyrics of those songs—bawled, hollered, shouted, or moaned out through phonograph, loudspeakers, and public address systems—have the sort of absolute importance that no public, surely, has attached to poetry since Shakespeare's groundlings whistled and whooped for Marc Antony's funeral oration over the dead Caesar. This is why writing rock lyrics has become such earnest business to so many. And this is why they have begun to load

*Another bad sign: more and more are dancing less and less. The way most dig the music today is sitting on the floor in front of the bandstand.

them with such heavy intellectual freight. After all, if you knew that you had an enormous public out there that was really listening to the words you wrote and really took them seriously, wouldn't you be tempted to be didactic? Of course you would. And since those who are doing the writing are no older or wiser, really, than those who are listening, we can hardly blame them for succumbing to temptation, nor can we expect much in the way of quality from their instruction.

This is just one indication of the power that rock wields over its audience today. And if its songs are now being used to preach sermons to the faithful, then this suggests that the whole phenomenon has taken on some of the characteristics of a religion. That seems to you to be stretching it a bit? Then you have probably never been to one of the Fillmores on a Saturday night and been swept up in that crowd of true believers. You can't really call them fans, for what they feel for the music clearly goes well beyond mere enthusiasm.

For the most avid of them, the rock thing is one with the drug experience. And it all came together in San Francisco during the middle 1960s. The groups that were playing at that time in and out of the Fillmore, the Matrix, and the Avalon Ballroom, were made up, for the most part, of musicians who lived in Haight-Ashbury and North Beach and were very deeply involved in the drug scene themselves. The Grateful Dead, Big Brother and the Holding Company, Jefferson Airplane, and a few others set about rather programmatically to translate the psychedelic experience into sound. The result, so-called acid rock, was louder, wilder, and freer than anything anyone had heard until then; those who played it were more skilled at improvisation and made better music simply because they were, on the whole, better musicians. The musical conventions of acid rock—shrill feedback guitar, tremendous volume, heavy crescendoes, and electronic sound for sound's sake—are now so much standard that it can be said that rock is acid rock. Nearly everything else—with the exception of some healthy and persistent strains that issue directly from country and blues sources—is justly dismissed as bubble-gum music, and if played at all is simply manufactured to the easy require-

228

ments of the pre- and early-teen record market. And as noted, the tendency for Bay area groups to propagandize for drugs and the new "free" life (Berkeley's Country Joe and the Fish were preaching fire, brimstone, acid, and revolution as far back as the days of the Free Speech Movement) has continued and intensified in the past few years as acid rock, alternatively known as progressive rock, underground rock, and hard rock, became the music's dominant mode. From the time these groups began to record and tour, and from the time the San Francisco hippie scene began to receive national publicity, rock began to take on the characteristics of a religion, one that, except for the addition of the music, was virtually indistinguishable from the one Timothy Leary was hawking on college campuses all around the country.

What sort of religion is it? It is one that offers a mass in the form of the rock concert, with drugs as the sacrament and the music functioning as a kind of ersatz liturgy. It is a religion that promises salvation by revolution and whose ethic consists of but one commandment: do what you will. Messiahs, shamans, and prophets it has in abundance, most of them performers (priests of the liturgy). Being a singer or musician, even an extraordinarily good one, seems to matter less and less in this cult context. What does matter is embodying and spewing forth the proper virtues—rebelliousness, moral liberation, and contempt for authority. As a result, some of rock's finest performers have all but turned their backs on the music and become shills for the revolution. Even those who have nothing to do with music may qualify for canonization in the cult if they possess the magic virtues in abundant measure. Thus Charles Manson has been exalted as a kind of messiah in long cover stories in two rock publications, *Fusion* and *Rolling Stone.*

What the congregation draws from all this is not just the excitement generated by the moment and the music, nor the easy counterfeit of mystic experience offered by drugs, but more important, a sense of group identity. The real joy of it all is in getting together with others like themselves and being involved in something big. *Together*—it has lately become a watchword, a term of enthusiastic and unqualified approval. Is it together? Then it's great. Does he know what's happening?

Is he really in touch? Then he's a very together guy. It is an odd formulation, isn't it? The underlying notion seems to be that mere assembly—part on part and body to body—is in itself an absolute good. But together for what? Whole in what sense?

With all this—the rise of rock, its recently acquired religious cult characteristics, and the generation's new desperate delight in togetherness—the three days of mud, drugs, and music they call Woodstock was simply bound to happen. It came as a logical consequence of all the be-ins, love-ins, pop festivals, and tribal convocations that prededed it. Yet it was more than all these, for it gave to an entire generation not so much a sense of who they are, but (much more important) who they would like to be. The reality of Woodstock mattered a good deal less to everyone—even perhaps to those who were present—than it did as symbol. The first Eucharistic Congress of the new rock religion.

This deserves emphasis. For only a year after the event, at a time when the many attempts to duplicate it in the interim had resulted only in spectacular flops and dismal failures, people were perplexed at the reasons and journalists sought—as they always will—explanations. Why couldn't Woodstock be made to happen again? The answer, though only whispered by a few, was a truth plain enough, but like so many truths, this one was a little unpleasant to face up to. It was simply that Woodstock couldn't happen *again* because it had never happened the first time. It was a myth.

The reality of Woodstock had little to do with that glorious Aquarian Exposition that was described so breathlessly in magazines and newspapers at the time. And it had even less to do with the Michael Wadleigh film, *Woodstock,* from which all but about 400,000 of the under-twenty-five generation have drawn their own impressions. This discrepancy has to do with the very limitations of reporting. For the best that even an honest writer can hope to do is to communicate the general shape of any event. He takes what seems salient and neglects (sometimes ignores) the rest. In most circumstances this will do the job. Although when an event has taken on its own life after the fact, as has Woodstock, the writer may sometimes see the outline he himself helped sketch out colored and embellished beyond the point where he can recognize it. Then he begins to wish he had included a few more details of the kind that at the time didn't seem to fit into the larger pattern of the story. He begins to wish that he had had the time and opportunity to sit back and ruminate a bit on the meaning of it all instead of shooting his impressions from the hip. And he then feels a terrific desire to restore the balance—to introduce new evidence somehow, without invalidating his earlier testimony. This is why most of the revaluations of Woodstock have been somewhat more negative in tone than the original reports.

Even before the film appeared, there was a general uneasiness that the beauty of it all had been slightly oversold. But when *Woodstock* was released, and the whole generation was invited on that trip to the never-never land portrayed there, it was apparent that Mr. Wadleigh had simply to take the myth that had been propagated by the print people and to explode it many times over as only film can do. What seemed pretty at the time was made absolutely gorgeous by Mr. Wadleigh's color photography. What seemed exciting in the music heard dimly over that overworked sound system there in the cow pasture was positively overwhelming when piped in stereophonically from all sides of the theater. And you could actually *see* the musicians in the film, when at the event one took it on faith that they were really down there on that tiny stage making the sounds. There were no bad smells in the film. No bad trips. And the only mud we saw—well, it looked kind of fun sliding down that hill, didn't it?

All of which sounds as though I were about to take out after Mr. Wadleigh for not making his film *Woodstock* more true to life. Nothing of the kind, however. For after all, it is the business of the film maker to create myths; one can hardly object that the job was done too well on this one. But it is also the business of the journalist who is plagued by second thoughts to express them when given the opportunity. I take this opportunity.

What sort of second thoughts? First of all, a great deal has been made of the fact that Woodstock was free to those who attended. The impression seems to have gained currency that this marvelous weekend-long entertainment was offered to the 400,000 who attended as a kind of gift of love by the producers and by the performers who appeared there. The idea seems to be that their only hope of compensation for their generosity was the money they would make from the film and the soundtrack album. Thus going to the movie and buying the album became quite like acts of charity.

But what happened was this. Having been denied the site they had originally intended for the festival at Bob Dylan's farm in Woodstock, New York, the producers began casting about desperately for a new location, one that could accommodate a crowd of up to 100,000 and might be made secure against gate crashers. Advance ticket sales had not been at all strong enough to guarantee the festival; they needed the money from the gate. But they were evidently lucky to get both a new location and a deal on security through the same individual, Sam Yasgur, an assistant district attorney in New York City. His father, Max Yasgur, had a dairy farm in the Catskills; eighty acres of it that included a natural bowl and a nearby pond were offered to Woodstock Enterprises, Incorporated, at a good price. And as part of the package deal from Mr. Yasgur came the services of 300 off-duty New York City policemen who were to serve as paid security men, guarding the gate and policing the festival grounds. But that last part fell through. At the last minute, New York City Police Commissioner Howard Leary forbade men on his force to participate. And so the policemen stayed home.

On the first day of the festival there at Max Yasgur's farm, some effort was made to collect and sell tickets—this seemed only fair to those who had bought advance admissions—but when a faction of militants arrived and began making threatening noises outside the gates, the producers soon saw just how tight their position really was. The militants began trampling down the chain link fences that had been erected to keep out gate crashers. There were no security people present, except members of the Hog Farm commune whose job it was to move traffic along. And chief Hog Farmer Hugh Romney (ex-Beat poet, ex-Merry Prankster) was fundamentally in sympathy with those who wanted to liberate the festival, anyway. And so,

232

acting on the old principle that when rape is inevitable it is best to lie back and enjoy it, the Woodstock producers threw open the gates and made the three-day festival free to one and all (except, of course, those who were unlucky enough to have purchased advance tickets).

By the time I got to Woodstock on Friday evening of that August weekend, the fences were already down, stakes bent to the ground and the heavy chain wire quivering and snapping dangerously as the crowd streamed over it. It had been drizzling intermittently on the drive I made through the side roads of New Jersey and Pennsylvania, and although it hadn't rained yet in Bethel, a look at the sky told me that it soon would.

The rain started, a drizzle at first, then gaining in intensity during Ravi Shankar's performance, even as the Indian sitar virtuoso's intricate rhythms increased in tempo. Slacking off briefly, it began pelting down during Arlo Guthrie's set, and I, along with thousands of others, ran for cover. I had had quite enough for one night, but I wondered as I headed for a dry bed in a motel room just how long it would keep up. What would it look like tomorrow? If the driving rain were to continue through the night, I told myself, they would have whatever excuse they needed to cancel this "liberated" festival.

It did continue, but there was no talk of scrubbing the remaining two days of the event. And what it looked like the next morning, after nearly a night of rain, was a battlefield. I stood on the hill in that cow pasture at about the point where I had sat the night before and watched the armies stream by. Those who had braved the night in the festival preserve were now on their way out, hiking for the highway and the town of Bethel in hopes of getting food and fresh water, for this was just the start of Woodstock's second day, and already they were starting to run low. In the opposite direction came another long line that seemed about equally mixed between those who had suffered through the night in tents pitched along the highway and newcomers to the festival who had driven the night to get there. At that time there must have been about 250,000 at the festival. They kept coming in all day, however, until by nightfall Saturday the peak attendance was reached. Estimates of the size of that crowd differ, of course, but there must have been close to the 400,000 they were claiming that weekend. Or, as somebody put it about that time over the loudspeaker, "Welcome to the third largest city in the state of New York. And the only *free* city."

But it looked like a battlefield. Mud was everywhere. Viscous, brown, and dunglike, it seemed to cover everything in layers. The hill around me was littered with garbage. And in every depression and declivity in sight water hung in brown pools. The natural bowl of which Woodstock's producers had been so proud was now a natural sink. A heavy stink compounded of garbage, excrement, and country wet hung over the entire festival areas. And as the sun came out and the temperature went up through the morning, moisture began to rise from the rain-soaked ground, hanging in a kind of miasma-like vapor over the rolling Catskill landscape.

I had begun the march into the festival area about an hour before from five miles down the highway. Parking in front of the Yasgur office, I had located and talked to Sam Yasgur, who was in for the event, helping out as best he could. It would all have worked out fine, he said, if Commissioner Leary hadn't turned thumbs down on the off-duty cops. Max Yasgur was there, too, but unavailable for the moment. His eyes were red-rimmed. He needed a shave. He was shouting into the telephone that he had to have gas for the ambulances even if they had to copter it in, and at the same time he was shaking his head indicating no, he couldn't speak to me now and that I was to come back later and talk with him. Sam Yasgur said as I walked out that his father had been so involved with festival preparations that he hadn't slept for days.

And so I joined the long column of marchers who were moving past the farm office and down Highway 17 B. Cars were parked on both sides of the road, and in spite of the efforts of New York state troopers to keep open the middle lanes for traffic that continued to move through, the lines of young people clogged the road.

They seemed almost like refugees. Although they ranged from flaky hippies to clean-jim types, and included rain-soaked veterans of Friday night as well as recent arrivals, all of them seemed constrained and quiet as they continued on in the same somnambulistic manner. They were in couples and trios, for the most part, but they seemed to have little to say to one another.

"Please God, no more rain!" someone groaned from the roadside to nobody in particular.

And then nothing for minutes more as we moved along the highway—nothing except the strumming of a guitar and the sounds of waking up from the tents pitched in the fields nearby.

In back of me a young man asked, "Did you see that guy who ran wild through the crowd last night?"

And another answered, "Yeah, but he wasn't as bad as the one they carried out rigid. Like, man, he was stretched out like a board."

And then silence, long stretches of silence as the column moved on. There were young mothers who carried their babies in slings and in backpack devices. There was a young man on crutches who was hobbling along valiantly trying to keep up with the line of marchers. And turning off the highway on the road into the festival grounds, I even saw one blind boy being led along by a girl, in the line moving toward town. The lame, the halt, and the blind—all here. Yet something is peculiarly absent. I find myself troubled by this, unable at first to decide just what it is I miss.

It was not until I stood up on that hill, looking down at those two columns passing through what had been the gate down on the road, that it occurred to me that what it was that seemed out of order here. It was too quiet. That was what was wrong. Yes, and it was the silence out on the road that had bothered me during the long hike in. Many of those around me then had been new arrivals and were at least as fresh as I. They hadn't seemed physically tired, for they moved along at a good pace, but there was a kind of lassitude in their manner that made them appear to droop slightly. They seemed to lack both the energy and inclination to communicate with those around them. All were to a greater or lesser degree withdrawn.

And the odd silence persisted throughout the long weekend of Woodstock, giving a kind of subdued, restrained character to what must have looked to those who were reading about it in the papers and watching it on the television screens like a sort of frenzied, primitive orgy. It was nothing of the kind. There was applause, of course—ovations and clapping time for Sly and the Family Stone, the Who, and Jefferson Airplane (among others), but all this seemed to have more to do with crowd psychology, the releasing of tensions, and so forth, then it did with real musical appreciation. Some of the best music played during the festival was played by the Latin rock group out of San Francisco, Santana, late Saturday afternoon,—and it received only scattered applause.

What was absent, though, was the sense of open exchange between strangers, of young people coming together and truly enjoying themselves. And yet this was what Woodstock was supposed to be about, wasn't it?

> Come on people now,
> Smile on your brother.
> Everybody get together,
> Try and love one another right now.

But there were, strangely, not many brotherly smiles in evidence, nor was there much laughter or the sort of good-natured horsing around that seemed to characterize behavior when people of this age would assemble twenty, fifteen, or even ten years ago. To one of my age, a member of the so-called Silent Generation, there was a peculiar irony in finding oneself in this vast multitude of the young and surrounded by such silence. Where, I wondered, were the sounds of fun?

If they were not particularly demonstrative toward one another, then neither were they very hostile. For that, of course, they have deservedly been praised to the skies. However, a few objections have been raised. Residents of Bethel complained that the reason there was so little conflict was that they offered the young visitors no resistance, and that if the police had done their job, there would probably have been plenty of violence. Perhaps. But the state troopers and Sullivan

236

County and other police present seemed to keep the situation in Bethel and out on the highway pretty well under control. They made no effort to extend their jurisdiction to inside the festival grounds. This may well have been by previous arrangement with Woodstock's producers, for remember there were to have been 300 off-duty policemen keeping things under control there. In any case, the cops kept out. The nearest were those in the Duchess County mobile unit fifty yards or so from the gate.

What went on inside the gate was drugs. That, of course, was the aspect of Woodstock that drew the most attention from the press. It is true that marijuana was smoked openly and that at times the high, acrid smell of it seemed to hang over the hollow like a fog. It is also true—judging from the number (over 800) of bad trips treated by Dr. William Abruzzi and the Woodstock medical team—that there was plenty of acid and exotic amphetamine and psychedelic combinations being taken by those present there. From this, some have formed the opinion that the reason Woodstock was so quiet and peaceful was that the multitude was simply too stoned on drugs to do more than let out an occasional groan. And while such a view might square nicely with my description of rock as a religious cult whose sacrament is drug-taking, it is not quite consistent with what I saw there. For based on what I observed through those three days, I would say that estimates in the press that put the proportion of those present taking drugs of one kind or another at about 90 percent were terribly inflated. Sure, drugs were available, but prices were high. Remember, the Woodstock weekend fell right in the middle of the great marijuana famine of 1969. Word has it that a lot of oregano was sold—and probably smoked—that weekend. A lot of the acid that was being distributed was found to be horrendously bad stuff. "Don't take any of the blue caps," the voice on the loudspeaker warned. "An incredible situation has happened here and we've got to make the best of it. Maybe instead of taking acid and spacing out, you ought to save that for next weekend, so you can really dig what's happening." And not long after that someone was leading the audience in
Yoga breathing exercises "for a hyperventilation high." And

though nobody else seems to have noticed, judging from the number of empty bottles and the amount of open guzzling I saw, there must have been about as many high on wine as there were stoned on pot.

The point that should be made then on that silence at Woodstock is that it did not come merely as a result of drug use by those in attendance. There were deeper reasons. It seemed to stem from a sense of separation that is felt by many members of the so-called Woodstock Generation. There seems to be a feeling of distance there, a feeling of aloneness that keeps each apart from his fellows. Maybe this is why they like to be together so much. It is then, it seems, when they feel most complete—when they are with others like themselves, immersed in the multitude, hidden in the many.

Does that constitute a religious experience? For some it does. Wrap up all that togetherness with bright ribbons of rock, tie it tight with promises that what is happening here and now has never happened before—that this is the beginning of the new life, the start of the revolution—and you've got going the next best thing to the beatific vision. For some. For others none of this mattered quite so much as the miserable conditions in which they were forced to live that weekend and the music they never heard quite as well as they had wanted. I talked to a number by the end of that weekend who were deeply disenchanted by what they had experienced. Yet the myth that grew out of it all was pure cult, and perhaps many of those who had been turned off by the realities of Woodstock were eventually won over by the myth—the feeling of pride in having taken part in something so big and (as everyone kept telling them) so important. And as for those who had not been there—those of the rock cult who for one reason or another had not been able to make the scene at Bethel—there could be no doubt that they regarded the Woodstock experience as essentially religious in nature. A year after the event, writer Michael Putney of the *National Observer* visited the site of the festival and found pilgrims from as far away as California who had come to visit the shrine. One of them grew misty-eyed and nostalgic (though there for the first time), and looking out over Max Yasgur's alfalfa field, he said aloud to nobody in particular,

"You know, I can still catch some of those good, year-old vibes."

It rained again on Sunday. And I, having picked up only a few hours sleep early that morning, surrendered rather shamefully. I got soaked in the driving rain that came late in the afternoon. And when the music started again I found there was no place to sit except in the mud, no place to drip dry as I splashed and slipped about looking for somewhere to settle. Even though the music had started again and would continue, I decided to leave. I had been invited to spend the day after Woodstock at Allen Ginsberg's farm, which is in upper New York, not too far away. Perhaps he would not mind if I were to show up a little early. And so I began the drive and pushed my arrival so that there might (I hoped) be some time left to talk.

I was made to feel welcome. Allen Ginsberg met me and while there was still a little light left, took me on a brief tour of the farm. He lives in what amounts to a commune, a farm that is the property of the Committee on Poetry, Inc., the "amateur foundation" that Ginsberg has formed to dispose of the royalties and fees that come his way. His is an amateur farm, too. There is nothing here of the food factory that has all but supplanted the family farm of a generation back. Ginsberg and those who live with him there want only to get from the farm the food they eat. No profits and no government subsidies. They have a vegetable garden and a small mixed herd of livestock, the latter in Peter Orlovsky's care. "What we're trying to do," Ginsberg explained, "is to take from his place what we need to live without disturbing the ecology. And to do this we've had to go back and relearn nineteenth-century technology." He took me into the field some distance from the farmhouse and showed me the old-fashioned vacuum ram pump they were building there to bring water up the hill from the well to the house. He was proud of that, and all the rest of the farm, and what it meant to them in independence and self-reliance.

They wanted to hear about Woodstock. And I told them
what I had seen and heard there. Though I admit that at first

I suppressed a few of my negative impressions, I did voice, in a neutral way, my opinion that most of those at the festival regarded the whole experience as essentially religious, a sort of cult rite.

Allen Ginsberg agreed enthusiastically. "Yes," he said, "I'm sure you're right. And the model for gatherings of this kind is the *Kumbah Mela* convocations that the Hindus hold every twelve years. It means literally a 'full pitcher,' and it refers to a myth in which the nectar of immortality is dropped from Shiva's pitcher onto those of the earth below. What it is is a gathering of all the holy men in India and their disciples in one spot. This is the sort of thing we were trying to do at the great Be-In in Golden Gate Park—to make a rite of it—and I'm sure this is how they looked at it at Woodstock. Imagine! Four hundred thousand of them there together in a cow pasture!" (Incidentally, Max Yasgur was incorrect when he told the multitude at Woodstock that they comprised the largest group who had ever assembled in one place for a single event. That distinction goes to a three-week religious festival of the kind described by Ginsberg that was celebrated on the banks of the Ganges in 1966. Five million attended.)

I asked Ginsberg if he felt that such gatherings of the faithful here in America had political, as well as religious, significance.

"Certainly. In the larger sense. Because it's *communal*, dig." He stressed "communal" and paused a moment for effect, like a teacher in the classroom. "And anything *communal* is thus political. Certain people have tried to direct all this tremendous communal energy toward specific ends, things they're interested in accomplishing. SDS tried this, but they had the wrong vibrations. The one sort of spontaneous movement that has come out of all this is the sudden awareness of the menace to ecology. There's been a complete shift of attention to this really important problem that concerns us all deeply. That's spontaneous communal interest. And if that isn't essentially political, then I don't know what is."

It is impossible to talk even indirectly about politics with Allen Ginsberg without soon discussing seriously with him his experiences at the 1968 Democratic convention in Chicago.

240

He had attended as an accredited member of the press, a correspondent for the now defunct *Eye* magazine, but the treatment he received in the convention hall corresponded roughly with that handed out to the young radicals in Grant Park.

"That part of it has been pretty well reported. After all, Burroughs and Genet were right up at the head of the column of marchers. They were there for *Esquire.* But inside the convention it was just as bad. In fact, it was unbelievable. It was a classical putsch scene from the Thirties. The gallery was packed. There were police agents everywhere, and there was terrible harassment of the McCarthy followers even *inside* the convention hall. It went as far as virtual kidnapping of delegates in order to silence free discourse. I know because I was kidnapped, too."

He explained that he had been picked up by the Chicago police inside the convention hall, and he had clear evidence, he said, that they were acting in collusion with the Secret Service. "The whole thing was their show," he said. "It was up to them to keep McCarthy from being nominated, because if he had been, everyone would have jumped on the movement, and we would have seen the end of the police state. And naturally the Secret Service couldn't have permitted that.

"I think that McCarthy, like all of us, is afraid of the authoritarian police state. He saw the putsch was in Chicago, that it had to be recognized as a historical moment. So I think this semiretirement he has now gone into is a general reflection of his feeling that, well, it's over now, there's nothing more that can be done. After all, they literally beat up his close aids."

What happened to Allen Ginsberg when he was arrested in the convention? "Well, I was picked up by Daley's police. They brought me to the Secret Service who treated me in exactly the same way. I thought going in there, 'Well, you can't trust the Chicago cops. They're stupid. They're not used to handling these political things.' But when I got to where they were taking us, there were eight black-suited guys waiting for us—Secret Service men. They examined my credentials. I pointed out to them that I was properly accredited as a press representative. And then a very slick one fixed me with a kind of sneer and said, 'Well, Allen . . .' He knew who I was, I'm sure of it. 'Your credentials are no good anymore.' Believe me, it wasn't a joke. It was Kafka. Every reporter got the same treatment. The police were working hand-in-hand with the government men. Daley and Hoover. The cops got all the information on Jerry Rubin and Abbie Hoffman from the FBI. It was just what happened in Czechoslovakia when the Russian-trained secret police remained loyal to the Russians. Let me tell you, when I was talking with that Secret Service man, I suddenly realized that I was living in a police state then and there. It's not just that we were going in that direction. We're already there. A drive through America will tell you that. Just look at those empty expressions on the faces of the state police. They're like machines in the service of the state."

I said that some of this seemed to be foretold in "Howl." Did he think when he wrote that almost fifteen years ago that things would go as far as they have in this direction?

"In a way. You know, that reading for *Big Table* you mentioned you attended was like a crossing of the Rubicon for us then. It was really important. And being there in Chicago that first time it seemed to me that I could sense the same feeling of confrontation that came through to me so clearly ten years later at the convention. Maybe it was all there in an implicit, prophetic way earlier. But as a literary movement, well, we came and we went. Paul Carroll, for instance, thought the revolution that we intended to create in prose and poetry really had been successfully accomplished by 1963. And in a way it had.

"But in another way it went beyond anything we had 'planned.' And in that way, yes, it did surprise me. I'm old enough to be surprised at major alterations in human consciousness. And that's what we've seen happen. I'm surprised that what was with the Beat thing a hieratic, gnostic thing is now so widespread. It was a visionary experience in 1948, when we started. Now everybody sees and understands these things."

He sighed and took a moment to adjust the glasses that never seem to leave his face except to be wiped. "Yes, it is
242    different, isn't it? It has taken on the characteristics of a mass

movement. There has been a terrific increase in antiwar consciousness. Do you know that 52 percent of the people they questioned in a poll recently said that they think that war is always a mistake? If it is possible that McCarthy could have been elected—and I think it is—then this really is a mass movement. You wonder at what point the McCarthy people shade into those who drive around now with flower decals on their car. And what does *that* mean in sympathy or commitment?

"Yes, it's different, but the nature of the planet is different. Things are changing so rapidly that with or without the movement I think there would have been a generation of young people who would have grown up thinking differently from the way people were thinking when we were trying to assert ourselves, trying to prove there were other ways of thinking, other ways of perceiving."

It was then I expressed to Ginsberg my misgivings regarding mass movements in general and in particular the aspects that had been shown me that weekend at Woodstock. There seemed, I said, to be distinct evidence of a loss of individuality, of personality diminished and merged. I described the silence at Woodstock, the evident lack of communication, and that, I told him, had bothered me.

"You mean communication with words?" he asked, slightly vexed. "How important is that? Let me quote McClure to you. He says we are all 'spores and tendrils of gentle leviathan.' And we get this image of leviathan winking his galactic eyebrows, a pupil flashing out of the spiral nebula, a kalpic wink that may close an eon. It's this sort of cosmic perception that this generation has today. They feel themselves members of a giant body. The kids who get together for rock festivals are assembling to manifest leviathan, this gentle leviathan that McClure describes. You don't need words for that."

Is that why they seem less interested in writing? "Listen, literary articulation, even of the long-haired generation, is just a ripple of the giant wave of the evolution that is taking place. What this whole generation feels is a cosmic consciousness, an awareness of being in the middle of the cosmos instead of this town or that valley or city. So if they perceive this big breath
243 of this giant being, then there are real differences between

them and previous generations who thought of themselves as individuals. Now it's as leviathan tendrils that the members of this generation see themselves.

"And that's what comes through on LSD. Psychedelics have been there for a long time. Hashish, for instance, is ancient, known for centuries in the East. In the New World they had the magic mushrooms and peyote. So why is it suddenly in this century, today, that they have taken on such importance? Why, if not because now they express something of this new cosmic consciousness? LSD is the Christ of the Kali Yuga. It seems that out of the enormous mercy of the creator he has manifested himself to us in the material form of a pill. Isn't this *amazing?*

"I got this from a teacher in India. To put it in more abstract language, it is the Christ or Messiah because it's the Creator interfering in history. That's why some people freak out, dig, because they perceive this, and it's just too much for them to handle. They're certain the world's coming to an end, and sure, of course it is. With LSD, the apocalypse becomes an everyday occurrence. But that's not a good thing, either. That's what the teacher was warning against, that with a pill these vast perceptions could become just a bore, like marriage, something great repeated over and over again becoming a bore. That's abuse of the infinite."

Allen got up suddenly then and beckoned me away from the kitchen table where we had been talking. "Come over here," he said, "I want to show you something." The something turned out to be the *Life* magazine cover picture of the earth that had been taken from the moon by the Apollo 11 astronauts. It was taped prominently to one wall of the kitchen. "This is an apoca'yptic age, all right. If you don't think so, just take a look at this. The earth. Look." He waited in an attitude of silent insistence for a long moment as I studied the photograph of the greenish-blue sphere with the swirls of white surrounding it.

"It's alive!" he said.

And it was true enough. There was something about the photo, perhaps in the way that the filmy layers of white that are the atmosphere seemed to have been stopped in sudden, swift motion. Or perhaps it was just the warm, beautiful color of that globe that made it seem alive.

"It's a living being. Don't you feel like one cell, one being, looking at another? Probably it thinks. Do you suppose it's conscious? When you look at it like this you get the feeling that it's we who are not conscious. She's more conscious than we are. Everything in human experience, everything in the higher philosophy that we pay lip service to has considered that yes, it is a person there. Think of what Wordsworth kept trying to tell us—wasn't it this?

"We are becoming more conscious of what it is and what we are in relation to it. LSD is precisely that—a way of increasing this consciousness. It was necessary and inevitable in a highly rigid and brainwashed civilization such as ours to help us find what was always there. To us the LSD thing was just as important as the trip to the moon. LSD equals the moon in terms of the expansion of human possibilities. The moon thing is a technological manifestation of cosmic consciousness. It all fits together and it was there all the time. It's implicit in the text of "Howl." It was what we meant when we used to tell them that Beat was short for Beatific."

# Epilogue

Jack Kerouac died two months later in St. Petersburg, Florida, at the age of forty-seven. Not long before he had moved down there with his wife and mother so that *Memere* might have the benefit of the sun and the mild climate. She had gone into a local hospital for care they couldn't give her at home, and when he was suddenly taken with a seizure, an awful pain inside, he was rushed into the same hospital and died there of internal bleeding. The drinking did it, of course.

Although down there in Florida he felt just as much out of it as he had in Lowell and nursed the same resentments, he continued to be to the end what he had been through all his adult life: a writer. He began working on a novel he had begun in 1951, finished it in a sudden rush of inspiration, and sent it off to Sterling Lord. And then a couple of weeks after that, he died.

They took him up to Lowell to bury him. A few of his old friends were there for the funeral—John Clellon Holmes, Allen Ginsberg, Gregory Corso, perhaps one or two more who might not have been so easily recognized. But for the most part, it was a local funeral, a Canuck Catholic affair in an old New England mill town. And perhaps that was as it should have been: "Remember, man, that you are dust and unto dust you shall return."

# INDEX